First Peter

Standing Fast in the Grace of God

First Peter

Standing Fast in the Grace of God

DANIEL L. SEGRAVES

I Peter: Standing Fast in the Grace of God

by Daniel L. Segraves

©1999, Word Aflame Press
Hazelwood, MO 63042-2299

All Scripture quotations in this book are from the King James Version of the Bible unless otherwise identified. Scriptures noted NKJV are from The New King James Bible, Copyright 1990 Thomas Nelson Inc., Publishers.

All rights reserved. No portion of this publication may be reproduced, stored in an electronic system or transmitted in any form or by any means, electronic, mechanical, photocopy, recording, or otherwise, without the prior permission of Word Aflame Press. Brief quotations may be used in literary reviews.

Printed in United States of America.

Printed by

Library of Congress Cataloging-in-Publication Data

Segraves, Daniel L., 1946–
   I Peter: standing fast in the grace of God / Daniel L. Segraves.
      p.   cm.
   Includes bibliographical references.
   ISBN 1-56722-225-0
   1. Bible.   N. T.   Peter, I—Commentaries.   I. Title.   II. Title:
First Peter.
BS2795.3.S44   1999   98-55256
227'.92077—dc21   CIP

Other Books by DANIEL L. SEGRAVES

I Peter: Standing Fast in the Grace of God

Ancient Wisdom for Today's World: Proverbs

Hair Length in the Bible

Hebrews: Better Things, Vol. 1 & 2

Living by Faith: A Verse-by-Verse Study of Romans

James: Faith at Work

Marriage: Back to Bible Basics

Messiah's Name

Themes from a Letter to Rome

You Can Understand the Bible

Order from:
Pentecostal Publishing House
8855 Dunn Road
Hazelwood, MO 63042-2299

Contents[1]

Preface 9
Introduction 13

I. Salutation (1:1-2) 25
   A. Author (1:1a) 25
   B. Recipients (1:1b-2a) 28
   C. Greetings (1:2b) 38

II. The Blessing of Salvation by Faith (1:3-12) 41
   A. The Origin of Salvation (1:3) 41
   B. The End of Salvation (1:4) 45
   C. The Keeping Power of Salvation (1:5) 47
   D. The Trial of Faith (1:6-7) 48
   E. The Certainty of Faith's Reward (1:8-9) 50
   F. Salvation Foretold by Hebrew Prophets (1:10-12) ... 52

III. Exhortations in View of Salvation (1:13-2:10) 59
   A. Call to Hope (1:13) 59
   B. Call to Holiness (1:14-16) 62
   C. Call to Reverence (1:17-21) 66
   D. Call to Love (1:22-25) 86
   E. Call to Spiritual Growth (2:1-10) 97

IV. Exhortations in View of Social Groupings (2:11-3:12) . 119
   A. Responsible Conduct among Unbelievers (2:11-12) . 119
   B. Responsible Conduct toward Civil Authority
      (2:13-17) 125

    C. Responsible Conduct of Slaves toward Their
       Masters (2:18-25)............................. 140
    D. Responsible Conduct in Marriage (3:1-7) 161
    E. Responsible Conduct in the Family of God (3:8-12) . 180

V. Exhortations in View of Suffering (3:13-4:19) 189
    A. Call to Boldness in the Face of Persecution
       (3:13-4:6) 189
    B. Call to Mutuality in Ministry in View of the Critical
       Hour (4:7-11).................................. 236
    C. Call to Accept Suffering As Normative (4:12-19) ... 253

VI. Exhortations to Elders and Younger Believers (5:1-9) . 267
    A. Call to Elders to Serve As Shepherds (5:1-4) 267
    B. Call to Younger Believers to Submit to Elders
       (5:5a)... 275
    C. Call to Mutual Submission and Humility (5:5b-7) ... 277
    D. Call to Spiritual Vigilance (5:8-9) 283

VII. Closing (5:10-14)...................................... 289
    A. The Reward for Suffering (5:10).................. 289
    B. Doxology (5:11)................................ 292
    C. Delivery of the Letter (5:12a) 293
    D. Purpose of Composition (5:12b) 294
    E. Greetings (5:13-14)............................. 295

Endnotes 299

Preface

Those who track the persecution of Christians around the world report that more people were martyred for their faith in Christ during the twentieth century than during the previous nineteen hundred years.[2] David Barnett, editor of *World Christian Encyclopedia*, estimates that as many as 160,000 people are slaughtered each year for their faith in Christ.[3] During 1996, two issues of *Christianity Today* were devoted to the theme of the suffering church and modern martyrdom.[4]

This situation makes Peter's first letter especially pertinent to our generation. As Edwin A. Blum has pointed out, the challenge facing the original recipients of this letter was "to live for God in the midst of a society ignorant of the true God."[5] Even if we define Christianity in the broadest terms, it is still a minority religion in today's world. As such, it is subject to the vehement disapproval of private and public forces worldwide. This disapproval frequently translates into oppression, denial of basic human rights, imprisonment, and even torture and death. For example, the great revival in Ethiopia was preceded by a time during which no pastor escaped imprisonment, beating, or death.[6]

The central theme of I Peter is the appropriate Christian response to suffering. (See 1:6-7; 2:19-21; 3:13-19; 4:1, 12-16, 19; 5:10.) This suffering is the result of "various trials" (1:6, NKJV), including the abuse of servants by their masters (2:19-21) and defamation by unbelievers (3:13-19). I Peter sees this suffering as normal for

First Peter

a believer (4:12). Christians simply share in Christ's sufferings because of their identification with Him (4:13-16). This suffering is nothing less than the will of God (4:19). To suffer patiently is commendable before God (2:20). Christians are called to submit to unjust suffering; our Lord set the example in His suffering for us (2:21). The result of this suffering, faithfully endured, will be "praise, honor, and glory at the revelation of Jesus Christ" (1:7, NKJV). Those who keep their faith in Christ will survive the suffering perfected, established, strengthened, and settled (5:10).

The increasing secularization of Western culture and the increasing intolerance of Christianity by non-Christian religions in the world today have created an environment for Christians at the dawn of a new millennium much like that of the last half of the first century. We can draw instruction, comfort, and hope from Peter's letter to believers scattered over northern Asia Minor (modern Turkey). If our spiritual ancestors could endure suffering victoriously, so can we. The same God they served will strengthen us.

Many commentaries have been written on I Peter throughout the history of Christianity. Little has been written, however, from the perspective of Oneness Pentecostal theology. This work is intended to be an analysis and exegesis of the text, not simply an attempt to defend a denominational view, however.

This commentary is based on the King James Version (KJV) of the Holy Bible. Where the wording of the KJV may tend to obscure the meaning for some modern readers, the reading of the New King James Version (NKJV) will be consulted. Where the critical Greek text (as seen

Preface

in Nestle-Aland's twenty-sixth edition and the third edition of the United Bible Societies' Greek New Testament) has a significantly different reading from the text upon which the NKJV and KJV are based, it will be discussed.

Introduction

Peter's first letter encourages believers who live as "sojourners and pilgrims" among those who do not share their faith (2:11, NKJV), and it instructs them concerning the appropriate Christian response to unbelievers. The encouragement comes in the form of reminding the readers about the certainty of their eternal inheritance. (See 1:3-7, 13; 4:13; 5:4.) The instruction centers on the responsibility of believers to conduct themselves so as to deflect unwarranted criticism of the church (2:11-12, 15; 3:15-16; 4:14-16) and on the reality of their suffering (2:21; 3:14, 17; 4:1, 12-14, 16, 19; 5:9).

The letter is written to a specific audience (1:1), but its message makes it just as relevant to believers of all times and places who live among unbelievers and who find themselves in need of encouragement and specific guidance as to how to respond to a hostile, non-Christian environment. Thus, the letter is specifically useful to believers at the beginning of the third millennium since our Lord walked on this earth.

Inspiration and Place in the Canon

Early Christian writers of the late first century and second century gave rich testimony to the authenticity and canonicity of I Peter. References to the book appear in *I Clement*, written in A.D. 96, and in the early second-century works of Ignatius, Hermas, and Pseudo-Barnabas. Polycarp, martyred in the mid-second century, referred to I Peter in his *Epistle to the Philippians*. Following Polycarp, Irenaeus, Clement of Alexandria, Tertullian, and Origen all confirmed the authenticity of the book.

First Peter

In his *Ecclesiastical History*, Eusebius of Caesarea, who lived in the late third and early fourth centuries, declared that I Peter was among the books accepted by the church without any doubt. Eusebius also referred to Papias (c. 60-130) as relying on the book. The *Gospel of Truth*, which seems to use the books considered authoritative in Rome in approximately A.D. 140, includes I Peter.[7]

In short, I Peter has been accepted from the earliest days of the church because believers from that time recognized its apostolic authority.

The letter also contains an internal witness as to its authority. The author claimed to be "an apostle of Jesus Christ" (1:1). He asserted that this brief letter is an exhortation and testimony to the "true grace of God in which you stand" (5:12, NKJV). The book abounds with quotations from and allusions to the Hebrew Scriptures. (See 1:16, 24-25; 2:3, 6-10, 22-25; 3:6, 10-12, 14; 4:8, 18; 5:5.)

Author

The book claims Peter as its author (1:1). Significant parallels exist between this book and speeches made by Peter and recorded in Acts. (Compare 1:20 with Acts 2:23; 2:24 with Acts 5:30 and 10:39; 4:5 with Acts 10:42; and 2:7-8 with Acts 4:10-11.) The author saw the sufferings of Christ (5:1). Similarities between the content of the book and the teachings of Jesus confirm that the author was personally acquainted with Jesus. (Compare 1:13 with Luke 12:35; 1:17 with Luke 11:2; 2:12 with Matthew 5:16; 3:9 with Luke 6:28; and 3:14 with Matthew 5:10.)[8]

Introduction

The evidence for Peter's authorship is so strong that it was not questioned until recently. Some have suggested that Peter's lack of education (Acts 4:13) precludes the possibility that he wrote this book, which indicates a mastery of Greek prose. But this argument assumes too much about what it meant for Peter to be "ignorant" and what his linguistic abilities were. Apparently, the statement in Acts 4:13 refers to his lack of formal rabbinical training, not to his ignorance of the Hebrew Scriptures. It was common for all Jewish boys in the first century to receive a rich biblical education.[9] Moreover, Greek was a common language in first-century Galilee, Peter's home. The same Jewish leaders who perceived that Peter and John were "uneducated and untrained" (NKJV) also marveled at Peter's defense. This does not suggest that Peter lacked biblical or communication skills.

Another attempt to dislodge Peter as the author of the book is the allegation that the persecutions it alludes to did not occur until the reign of Domitian (A.D. 81-96) or Trajan (A.D. 98-117). This was after Peter's death. But nothing in the book suggests that the persecution of the believers was official persecution by the Roman government. The allusions may be simply to the general and universal tension that has always existed where believers find themselves living in a faithless society. It may also be that I Peter was written on the eve of the persecution of the church by Nero, which began after much of Rome was destroyed by fire on July 19, 64.

Some have suggested that if Peter were the author, given his stature in the church, the letter would not have such a Pauline flavor. This argument is hardly convincing. Peter acknowledged Paul's authority (II Peter 3:15-16)

First Peter

and both were inspired by the same Holy Spirit. In any case, Peter does not follow Paul slavishly. For instance, the reference to Christ's preaching to the "spirits in prison" (3:19) has no parallel in Paul's writings.

Since the text claims Peter as the author, since the internal evidence agrees with this claim, since the earliest Christians accepted this claim, and since those who have recently questioned Peter's authorship have been unable to advance any convincing evidence to the contrary, we accept the testimony of the book itself: Peter is the author.

Date of Composition

Most scholars hold that I Peter was written in approximately A.D. 62-64. Under Nero, official persecution broke out against the church in A.D. 64. The book does not seem to suggest that such persecution had already begun but that more intense suffering was near. (See 4:1, 7, 12.) It seems likely that Peter issued his call to "submit . . . to every ordinance of man"—a call to obey civil rulers who were "sent . . . for the punishment of evildoers, and for the praise of them that do well" (2:13-14)—prior to the outbreak of official persecution. When Nero began his campaign against Christians on trumped up charges of burning the city of Rome, he certainly was not fulfilling his God-given responsibilities. Instead, he was punishing those who had done good and was rewarding evildoers.

The book of *I Clement*, written about A.D. 96, describes the martyrdom of Peter and Paul.[10] Most scholars believe their martyrdom took place under Nero at Rome, during the persecution that began after fire destroyed much of the city on July 19, 64.[11] If so, Peter could not have written the book of I Peter later than this persecution.

Scot McKnight suggested that "Peter wrote this letter near the beginning of Nero's persecutions and that it is an early strategy for coping with serious problems from the state."[12] In any case, it is clear that Peter recommended submission and love in the face of persecution.

Place of Origin

Peter's location when he wrote this letter is indicated in 5:13: "She who is in Babylon, elect together with you, greets you; and so does Mark my son" (NKJV). It seems likely that "Babylon" here is "a symbolic way of referring to Rome, a name that expressed something of Rome's pride, luxury, immorality, and godlessness."[13] It is not unheard of for Scripture to refer to a city by a symbolic name. Revelation 11:8 says that Jerusalem is "spiritually called Sodom and Egypt." It seems unlikely that Peter would have been in the declining Mesopotamian Babylon of Old Testament history, for Jews had been expelled from that city well before the New Testament era. There is no evidence that Peter's missionary journeys ever included this area, and it would be difficult to conceive of Peter, Mark, and Silvanus all being there at the same time. There was also a military post in Egypt called Babylon, but there is no evidence that Peter was ever there either.[14]

Revelation seems to use "Babylon" as a cryptogram. (See Revelation 14:8; 17:18; 18:2, 10, 21.) If Peter was in Rome when he wrote this book, it would be sensible for him to disguise his location if the persecution under Nero had begun or was at hand. At any rate, Eusebius, in his *Ecclesiastical History*, quoted Papias, an early bishop of

Hierapolis, as saying that "Peter makes mention of Mark in his first epistle which they say that he wrote in Rome itself, as indicated by him, when he calls the city, by a figure, Babylon."[15] A few Greek minuscules (manuscripts written in a cursive script) actually read "Rome" in 5:13 rather than "Babylon."[16] Either they rely on older manuscripts that read "Rome" or on the ancient tradition that the "Babylon" in view was actually Rome.

Original Audience

The letter is addressed to "the pilgrims of the Dispersion in Pontus, Galatia, Cappadocia, Asia, and Bithynia" (1:1, NKJV). This "dispersion" language is distinctively Jewish and gives the immediate impression that Peter wrote to Jewish Christians scattered in the specific areas he named. Because of other internal evidence, however, various views have arisen as to the identity of the original readers. Since knowing the original audience greatly aids the interpretation of Scripture, we will consider these views.

1. Peter wrote to a mixed audience of believing Jews and Gentiles. In 1:18, Peter stated that his readers had been redeemed "from [their] aimless conduct received by tradition from [their] fathers" (NKJV). Some, who recognize the Jewishness of the dispersion language, think that this verse indicates a Gentile audience. In this view, Peter would not describe Jewish believers as receiving from their fathers the tradition of "aimless conduct." Those who hold this view see 4:3 as suggesting a Gentile audience: "For we have spent enough of our past lifetime in doing the will of the Gentiles" (NKJV).

2. Peter wrote to an almost exclusively Gentile

audience. McKnight, who holds this view, believes "that the readers were mostly Gentiles who had probably previously become attached to Judaism through local synagogues and other forms of Judaism."[17] As evidence, he appeals to 1:14, which describes the lives of the readers before they came to Christ as "former lusts in . . . ignorance." He also appeals to 1:18, noted in point one above. To this, McKnight adds 2:10, which indicates that the first readers of this letter were "once not a people" but that they were "now the people of God." Once they "had not obtained mercy," but now they "have obtained mercy." McKnight also appeals to 4:2-4, which he sees as pointing to an "earlier pagan lifestyle."[18] According to this view, Peter addressed the original Gentile audience of the letter "as if they were Israel. That is, they have in some sense 'replaced' national Israel as the people of God and are now the new and true Israel. . . . This is the language of fulfillment and replacement."[19]

3. Peter wrote to an almost exclusively Jewish audience. In this view, taken in this commentary, the dispersion language of 1:1 sets the tone for the entire letter, and it is uniquely appropriate to a Jewish audience. James used precisely the same language to write to Jewish readers (James 1:1). Peter frequently quoted from the Septuagint, a Greek translation of the Hebrew Scriptures used widely among the Jews. Although Peter certainly ministered to Gentiles (Acts 10), he was specifically the apostle to the Jews. (See Galatians 2:7-8.)

Nothing in the book demands a predominately Gentile audience. Jesus Himself often rebuked the prevalent Judaism of the first century for ignorance and vain behavior. (See Matthew 15:1-9; 23.) Paul warned unbelieving

Israel repeatedly, accusing them of having a "spirit of stupor," ears that could not hear, and eyes that could not see. (See, e.g., Romans 9:30-32; 11:7-10.) Thus, the description of the readers' "former lusts" and "ignorance" (1:14) and their "aimless conduct received by tradition from [their] fathers" (1:18) does not demand a Gentile audience. The origin of 2:9 in Deuteronomy 7:6 and of 2:10 in Hosea 1:10 is specifically Jewish. The view that 4:3 indicates a Gentile audience is open to question. Indeed, it seems to suggest just the opposite; before they came to Christ, the Jewish believers had been living like Gentiles, walking in "lewdness, lusts, drunkenness, revelries, drinking parties, and abominable idolatries" (NKJV). If one doubts that Jews were capable of this lifestyle, or thinks it unlikely that they would engage in these things, a reading of the Hebrew prophets should make it clear that Jews were just as apt as Gentiles to walk in the lusts of the flesh.

Certainly there was a Gentile component in the churches of northern Asia Minor, and Peter's letter would have been just as useful and authoritative for them as it is for Gentiles around the world today. But the letter, as it claims for itself, was written specifically to Jewish Christians dispersed throughout the region. No doubt some of them had actually heard Peter's first message on the Day of Pentecost. (See Acts 2:8-11.)

Purpose

Peter revealed his purpose in 5:12: "I have written to you briefly, exhorting and testifying that this is the true grace of God in which you stand" (NKJV). The phrase translated "in which you stand" (Greek, *eis en stete*) is actually an imperative of command. The idea is something like, "Stand firm in it!" The letter is characterized by imperatives.

The persecution that the readers were already experiencing, and the greater persecution looming on the horizon, apparently made it necessary for Peter to firmly exhort them to stand fast in the grace of God. Otherwise, they may have been tempted to question the gospel message as they endured the suffering associated with it.

Style and Structure

The literary form of I Peter is that of a normal first-century letter. Though there have been recent attempts to describe the letter as a sermon or baptismal liturgy, they are not completely convincing.[20] Peter may have intended for the letter to be read aloud in the churches to which he sent it; this practice has precedence. (See Colossians 4:16; I Thessalonians 5:27; Revelation 1:3.)

One could argue that the letter includes "material that had previously existed in other forms (possibly material from [Peter's] past teaching and preaching activity), yet these materials now form a letter [Peter] intends to be intelligible apart from the knowledge of previously existing forms."[21]

Summary of Content

The letter begins with a claim of apostolic authority and is addressed to a specific audience scattered throughout northern Asia Minor (1:1). These scattered believers are the elect; they have been sanctified by the Spirit and sprinkled with the blood of Jesus, and they are called to obey Him (1:2).

After this initial salutation, the letter describes the

hope of salvation (1:3-12). New Testament salvation provides an inheritance and sustains its heirs (1:3-5). Though faith may be tried, faith that endures receives a rich reward (1:6-9).

The Hebrew prophets were very interested to know when the grace of which they prophesied would come (1:10-11). God revealed to them, however, that their prophecies would not be fulfilled in their days; the fulfillment was for the future (1:12).

In 1:13-5:11, we find the expected behavior of those who enjoy new covenant salvation. In view of redemption, there is a call to holiness (1:13-21). In view of the incorruptibility of the Word of God, there is a call to brotherly love (1:22-25). In view of the graciousness of the Lord, there is a call to spiritual growth (2:1-3). In view of the chosenness of the believer (1:9-10), there is a call to come to Christ (1:4-8).

The specific behavior expected of believers includes honorable conduct and abstinence from fleshly lusts (2:11-12), submission to civil authority (2:13-17), submission of slaves to their masters (2:18-25), submission of wives to their husbands (3:1-6), honorable treatment of wives by husbands (3:7), empathy with the brotherhood (3:8), and doing good in the face of maltreatment (3:9-12).

Believers are to prepare for suffering (3:13-14). Not only are they to submit to suffering for the sake of the gospel, they are also to be ready to defend their faith to all who question them (3:15-4:6). In view of the certainty of future events, I Peter warns its readers to be serious and watchful in prayer (4:7). They are to love one another fervently, mutually ministering spiritual gifts (4:8-11).

Suffering is seen as normal (4:12-19).

Spiritual leaders are to function willingly and selflessly as shepherds over the flock (5:1-4). Younger believers are to submit to their elders, casting their cares upon Christ (5:5-7). Believers are to be alert to Satan's attempts to destroy them; they are to resist him in faith (5:8-9). They should also understand that they do not suffer in isolation (5:9).

Believers have the promise that their suffering will terminate in the intervention of God, who will bring to pass in their lives the things that glorify Him (5:10-11).

Silvanus carried this letter to its recipients (5:12); it was written in "Babylon" (Rome) (5:13). The believers in the dispersion were to greet one another with love, and Peter wished them peace (5:14).

I

Salutation
1:1-2

A. Author (1:1a)

(1a) Peter, an apostle of Jesus Christ.

Verse 1a. The letter begins with a claim to apostolic authority. The author is Peter, one of the first to follow Jesus. (See John 1:40-42.) His brother Andrew brought him to Jesus. When Jesus saw him, He said, "You are Simon the son of Jonah. You shall be called Cephas" (John 1:42, NKJV). The original name of this disciple, Simon (from the Greek *Symeon*, Acts 15:14), is transliterated from the Hebrew *Shimeon*. It is a form of the word *shama*, which means "to hear," "to listen," or "to obey." A form of *shama* appears in Deuteronomy 6:4, translated "hear" in the command, "Hear, O Israel: The LORD our God is one LORD." Peter's original name indicated his Jewishness, and it meant something like "hearing" or "heard."

Jesus declared that Peter would be called "Cephas." "Cephas" (Greek, *Kephas*) is transliterated from the Aramaic *kêp'*, which means "stone" or "rock." The Greek name "Peter" (*petros*) has the same meaning. (See Matthew 16:18.)

In view of the significance of names among the Jewish

people,[22] this change of Simon's name to Cephas was an important development. Generally, a new name symbolized a change of character. Peter's destiny was to be a pillar and foundation stone in the church (Galatians 2:9; Ephesians 2:20). His name will appear on the foundation stones of the New Jerusalem (Revelation 21:14).

After Andrew introduced Peter to Jesus, Jesus called Peter—a commercial fisherman—to be a fisher of men (Luke 5:10). When Jesus later chose, empowered, and commissioned His twelve apostles from among His disciples, Peter was the first one listed. (See Matthew 10:1-4; Mark 3:13-19; Luke 6:13-16.) On special occasions, Peter was one of only three apostles permitted to accompany Jesus. (See Mark 5:37; 9:2; 14:33.) On one occasion, Andrew was permitted to join this select group. (See Mark 13:3.)

After the ascension of Jesus and before the church was born on the Day of Pentecost, Peter still occupied a leading role among the Twelve. (See Acts 1:13.) He was the recognized leader of the waiting believers as they chose a replacement for Judas. (See Acts 1:15-22.) After the outpouring of the Holy Spirit, it was Peter who explained the phenomenon to the gathered multitude and who responded to their question, "Men and brethren, what shall we do?" (Acts 2:14-39, NKJV).

Peter's leadership in the church seems to be linked to his confession that Jesus was the Christ—the Messiah—the Son of the living God. (See Matthew 16:13-19.) Jesus gave him the "keys of the kingdom." The Jewish background of this phrase suggests that Peter would have the spiritual insight to lead others through the door of revelation through which he had passed.[23]

Salutation

Peter's spiritual insight did not render him inerrant, for shortly after his dramatic confession of faith he attempted to dissuade Jesus from His destiny. Jesus said to him, "Get behind Me, Satan! You are an offense to Me, for you are not mindful of the things of God, but the things of men" (Matthew 16:23, NKJV). Peter's frailties are well known. He was sometimes at a loss for words, but that did not keep him from speaking up. (See Mark 9:5-6.) He at first refused Jesus' ministry of washing his feet, but soon he swung to the opposite extreme (John 13:6-9). In spite of his protests that he would die before he would deny Jesus, he did deny Him three times, even cursing and swearing (Mark 14:29-31, 66-71). Jesus singled him out for rebuke for his inability to prayerfully support Him in the Garden of Gethsemane (Mark 14:37-38).

To Peter's credit, he recognized his sins (Mark 14:72). It is evident that Jesus forgave him, for after Jesus' resurrection an angel sent him special greetings (Mark 16:7) and then Jesus appeared personally to him (Luke 24:34; I Corinthians 15:5). Later, Jesus gave Peter a special commission, offering him an opportunity to recover himself from his three denials (John 21:15-17). He also foretold Peter's martyrdom (John 21:18-19).

In the first twelve chapters of Acts, Peter is the dominant apostolic influence. He conducted the replacement of Judas (Acts 1:15-22), preached the first message after the birth of the church (Acts 2:40), was instrumental in working miracles (Acts 3:1-11; 5:15), proclaimed Jesus to be the fulfillment of Messianic prophecies (Acts 3:12-26), defended the faith before the Sanhedrin (Acts 4:5-12), protected the purity of the young church (Acts 5:1-11), represented the Jerusalem church (together with John) to the

Samaritan believers and was instrumental in ministering the Holy Spirit to them (Acts 8:14-17), conducted a missionary ministry accompanied by remarkable miracles (Acts 9:32-43), introduced the gospel to Gentiles (Acts 10-11), and was miraculously released from prison (Acts 12:1-19).

Peter's apostolic authority and his high profile in the early church still did not render him inerrant. At Antioch, he suffered a stern public rebuke from Paul for his hypocrisy in withdrawing from Gentile believers in the face of Jewish disapproval. (See Galatians 2:11-21.) But at the Jerusalem Council, which apparently occurred after this event, Peter stood in agreement with Paul on the issue of Gentile freedom from the law of Moses (Acts 15:2-12).

Letters in the first century typically began with the writer's name and any needed descriptions. Following that pattern, Peter identified himself as an apostle of Jesus Christ. The word "apostle" is transliterated from the Greek *apostolos*, which means something like a "messenger" or "delegate" or "envoy."[24] By definition, apostles authoritatively represented someone else. In this case, Peter represented Jesus Christ. Not only was Peter one of the original twelve apostles, he was specifically an apostle to the Jewish people. (See Galatians 2:7-8.) Though Peter occasionally ministered to Gentiles, the bulk of his ministry focused on taking the gospel to the Jewish communities.

B. Recipients (1:1b-2a)

(1b) To the strangers scattered throughout Pontus, Galatia, Cappadocia, Asia, and Bithynia, (2a) elect

according to the foreknowledge of God the Father, through sanctification of the Spirit, unto obedience and sprinkling of the blood of Jesus Christ.

Verse 1b. The word translated "strangers" (*parepidemois*) is translated "pilgrims" by the NKJV. Like the word translated "scattered" (*diasporas*), which is translated "dispersion" in the NKJV and other modern English translations, this word evokes the Jewish aura of I Peter.[25] The faithful people of ancient Israel were "strangers and pilgrims [*parepidemoi*] on earth" (Hebrews 11:13).

The idea communicated by "pilgrims" is that of "resident aliens." In the first century, Jews throughout the Roman Empire generally had the status of resident aliens, distinguished from local citizens but legal residents.[26] The symbolism of this word is significant. Pilgrims had a homeland elsewhere. If the Jews of the Old Testament era were pilgrims as they wandered from place to place seeking a country (Hebrews 11:14), the believing Jews of the first century were even more so. They belonged to another realm. (See Ephesians 2:19; Philippians 3:20.) So, of course, do Gentiles whose faith is in Christ Jesus. They may legally reside in this world, but they are not at home here.

The arrangement of the Roman provinces mentioned here suggests that the letter may have been a circular, intended to circulate from one believing community to another. This was not uncommon for the New Testament letters. (See Colossians 4:16.[27]) Keener points out that the "sequence in which Peter lists the provinces of his intended readers reflects the route a messenger delivering the letter could take if he started from Amastris in Pontus."[28]

First Peter

These provinces were in northern Asia Minor, north of the Taurus Mountains. The region is known today as Turkey. If Paul's letter to the Galatians was addressed to the churches in south Galatia, Peter's letter was addressed to different churches. Jews from at least some of these areas were present on the Day of Pentecost in Jerusalem to hear Peter's first message after the outpouring of the Holy Spirit. (See Acts 2:5-11.)

Verse 2a. The scattered pilgrims to whom this letter was addressed were "elect" (*eklektois*). Although the New Testament uses this term of both Jewish and Gentile believers, its appearance here further suggests the Jewishness of the original recipients of this letter. Like "pilgrims" and "dispersion," the word "elect" finds its roots in the Hebrew Scriptures. As a nation, Israel was God's elect. (See Isaiah 45:4; 65:9, 22.) That is, He chose the entire nation for special purposes. The Gospels continued to use the word in discussions of the future of national Israel. (See Matthew 24:24, 31; Luke 18:7-8.) After the birth of the church, the Epistles broadened the use of "elect" to include both Jewish and Gentile believers. (See Romans 8:33; Colossians 3:11-12; Titus 1:1; I Thessalonians 1:4; II Peter 1:10.) Although Gentiles are included in the election of the new covenant, the contextual connection here between "pilgrims," "dispersion," and "elect" supports the view that Peter, the apostle to the Jews, addressed this letter primarily to Hebrew Christians.

In the Greek text, the word "elect" actually appears in verse 1, modifying "pilgrims." Thus, the letter is addressed to "elect pilgrims" dispersed throughout northern Asia Minor. In terms of the new covenant, the word "elect" takes on a significance beyond its use in the old covenant. Under the old covenant, the entire nation of Israel was elect by natural birth. Individuals had no choice as to whether they were included in this election. But in the new covenant, election is connected not only to God's foreknowledge but also to sanctification, obedience, and the Atonement. The elect to whom Peter wrote were not elect on the basis of their ethnic heritage but on the basis of their obedience to the truth through the Spirit (1:22). They had been "born again" (1:23). They were "newborn babes" (2:2). Under the old covenant, one could be elect only if he was born by natural birth into the nation of Israel. Under the new covenant, the basis for election is not the natural birth but the second birth. Regardless of their ethnic backgrounds, all those who have obeyed the truth through the Spirit and who have thus been born again are included in the elect.

The election of the new covenant is "according to the foreknowledge of God the Father." The word "foreknowledge" (*prognosin*) means "to know beforehand." There is no suggestion here of predestination of individuals prior to the active exercise of faith. Instead, these are people who are kept by faith (1:5), who will receive the end of their faith (1:9), who responded to the preaching of the gospel (1:12), who believed in God (1:21), who obeyed the truth (1:22), who had been born again (1:23) and who had "returned to the Shepherd and Overseer" of their souls (2:25, NKJV).

Peter's reference to the foreknowledge of God is the same as that of Paul in Romans 8:28. God certainly can and does predestine certain events to happen; much of Old Testament prophecy falls into this category. Christ was "foreordained before the foundation of the world" (I Peter 1:20). Both the word translated "foreordained" (*proegnosmenou*) and the word translated "foreknowledge" in 1:2 are from the same root. The coming of Christ was a certainty based on God's decision alone; He was the only one involved in this decision. God has also predetermined the salvation of those who obey the gospel, but since human beings are made in the image of God with the power of choice, the salvation of individuals is based on their free response to the gospel. (See Revelation 22:17; II Peter 3:9; Isaiah 55:1; John 7:37-38.)

God is a rational Being. Since humans are made in His image, they are also rational beings. When only one rational being is involved in a decision, he can make that decision unilaterally. This is the manner in which Christ was foreordained before the foundation of the world. But when two rational beings are involved in a decision, the decision must be made bilaterally. This is the case with the salvation of humans. It is the will of God that all people should be saved, but each individual must also be willing. Any other view compromises the genuineness of the image of God in man with its inherent power of choice and makes God the ultimate cause of sin.

God has predestined and elected the corporate church (Ephesians 1:4), just as He did the nation of Israel. But the membership of the church is based on the free choice of individuals. This makes the relationship of the church to God superior to that between Israel and God. Individuals had no choice as to whether they were included in national Israel. But genuine love can be experienced only when there is freedom not to love. Love cannot be forced. Israel was made up of those willing and unwilling to serve God. The church is made up only of those willing to love Him.

Upon the basis of His foreknowledge, God has included in His elect those whom He knew would exercise their faith to come to Him. This is not at all the same thing as the predestination taught by Calvinism. In the latter view, individuals are predestined, even before birth and thus apart from any conscious response to the gospel, to be saved. Depending on the particular Calvinistic perspective, all others are either predestined to be lost or simply passed over and thus abandoned to an eternity without God. But the Scripture teaches that the Atonement was motivated by the love of God for the entire world (John 3:16) and that the blood of Jesus satisfied the righteous judgment of God against the sins of the whole world (I John 2:2).

It is one thing for God to make a prior decision to treat in a certain way those who freely choose to come to Him; it is another thing for God to make the decisions of individuals for them.

The pilgrims of the dispersion were "elect according to the foreknowledge of God the Father, through sanctification of the Spirit, unto obedience and sprinkling of the blood of Jesus Christ." Grammatically, it seems best to see the three prepositional phrases in this statement as all modifying "elect."[29] That is, believers are "elect according to the foreknowledge of God the Father," they are "elect . . . through sanctification of the Spirit," and they are "elect . . . unto obedience and sprinkling of the blood of Jesus Christ."

This understanding further suggests that the focus is not on an idea of unconditional election but on the basis, means, and purpose of election. Believers are elected (chosen) *according to* the foreknowledge of God the Father (i.e., on the *basis* of their decision to come to God, which decision He knew they would make), they are elected *through* sanctification of the Spirit (i.e., by *means* of the Holy Spirit in setting them apart unto God and from the unbelieving world around them), and they are elected *unto* obedience and sprinkling of the blood of Jesus Christ (i.e., the *purpose* for which they are elected is that they might be obedient to the gospel and that they might enjoy the provisions of the new covenant established in Christ's blood [Matthew 26:28]).

The Spirit's work of sanctification (*hagiasmoi*) involves setting God's people apart. It is related to the Greek word frequently translated "holy."[30] On the sanctifying influence of the Holy Spirit, Peter was in agreement with Paul. (See II Thessalonians 2:13.)

There is a sense in which sanctification is instantaneous and complete at the moment of salvation. (See Hebrews 10:10; I Corinthians 1:2, 30; 6:11; Acts 20:32; 26:18). This could be called positional sanctification. In other words, at the moment they obey the gospel and are born again (I Peter 1:22-23), believers are fully the children of God (2:2), separated by the power of the Holy Spirit unto their Father and from their sins.

There is another sense in which sanctification is an ongoing process as the believer seeks daily to come into greater conformity to the character of Christ. (See I Thessalonians 4:4; 5:23; II Corinthians 7:1; Hebrews 10:14, NKJV; 12:10, 14.)

In a third sense, there is a final act of sanctification that will occur when Christ presents the church to Himself as a spotless bride free of any wrinkle or blemish.

(See Ephesians 5:26-27.) This will be the culmination of the ongoing sanctifying and cleansing effect of the "washing of water by the word."

The purpose for which believers are elected includes their obedience. This is the obedience to the gospel (II Thessalonians 1:8), which springs from genuine faith (Romans 16:26). We cannot separate the biblical concept of faith from behavioral response. James emphasized the necessity of works to validate faith. (See James 2:14-26.) Even Paul, who emphasized the priority of faith over works, saw genuine faith as inseparably connected to specific responsive actions.[31] Peter agreed (1:22; 2:8; 4:17).

The purpose for which believers are elected also includes the "sprinkling of the blood of Jesus Christ." This purpose, together with obedience, would certainly remind the Jewish readers of their Hebrew heritage. When he completed the writing of the law, Moses read it to the people of Israel. They said, "All that the LORD has said we will do, and be obedient" (Exodus 24:7, NKJV). Then Moses took the blood of oxen, "sprinkled it on the people, and said, 'This is the blood of the covenant which the LORD has made with you according to all these words'" (Exodus 24:8, NKJV).

Although the sprinkling of blood was frequently associated with Tabernacle service (Leviticus 7:14; 14:7, 16, 51; 16:14-15; Hebrews 9:13; 12:24), the people were sprinkled with blood only at the inauguration of the law of Moses, after they had pledged obedience to the law. Just as the sprinkling of the blood of oxen was the harbinger of the Mosaic covenant, so the shedding of the blood of Jesus ushered in the new covenant. (See Matthew 26:28; I Corinthians 11:25; Hebrews 9:11-14,

18-22; 10:19; 12:24; 13:12.)

The "sprinkling" of the blood of Jesus is a metaphor drawn from the account of the sprinkling of the blood of oxen upon the people at Mount Sinai. The literal sprinkling of the blood of animals under the law of Moses was but a shadow of the reality of the atoning work of Christ's death. (See Hebrews 10:1-10.) It is not necessary for believers to come into physical contact with the literal blood of Jesus for them to enjoy the redemptive work of Christ. Rather, they appropriate the marvels of the Atonement by faith.[32]

Christ's blood does not cleanse only at the inauguration of the new covenant, or when a person first comes to Him in faith, however. It continues to cleanse from sin those who walk in the light, which means to walk by faith in Christ Jesus. (See I John 1:7; John 8:12.)

Some trinitarians think that the reference in verse 2 to "God the Father," the "Spirit," and "Jesus Christ" indicates that the one God exists as three distinct persons.[33] But our goal is to understand the Scriptures as did the original readers, not to read back into them the philosophical or theological speculations of the first five centuries of the Christian era. How would the strictly monotheistic Jewish audience to whom Peter wrote have understood his words? How did Peter—himself a devout Jew—intend them?

In his second letter, Peter identified Jesus Christ as "our God and Savior" (II Peter 1:1, NKJV). He identified the Holy Spirit as the Spirit of Christ (1:11; II Peter 1:21). On the Day of Pentecost, Peter quoted Joel's prophecy that the Spirit poured out upon the waiting believers was actually the Spirit of the LORD (Hebrew, *Yahweh*) (Acts 2:16-18).

He connected the identity of Jesus Christ with the Incarnation and declared that Jesus Himself had poured out the Holy Spirit (Acts 2:22, 30-33). He proclaimed that the gift of the Holy Spirit comes in conjunction with identification with Jesus Christ in baptism (Acts 2:38). He apparently saw baptism in the name of Jesus Christ to be the equivalent of baptism in the name of the Father and of the Son and of the Holy Spirit (Matthew 28:19). He equated lying to the Holy Spirit with lying to God (Acts 5:3-4). He declared the Holy Spirit to be the gift of God (Acts 8:17, 20). He identified the voice of God as the voice of the Spirit (Acts 10:13, 14-15, 19-20; 11:8, 12, 17).

None of this language sounds as if Peter departed from the strict monotheism of the Hebrew Scriptures. Had that been Peter's intent, he surely could have done so with far greater clarity. Instead, under divine inspiration, he proclaimed that God is our Father, that God has come among us in the Incarnation in the person of Jesus Christ, and that He has given us the gift of His Holy Spirit. Indeed, I Peter 1:2 does not reflect the trinitarian formula developed later (i.e., God the Father, God the Son, and God the Holy Spirit). Instead, it mentions God the Father first, the Spirit second, and Jesus Christ third. The point is not to establish theology but to describe the various aspects of the salvation experience. We should read nothing more into the verse. I Peter does not imply that God the Father is the first person, the Spirit the second, and Jesus Christ the third. It simply indicates that the one true God, who is our Father and whom we know redemptively in Jesus Christ, has sanctified us by His Spirit.

Other references say that Jesus Christ performs the work of sanctification (Ephesians 5:25-26; I Corinthians

1:2, 30; Acts 26:18). The Bible also says that Christians are sanctified by the name of Jesus and the Spirit of God (I Corinthians 6:11). It further says that God Himself sanctifies believers (I Thessalonians 5:23; Hebrews 12:10).

If I Peter taught that three distinct persons compose the one God, then it seemingly would connect foreknowledge to the Father alone, sanctification to the Spirit alone, and the requirement for obedience and the work of atonement to Jesus Christ alone. As we have seen, this cannot be, for the Bible does not attribute sanctification to the Spirit alone. In addition, the church was purchased by the very blood of God (Acts 20:28).

The teaching of Scripture is that there is one God (Deuteronomy 6:4) who is Spirit (John 4:24) and who is manifest in the flesh in the person of Jesus Christ (I Timothy 3:16). We will never on this earth fully understand God or the Incarnation, but we should not resort to extrabiblical or postbiblical speculations in an attempt to satisfy our curiosity. We must joyfully confess all that the Bible declares to be true without confounding scriptural statements with human conjecture.

C. Greetings (1:2b)

(2b) Grace unto you, and peace, be multiplied.

Verse 2b. Peter's greeting of "grace" was typical in the Greco-Roman world, but—like the writers of other New Testament letters—he also incorporated the common Jewish greeting "peace" (Greek, *eirene*, the equivalent of the Hebrew *shalom*).

Peter's wish for grace (Greek, *charis*) to be multiplied to his readers was not a mere formality. Like Paul, Peter saw the grace of God as far more than simply unmerited favor.[34] The grace of God is a powerful force by which God motivates and enables people of faith to do what pleases Him. Peter made this clear in his repeated references to grace. (See 1:10, 13; 2:19-20 [where *charis* is translated "thankworthy" and "acceptable" by the KJV]; 3:7; 4:10; 5:5, 10, 12.) According to Peter, believers should grow in grace (II Peter 3:18).

The Hebrew idea of peace goes far beyond similar expressions in Western culture. *Shalom* essentially refers to holistic well-being. The Western view of peace is fragmentary; it splits people up so that one can express concern for a person's physical well-being with no regard for spiritual well-being. This idea does not occur in Hebrew thought. *Shalom* embraces both material and spiritual wellness. (See Isaiah 48:22; 57:21; Psalm 34:14; 119:165.)

II

The Blessing of Salvation by Faith
1:3-12

The Greek text behind this section is grammatically in the form of one sentence. It would be considered unwieldy in modern English, but it expresses in a profound way the full-orbed salvation provided by Christ's resurrection from the dead. The new birth leads to a living hope of assured salvation (verses 3-5), which leads believers to rejoice even in the face of suffering as they anticipate the revealing of Jesus Christ (verses 6-7), whom they love and in whom they believe even though they have not seen Him, which leads to inexpressible joy as they anticipate faith's ultimate reward, salvation (verses 8-9), which the Hebrew prophets foretold (verses 10-12).[35]

A. The Origin of Salvation (1:3)

(3) Blessed be the God and Father of our Lord Jesus Christ, which according to his abundant mercy hath begotten us again unto a lively hope by the resurrection of Jesus Christ from the dead.

Verse 3. As we would expect from a Jewish author writing to a Jewish audience, Peter used the form of a common Jewish blessing, the Hebrew *berakah*, which began, "Blessed be God who . . ."[36] In this context,

First Peter

"blessed" means "praised." We are to praise God for the rich salvation He has provided.

This verse identifies God as the Father of our Lord Jesus Christ. As we noted in the discussion on verse 2, Peter—a devout Jewish monotheist—did not establish an idea of distinct persons who together compose the one God. Verse 3 not only identifies God as the Father of Jesus Christ, but also the Father as the God of Jesus Christ. The complete description is "the God and Father of our Lord Jesus Christ." The Greek phrase cannot be translated "God and the Father of our Lord Jesus Christ," which would eliminate the potentially troublesome idea that someone is the God of the Lord Jesus.

If God indeed did exist as more than one person, it would be difficult to understand how one of the persons could be a God to another. This notion would certainly imply inequality among the persons, not just in economic or functional subordination but in essential subordination.[37] It would be one thing for a person in such a Godhead to be the Father of another; it would be quite another thing for one person to be the God of another.

In view of the truth that Jesus is God Himself (II Peter 1:2), there must be a more satisfactory understanding of this reference to "the God and Father of our Lord Jesus Christ." This understanding focuses on the Incarnation. Contextually, we have been born again by "the resurrection of Jesus Christ from the dead." The work of the Atonement—the death, burial, and resurrection of Jesus Christ (I Corinthians 15:1-4; Isaiah 53)—requires the Incarnation, or the manifestation of God in human existence (I Timothy 3:16; John 1:14). In order to redeem us, it was necessary for Him to become one of us. (See

The Blessing of Salvation by Faith

Hebrews 2:14, 17-18; 4:15; Philippians 2:5-8; I Timothy 2:5-6.)

When Scripture declares God to be the Father of Jesus Christ, the focus is not on an eternal paternal-filial relationship between two persons, which requires speculation about the Son being "eternally begotten," but on the coming of the Holy Spirit upon the virgin Mary, miraculously causing her to conceive and give birth to the "Son of God" (Luke 1:35). The Son of God is made "of" (*ek*, which means "out of" or "from") a woman (Galatians 4:4). This does not mean, however, that the term "Son of God" as it relates to Jesus describes His human existence in isolation from His deity. He is one integrated person. Rather, "Son of God" describes God *as He is manifest in human existence*. In other words, just as Scripture never uses "Son of God" to describe His deity in isolation from His humanity (e.g., in a preincarnate state), so the term does not describe His humanity in isolation from His deity. We cannot fragment our Savior.

Since He was God in human existence, Jesus shared fully in the human experience, including the need to pray and to relate to God as His Father. (See Hebrews 5:7.) This relationship was real, not just a charade; it arose from the fullness and completeness of His authentic humanity. Otherwise Jesus would have been less than human. Precisely how this worked is a mystery to us, because the Incarnation is the greatest miracle ever to occur. But we certainly cannot explain it by attributing the relationship of the Father and Son to "eternal generation."[38]

Believers have been "begotten again" in accordance with the abundant mercy of God. The Greek *kata*, translated "according to," reveals the ground of the new birth:

it is the mercy of God. The abundant mercy of God is the favor He extends to the human race, even though we are completely and hopelessly undeserving of it. Peter perfectly agreed with Paul: salvation is by grace (*charis*, "a free gift") through faith; it is not on the basis of human merit. (See Ephesians 2:8-9.)

God has "begotten us again" (*anagenneas*). This is a reference to the new birth, which Jesus explained to Nicodemus. (See John 3:1-5.) Peter used the word again in verse 23. Since our first and natural birth identifies us with Adam in condemnation, it is necessary for us to experience a second and supernatural birth that identifies us with Jesus Christ in redemption. (See Romans 5:12-21; I Corinthians 15:22, 45-50.)

The new birth has produced in us a "living hope" (NKJV). Biblically, hope is not mere wishful thinking. It is assurance that arises from the promises of God. Life is inherent in this hope, in contrast to the spiritual death inherent in the vain hope of those who have no faith in Christ.

Gene Getz has pointed out that the measure of the New Testament church is its faith, hope, and love and that we can determine the strengths and weaknesses of an individual church by the mention or lack of mention of these virtues in the early verses of the letter to that church.[39] This certainly seems to be the case in Paul's letters.[40] I Peter also emphasizes the virtues of faith (1:5, 7, 9, 21; 5:9), hope (1:3, 13, 21; 3:15), and love (1:8, 22; 2:17; 3:8). Faith is trust in God regardless of the circumstances of life. Hope, as opposed to mere wishful thinking, is confidence that God will fulfill His promises. Love is the unconditional commitment to invest one's life in others. (See I Corinthians 13:4-8.)

The event that makes possible the new birth is "the resurrection of Jesus Christ from the dead." Had Jesus remained in the tomb, salvation would not have been possible. The gospel message is not complete with the death and burial of Christ. (See I Corinthians 15:1-4.) Believers are identified with Him not only in His death and burial but also in His resurrection. (See Romans 6:3-5; I Peter 3:21.) The death of Christ paid the penalty for the sins of the human race (Hebrews 9:12-15; 10:10-12, 19-21, 29; I John 1:7; 2:2); His resurrection imparts new life to those who believe on Him (I Corinthians 15:20-23; Colossians 2:11-13).

The resurrection of Jesus Christ from the dead was positive proof of His deity (Romans 1:4). Though there were others raised from the dead, Jesus was raised to die no more (Romans 6:9-10). He was the prototype of all who would eventually be raised from the dead to eternal life (I Corinthians 15:20). His resurrection from the dead was conclusive proof that He was who He claimed to be. (See Matthew 12:39-40.)

B. The End of Salvation (1:4)

(4) To an inheritance incorruptible, and undefiled, and that fadeth not away, reserved in heaven for you.

Verse 4. The living hope resulting from the new birth focuses on an inheritance that is incorruptible, undefiled, and unfading. This inheritance is reserved in heaven for believers.

We see the Jewish flavor of this letter in that the word

translated "inheritance" (*kleronomian*) is used in the Septuagint for the land God promised to Israel. (See Numbers 26:54, 56; 34:2; Joshua 11:23.) Under the old covenant, the promised inheritance was earthly; under the new covenant, the promised inheritance is heavenly. (See Hebrews 11:8-9, 16.)

That our heavenly inheritance is incorruptible means it cannot be destroyed. Peter used the same word (*aphtharton*) again in verse 23, when he declared that the Word of God—the seed by which we have been born again—is incorruptible. That it is undefiled means it is not negatively affected by evil. That it does not fade away means it is not negatively affected by time. Thus, the believer's inheritance is permanent and pure.

Blum points out that the "concept of inheritance is one of the major Bible themes and stresses family connection and gift."[41] (See 3:9; Galatians 3:18; Matthew 5:5; 19:29; 25:34.) In other words, the promise of an inheritance indicates that we are the children of God. We became His children by means of being "begotten . . . again" (verse 3), or by means of the new birth. (See verse 23; 2:2.) Since it is an inheritance, it is also a gift. That is, it is not something we earn or deserve. God gives it on the basis of family relations, not on the basis of performance.

This permanent, pure, and free inheritance is "reserved in heaven" for the believer. God Himself protects and watches over it. The perfect passive participle translated "reserved" (*teteremenen*) indicates that God is guarding this inheritance so that it is certain. For this reason, it cannot be destroyed or defiled and it cannot fade away. Verse 5 reveals the only condition attached to this inheritance: the faith of the believer.

As wonderful as the inheritance of the Promised Land was for ancient Israel, even it will pass away. (See II Peter 3:10-13.) Thus, as opposed to the inheritance of the new covenant, it is not "incorruptible."

C. The Keeping Power of Salvation (1:5)

(5) Who are kept by the power of God through faith unto salvation ready to be revealed in the last time.

Verse 5. On the basis of their faith, believers are kept by the power of God to the extent that they will certainly receive the ultimate reward of salvation.[42]

The word translated "kept" (*phrouroumenous*) "is a military term used to refer to a garrison within a city."[43] The idea is to be protected by being shielded. Philippians 4:7 uses the same word, where Paul declared that "the peace of God . . . will guard [*phrouroumenous*] your hearts and minds through Christ Jesus" (NKJV).

Just as God watches over the believers' inheritance to protect it from corruption, defilement, and the ravages of time (verse 4), so He guards believers by His power so that they will not lose their inheritance through any distraction, including the various trials they confront in life. (See 1:6-7; 2:20-21; 4:12.) The only condition upon which this protection depends is the believers' faith.

Though not stated, the implication is that if the believer abandons faith, he will lose the inheritance. This is apparently the issue that gave rise to the writing of this letter. It is essential that believers keep faith in the face of trials. Otherwise, they will lose their inheritance. (See

Hebrews 10:26-31, 35-39.) Regardless of the circumstances of life, it is essential to continue to trust in God. When there is no trust in Him, there is no basis upon which He can legitimately grant eternal life. (See John 3:16, 18; Hebrews 11:6; I John 5:1-5, 13.)

The inheritance in store for believers is "the salvation ready to be revealed in the last time." Though there is a sense in which we have already experienced salvation (Ephesians 2:8), we have not yet experienced the ultimate reward of salvation. The ultimate outworking of salvation will not be revealed until the "last time" (*eschaton*). This "last time" is the appearing of Jesus Christ. (See verses 7, 13.)

The biblical idea of salvation (*soter*) has to do with some kind of deliverance. The context defines the nature of the deliverance. I Peter defines faith's ultimate reward as "the salvation of your souls" (verse 9). At the appearing of Jesus Christ, believers will be finally and completely delivered from all of sin's consequences, including the "various trials" (verse 6, NKJV) they now experience.

D. The Trial of Faith (1:6-7)

(6) Wherein ye greatly rejoice, though now for a season, if need be, ye are in heaviness through manifold temptations: (7) that the trial of your faith, being much more precious than of gold that perisheth, though it be tried with fire, might be found unto praise and honour and glory at the appearing of Jesus Christ.

Verse 6. It seems best to understand "wherein" ("in this," NKJV) as referring back to the *eschaton*, the "last

The Blessing of Salvation by Faith

time," which will reveal the ultimate outworking of salvation. As believers confront the "manifold temptations" ("various trials," NKJV) that come their way, their grief is tempered by joy when they contemplate the temporary nature of the trials ("for a season") and the certainty of their final and complete deliverance (verse 9).

I Peter uses the same words for "various trials" (*poikilois peirasmois*) as does James.[44] (See James 1:2.) Both see trials as cause for rejoicing. James recommends rejoicing because of the positive benefits that testing develops in one's character (James 1:3-4). I Peter recommends rejoicing for the same reason (verse 7), but also in view of the ultimate salvation that will result from the faith that trials prove to be genuine.

The "various trials" are apparently persecutions as opposed to the ordinary trials of life. (See 2:19-23; 3:14-18; 4:12-19; 5:10.) We can expect ordinary trials to endure throughout our lifetimes; they are the result of living in an imperfect world among imperfect people. But the trials in view here are immediate and brief ("though now for a little while," NKJV). The word translated "heaviness" (*lypethentes*) is an aorist participle, which de-emphasizes the duration of the grief.[45] The trials are, however, necessary ("if need be").

Verse 7. Persecution for the sake of Christ proves the genuineness of one's faith (4:12-16). Those who have a mere profession of faith in Christ will not endure persecution; those who truly trust Him will continue to trust Him regardless of life's circumstances. The persecution that tries the believer's faith is like the fire that purifies gold by purging out the impurities. Even though purified gold lasts a very long time, it will eventually perish. (See

1:18; James 5:3.) Genuine faith is more valuable than gold; it will never perish.

The imagery of the righteous being tested by fire like precious metals underscores the Jewishness of this letter, for it is a common theme in the Hebrew Scriptures. (See Job 23:10; Psalm 12:6; Proverbs 17:3; Isaiah 43:2; Jeremiah 11:4.) The point is that persecution tends to purify motives.

Faith that endures persecution will be "found to praise, honor, and glory at the revelation of Jesus Christ" (NKJV). Those whose faith has proven genuine will bring praise, honor, and glory to the Lord Jesus when He is revealed. (See Revelation 4:9-11; Titus 2:13.) They will also partake in some way in the glory that will accompany Christ's revelation (4:13-14; 5:1). At least in part, this will be due to the glorification of the believer's human body, which will be transformed so as to be like "his glorious body" (Philippians 3:21; I John 3:2).

E. The Certainty of Faith's Reward (1:8-9)

(8) Whom having not seen, ye love; in whom, though now ye see him not, yet believing, ye rejoice with joy unspeakable and full of glory: (9) receiving the end of your faith, even the salvation of your souls.

Verse 8. The recipients of Peter's letter had never seen Jesus. This may have been due to their geographical removal from Israel or to their being second-generation believers. This fact enables us today to identify with them even more closely. Their faith proved that it is possible to

The Blessing of Salvation by Faith

love Jesus even without seeing Him. Jesus Himself indicated that there is a special blessing for those who "have not seen and yet have believed" (John 20:29, NKJV). Indeed, Jesus prayed not only for those who followed Him while He was on earth, but He also prayed for those who would believe in Him through the word of the original apostles. (See John 17:20.)

The joy that arises in the hearts of believers as they contemplate faith's ultimate reward is "inexpressible and full of glory" (NKJV). (See 4:13.) We cannot adequately communicate this joy with human words. It is glorious.

There is a close connection here between loving Jesus and believing in Him. John made the same connection. (See I John 5:1.) It is impossible to respond to Him in a fragmented way, since He Himself is not fragmented. We must accept Him for all that He is, or we do not accept Him at all. Thus, it is impossible to accept Him as Savior without accepting Him as Lord. Likewise, it is impossible to love Him without believing in Him or to genuinely believe in Him without loving Him. There is no biblical support for the idea of accepting Jesus as the supreme ethical teacher while rejecting the necessity of putting all one's trust in Him for salvation.

Verse 9. The "end" (*telos*) or consummation of faith is "the salvation of your souls." Biblically, salvation is deliverance. Here, it is the final, consummate deliverance from all of sin's consequences, both temporal and eternal.

By referring to the salvation of our "souls," I Peter does not establish the "soul/body" dichotomy of Greek philosophy. Rather, it uses "soul" in the Hebrew sense of "self" or "person."[46] The biblical promise of redemption includes the redemption of our bodies. (See I Corinthians

15:12-23, 35-54; Philippians 3:21; Romans 8:23; II Corinthians 5:1-4.) Thus, Christianity is squarely opposed to nonbiblical religions that view the body as an inherently evil nuisance which must be discarded before human beings can experience the ultimate state for which they were intended. Even in the case of our Lord Jesus Christ, it was His bodily resurrection from the dead that proved Him to be the Son of God (Romans 1:4).

The word translated "receiving" (*komizomenoi*) is a present participle, indicating that even now the believer's salvation is in the process of being realized.[47] That is, believers do not have to wait until the revelation of Jesus Christ to enjoy the benefits of salvation. Although they will not experience full and final deliverance until the end, in a very real sense believers are cut loose from sin's consequences even now. Though the material man awaits final redemption, the immaterial man already soars into heights of inexpressible, glorious joy (verse 8).

F. Salvation Foretold by Hebrew Prophets (1:10-12)

(10) Of which salvation the prophets have enquired and searched diligently, who prophesied of the grace that should come unto you: (11) searching what, or what manner of time the Spirit of Christ which was in them did signify, when it testified beforehand the sufferings of Christ, and the glory that should follow. (12) Unto whom it was revealed, that not unto themselves, but unto us they did minister the things, which are now reported unto you by them that have preached the gospel unto you with the Holy Ghost

sent down from heaven; which things the angels desire to look into.

Verses 10-11. The Old Testament prophets foretold the grace that New Testament believers experience. This "grace" is the gift of salvation. (See Acts 11:23; 13:43; 14:3; 15:11; 18:27; 20:24, 32.) I Peter does not specify which Hebrew prophets are in view, but the promise of a Messiah who would deliver the people of God is the premier theme of the Hebrew Scriptures.[48]

Even though the Hebrew prophets prophesied of the salvation the Messiah would bring, they did not fully comprehend the time frame in which this would occur and the relationship between the Messiah's sufferings and glorification (verses 11-12). Daniel is an example (Daniel 8:27; 12:8-9). (See also Luke 10:24.) Though they "inquired and searched carefully" (NKJV), the extent of their understanding was that the prophecies would not be fulfilled in their time (verse 12). (See Matthew 13:17.)

The prophets' inquiry is described by two Greek words: *ekzeteo* (translated "enquired") and *exeraunao* (translated "searched diligently"). *Ekzeteo* means "seeking out and searching." *Exeraunao* means "inquiring carefully." Josephus used *exeraunao* to describe the way military invaders conduct a search by inquiring from house to house. The Septuagint uses both of these words in Psalm 119:2 to describe those who seek the Lord in obedience.[49] The prophets' search was not casual curiosity. Although they did not fully comprehend what they wrote, they understood enough to sense the grand magnitude of this grace. Naturally, they would hope to experience this grace themselves, but that was not to be. (See Hebrews 11:39-40.)

The first question in the minds of the prophets had to do with the prophecies of the Messiah's sufferings and glories.[50] The second question was when these prophecies would be fulfilled.

The Hebrew Scriptures proclaim both that the Messiah would suffer and that following His sufferings He would experience various glories. (See Luke 24:25-26.) His sufferings included His rejection by His own people (John 1:11) and His betrayal by a friend (Matthew 26:47-50). But no doubt I Peter has in view His ultimate suffering as He satisfied righteous judgment against sin on Calvary's cross. (See Isaiah 53; I Peter 2:21-24.)

The glories foretold by the Hebrew prophets focused primarily on the millennial era, when Christ will rule all nations as David's greatest Son. (See Isaiah 11, especially verse 10; Luke 1:32-33; Amos 9:11-15.) There were glorious events during Christ's life on earth, such as His transfiguration (II Peter 1:17; Luke 9:31) and His resurrection (1:21), but they were precursors of His ultimate glory.

The Hebrew prophets did not, however, discern the gap of time between Christ's sufferings and glories. The extent of their knowledge was that the glories would follow the sufferings. The dispensation of the grace of God—the era of the church age during which Jews and Gentiles are fellow heirs and of the same body—was not revealed to the Hebrew prophets, but to the New Testament apostles and prophets. (See Ephesians 3:2-11.) So although the Hebrew prophets saw that the Messiah would suffer and enter into glories, they did not discern that the sufferings would occur in conjunction with His first coming and

The Blessing of Salvation by Faith

the glories in conjunction with His second coming. (See Revelation 19:11-16; 20:4-6, 11.)

Indeed, although the Hebrew prophets proclaimed a suffering Messiah, by the time Jesus walked on the earth, the Jewish people had come to focus almost exclusively on the prophecies of Israel's age of glory. Thus, when Jesus discussed His coming sufferings, even His followers did not understand. (See Matthew 16:21-23; John 2:19-22; Luke 18:31-34; 24:13-27, 32; Acts 1:6.)

I Peter assumes the inspiration of the Hebrew Scriptures by the Holy Spirit. The purpose here was not to prove this point, but the statement that "the Spirit of Christ which was in them . . . testified" indicates that the Hebrew prophets wrote and spoke by inspiration of the Spirit. Peter's second letter underscores the truth of divine inspiration: "For the prophecy came not in old time by the will of man: but holy men of God spake as they were moved by the Holy Ghost" (II Peter 1:21). Peter also expressed this belief during the selection of a replacement for Judas: "Men and brethren, this scripture must needs have been fulfilled, which the Holy Ghost by the mouth of David spake before concerning Judas, which was guide to them that took Jesus" (Acts 1:16). In this belief, Peter was in perfect agreement with Paul (II Timothy 3:16).

Grammatically, the term "Spirit of Christ" in verse 11 is a genitive of description. It describes the way the Holy Spirit testified about Christ.[51] In other words, "Spirit of Christ" here does not mean the Spirit *possessed by* Christ but the proclamation of the Holy Spirit *about* Christ. When we speak of the Spirit *possessed by* Christ, we have the Incarnation in view, for Christ (*Christos*) is simply the

Greek equivalent of the Hebrew *Messiach*, and the Messiah's identification is inseparably connected to the Incarnation. The Messiah is God *as He is manifested in human existence*. (See I Timothy 3:16; John 1:14; Galatians 4:4; Luke 1:35.) The Incarnation had not occurred when the Hebrew Scriptures were being written.

Verse 12. God revealed to the writers of the Hebrew Scriptures that their prophecies concerning the sufferings and glories of the Messiah would not be fulfilled in their day. Indeed, some four hundred years elapsed between the last written revelation in the Old Testament and the coming of the Messiah.

Since the inauguration of the church was yet future when the Messiah came (Matthew 16:18), and since the church could not exist apart from the grace resulting from the Messiah's ministry, the church did not exist during the days of the Hebrew prophets.[52] In the church, God does a new thing, which the faithful people of the Old Testament era were not privileged to enjoy. (See Hebrews 11:39-40; Galatians 3:19-25; Ephesians 2:11-22; 3:1-12; Colossians 2:14-17.)

However, the Hebrew prophets were serving the church ("unto us they did minister the things"). This statement underscores the importance of the Hebrew Scriptures to the church, even though the church was not established during the era of the Old Testament and even though the church is not under the old covenant, the law of Moses. (See I Corinthians 10:11; Romans 4:23-24; 15:4; I Corinthians 9:9-10; I Timothy 1:8.) The Hebrew Scriptures contain the prophecies concerning the coming Messiah and the new covenant, and they offer a rich storehouse of examples and principles to discover and

The Blessing of Salvation by Faith

apply to the New Testament church.

Those who preached the gospel during the first century proclaimed the fulfillment of the Old Testament prophecies concerning the Messiah and the grace (salvation) He brought. (See I Corinthians 15:3-4.) Those who preached did so by the unction of the same Holy Spirit who had originally inspired the prophecies. There is an implication that those today who are led by the Spirit in their preaching ministry will incorporate into their proclamation not only the New Testament but also the Old Testament.

Not only were the Hebrew prophets curious about the message of grace connected with the Messiah's coming, so are the angels. They desire to look into what is preached by those who minister under the direction of the Holy Spirit. They rejoice over a sinner's repentance (Luke 15:10). They observed Jesus' life on earth (I Timothy 3:16). In some way, Paul was a spectacle to angels (I Corinthians 4:9). Angels were involved in the first century in bringing together believers and seekers (Acts 8:26). Angels will rejoice over the work of redemption (Revelation 5:11-14).

The verb translated "to look into" (*parakypto*) means "to stoop over to look." It indicates a "willingness to exert or inconvenience oneself to obtain a better perspective."[53] It is in the present tense, which indicates a "continuous regard rather than a quick look."[54] But, like the Hebrew prophets, the angel cannot fully satisfy their curiosity. The Hebrew prophets could not satisfy their curiosity because the prophecies were not for their day. The angels cannot satisfy their curiosity because they cannot share in the joys of redemption.

First Peter

No doubt Peter wanted his readers to understand that if glories followed the sufferings of Christ, then likewise glories would follow their own sufferings. (See 1:7-8; 4:13; 5:1; Romans 8:18; Hebrews 2:10.)

III

Exhortations in View of Salvation
1:13-2:10

To this point, Peter's letter focuses on the salvation provided by Jesus Christ. From this point, it focuses on practical issues related to living the Christian life.

The Greek *dio*, translated "wherefore" ("therefore," NKJV) in verse 13, indicates that the following exhortations are based upon the salvation discussed in the immediately preceding verses. It would be pointless to call those who are not born again (verse 3) to hope, holiness, reverence, love, and spiritual growth.

A. Call to Hope (1:13)

(13) Wherefore gird up the loins of your mind, be sober, and hope to the end for the grace that is to be brought unto you at the revelation of Jesus Christ.

Verse 13. The imagery of "girding up" the "loins of the mind" comes from the clothing worn by men during the first century and still worn by many today. The long robes worn by men hindered quick and agile movements, so they would tuck the folds of the garment into their belt (or "girdle") to shorten its length and get it away from their feet and ankles. (See I Kings 18:46; Jeremiah 1:17; Luke 12:35.)

The idea behind the metaphor of girding up the loins

is to prepare for unhindered action. The NIV, with a translational philosophy of dynamic equivalence, renders the phrase, "Prepare your minds for action." C. E. B. Cranfield suggested translating it as "rolling up the shirtsleeves of your mind."[55]

It could be that Peter, a Jew writing to a Jewish audience, had the imagery of the Passover in view. The blood of the Passover lamb represented their redemption from Egyptian bondage (Exodus 12:7, 12-13); they were to eat the lamb with a belt on their waist, sandals on their feet, and a staff in their hand. They were to "eat it in haste," prepared to leave Egypt. (See Exodus 12:11.)

Christians have been redeemed "with the precious blood of Christ, as of a lamb without blemish and without spot" (1:19). The close proximity of this reminder with the admonition to gird up the loins of the mind suggests the Passover background of the passage, especially since the Israelites were preparing for an exodus that would lead them to the land of their inheritance. Likewise, believers are preparing for an exodus that will occur at the "revelation of Jesus Christ" and will result in the ultimate inheritance (1:4).[56]

Next, Christians are commanded to "be sober." The Greek word here (*nephontes*) describes literal abstinence from intoxicating drink, but it is also used metaphorically to describe self-controlled behavior as opposed to behavior influenced by external circumstances. Although the word seems to be used here in a figurative sense, for the figurative sense to be true the literal must also be true. In other words, if believers must abstain from being "intoxicated" by circumstances that would hinder them from making sound judgments, they must certainly

Exhortations in View of Salvation

abstain from drinking intoxicating beverages that would also render them incapable of thinking clearly. (For further discussion of alcoholic beverages, see the endnote.[57])

The way verse 13 is often translated suggests that it gives three commands: (1) gird up the loins of your mind; (2) be sober; (3) hope to the end for the grace that is to be brought to you at the revelation of Jesus Christ. Actually, the word translated "gird up" (*anazosamenoi*) and the word translated "be sober" (*nephontes*) are both participles. The only finite verb is *elpisate*, translated "hope" ("rest your hope," NKJV). The grammar indicates that the participial clauses "gird up the loins of your mind" (literally, "girding up the loins of your mind") and "be sober" (literally, "being sober") are subordinate to the main verb, "hope," and therefore express the same idea in figurative imagery. "Girding up the loins of your mind" and "being sober" are metaphors for "hope." They are another way of saying the same thing.

Thus, we could translate the verse as follows: "Therefore, girding up the loins of your mind, being sober, set your hope fully on the grace being brought to you at the revelation of Jesus Christ."[58] By girding up the loins of our mind and by being sober, we set our hope. Thus, verse 13 does not actually give three commands, but one. The command is to focus our hope on the grace ("salvation," see comments on verses 10-11) that will come to us when Jesus Christ is revealed. This is a reference to the final and ultimate expression of salvation that we will experience when we see Him (1:4-5, 7, 9; 4:13). It includes, but is not limited to, the glorification of the believer's body. (See comments on verse 7.)

Believers have many opportunities to be distracted

from the appearing of Jesus. These distractions may include the sufferings of those who find themselves at odds with the society around them. But we cannot allow suffering or other distractions to cause us to lose focus on our present identity as the elect children of God (verses 2-3, 23), for all such distractions are temporary. The appearing of Jesus Christ is certain; it is part of what the prophets of old foretold (verses 10-12). We must "rest [our] hope fully" on the final outworking of our salvation (NKJV).[59] We do so by preparing our minds and embracing a lifestyle of disciplined self-control.

B. Call to Holiness (1:14-16)

(14) As obedient children, not fashioning yourselves according to the former lusts in your ignorance: (15) but as he which hath called you is holy, so be ye holy in all manner of conversation; (16) because it is written, Be ye holy; for I am holy.

By "girding up the loins" of the mind and embracing sobriety as a way of life (verse 13), believers are behaving as "obedient children," rejecting their former evil desires and developing a lifestyle of holiness. This action is necessary in order to enjoy fellowship with God, for He is holy. (See Hebrews 12:14.)

Verse 14. Since believers are in a relationship with God characterized by being "begotten again" (verse 3) or "born again" (verse 23) and are now "newborn babes" (2:2), they are to behave as "obedient children." In the first century, people highly valued the obedience of children to their parents; indeed, both Roman and Jewish law required it.[60] The first readers of Peter's letter had exercised obedience in coming to Christ (verses 2, 22); now they were to extend that obedience to a lifestyle of consistent holiness.

The word *syschematizo*, found in the participial phrase translated "not fashioning yourselves" ("not conforming yourselves," NKJV), appears elsewhere in the New Testament only in Romans 12:2, where it is an imperative translated "be not conformed." The implication seems to be that those who "live in sensual lusts take up the likeness of those lusts into themselves, and are made, not as man was at first, after the likeness of God, but after the likeness of those lusts of the flesh which are not of the Father, but are of the world."[61]

The "former lusts" we are to avoid are those that characterize a life of "ignorance." This reference to "ignorance" leads some to think that Peter addressed the letter specifically to a Gentile audience, or at least to the Gentile members of the churches, on the basis that ignorance would not characterize the Jews, who received the Hebrew Scriptures. But Peter himself had previously identified unbelieving Jews as ignorant (Acts 3:17). So did Jesus (Matthew 15:1-9; 23) and Paul (Romans 9:30-32; 10:3; 11:7-10; I Timothy 1:13). The description of the "former lusts" and "ignorance" of the original readers of this letter and of their "aimless conduct received by tradition from [their] fathers" (1:18) does not demand a predominately Gentile audience.

Some commentators identify the audience as Gentile by distinguishing "moral ignorance," which supposedly characterized the Gentiles, from ignorance of Christ, which supposedly characterized Jews.[62] But if anything,

First Peter

the context seems to discuss ignorance of the Messiah, Jesus Christ, for Peter commanded his readers to rest their hope fully upon the grace to come to them at the revelation of Jesus Christ (verse 13). It seems certain that he gave this command to oppose a genuine temptation: the temptation to abandon Jesus Christ as the only source of their hope. The wrong response to their trials would have been to lose faith in Christ; this would certainly have returned them to their former "ignorance." (See II Peter 2:20-22.[63])

One may think that "lusts" (*epithymiais*) have to do uniquely with temptations to moral impurity. But the word simply means "strong desires," and it appears in a variety of contexts. Though it often refers to evil desires, it sometimes refers to good desires. (See Matthew 13:17; Luke 22:15; Philippians 1:23; I Thessalonians 2:17.) In Romans 7:7-8, it refers specifically to passions aroused by the law of Moses. (See also Romans 7:5.) Due to the weakness of the fallen human nature, one of the problems with the law of Moses was the tendency for people to trust in the law rather than to live by faith.[64] The present context contrasts "ignorance" and "former lusts" with the need to place one's hope fully and exclusively in Jesus Christ and the ultimate salvation He will bring. Thus, it seems reasonable to see these lusts as including the natural desire of fallen humanity to trust in something or someone other than Jesus Christ. This is indeed a way of ignorance, and it characterized unbelieving Jews as well as Gentiles.

Nothing in verse 14, then, demands an exclusively Gentile original audience for this letter.

Verses 15-16. Since the God who calls sinners to

repentance is holy, those who come to Him must be "holy in all [their] conduct" (NKJV). This command is supported by a reference to the law of Moses. (See Leviticus 11:44.) God's holiness and the subsequent demand for holiness from God's people is a common theme in the law. (See Exodus 3:5; 19:5-6; Leviticus 19:2; 20:7, 26; Psalm 99; Hosea 11:9.) The New Testament identifies Jesus as the "Holy One of Israel." (See Luke 4:24; John 6:69, in the critical text.) The call to holiness from the people of God is just as pronounced in the New Testament as in the Hebrew Scriptures. (See Hebrews 12:14; II Corinthians 7:1; Ephesians 1:4; Revelation 22:11.) I Peter addresses the theme here and in 2:5, 9; 3:5.

The biblical idea of holiness is essentially separation unto God and from all that is unlike Him. It includes purity and moral integrity.[65] Under the law of Moses, holiness included issues like the dietary law and the sabbaths (Leviticus 11:41-47; 19:2-3). These specific commands are not binding on New Testament believers (Colossians 2:16-17). They were uniquely pertinent to the ancient Hebrew people as an aspect of their separation from the idolaters about them, who had their own holy days and holy foods. The holiness demanded under the new covenant focuses on issues of character and ethics. We see this concept of holiness in I Peter in the commandments regarding honorable conduct among unbelievers (2:11-12), toward civil authority (2:13-17), of slaves toward masters (2:18-25), in marriage (3:1-7) and within the family of God (3:8-12).

Believers are the newly born children of God. Children are to emulate the character and behavior of their parents. Therefore, we are to resist temptations to return to our former desires and ignorance, and we are to conform to the holy character of our heavenly Father.

C. Call to Reverence (1:17-21)

(17) And if ye call on the Father, who without respect of persons judgeth according to every man's work, pass the time of your sojourning here in fear: (18) forasmuch as ye know that ye were not redeemed with corruptible things, as silver and gold, from your vain conversation received by tradition from your fathers; (19) but with the precious blood of Christ, as of a lamb without blemish and without spot: (20) who verily was foreordained before the foundation of the world, but was manifest in these last times for you, (21) who by him do believe in God, that raised him up from the dead, and gave him glory; that your faith and hope might be in God.

The call to holy conduct in the previous verses (15-16) flows into the call to "conduct yourselves . . . in fear" (NKJV) as a consequence of the impartiality of the holy God, who is not only our Father but also our Judge. The knowledge that gives rise to this kind of conduct is the awareness of the infinitely significant price paid for our redemption. In view of the value of the blood of Christ, it is only reasonable that those who have been redeemed by His blood should embrace a lifestyle which honors that redemption.

Verse 17. The first word in the verse (*kai*) ties what follows with what precedes. Believers are to "rest [their] hope fully upon the grace that is to be brought to [them] at the revelation of Jesus Christ" (verse 13, NKJV). They do so by girding up the loins of their minds and being sober. This is an obedient response that rejects conformity to the desires that characterized life before faith, which was a life of ignorance (verse 14). By taking these steps, believers embrace a lifestyle of holiness, a lifestyle necessary to be in fellowship with a holy God (verses 15-16).

It is characteristic of believers to "call on the Father." (See Joel 2:32; Acts 2:21; Romans 10:13.) There seems to be an echo here of the prayer that Christ instructed His disciples to pray. (See Matthew 6:8-14; Luke 11:1-4.) There is a similar reference in II Timothy 4:18. To call on God as Father acknowledges that we are His children, a point I Peter repeatedly makes. (See 1:3, 23; 2:2.) If we are obedient children (verse 14), we will emulate our Father's character insofar as it is possible for fallen human beings to pattern their character and conduct after that of the supreme Holy One.

The phrase "if ye call on the Father" does not imply any uncertainty as to whether believers actually call on the Father. It is a first-class condition (*ei* with the indicative mood in the "if" clause), which affirms the reality of the condition. The idea is "since you call on the Father." In other words, since believers claim the holy God as their Father, and since His judgment is completely impartial, they should order their entire lives in view of His impartiality. He will show no favoritism.

The Scriptures repeatedly state that God is "without respect of persons," or impartial.[66] A supernatural vision confirmed this truth to Peter (Acts 10:34).

In several of the references to God as impartial, the point is that He treats Jews and Gentiles alike. (See

Romans 2:10-12; 3:29-30; 10:12-13; Acts 10:34.) All must come to Him on the basis of faith, and all who come in faith are acceptable to Him. This reference supports the idea that I Peter was written to a primarily Jewish audience. There would be little need to remind Gentiles of God's impartiality. The Jewish milieu of salvation in the first century would have been a constant reminder to any believing Gentiles that it was on the basis of God's impartiality that they were saved. In general, reminders of God's impartiality (e.g., Galatians 3:28; Colossians 3:11) seem intended to convince Jews that their exclusiveness was wrong. Gentiles did not so much need assurance that God could love them; they seem to have had a stubborn ability to believe that God would not turn them away.[67] Instead, the Jews needed to be reminded that the love of God was without condition, ethnic or otherwise.

The statement about God's impartiality, then, seems to be a reminder to a Jewish audience that they will have no special privileges when they stand before their Father to receive His judgment. The same is true, of course, for Gentiles.

In John 5:22-23, Jesus said, "For the Father judges no one, but has committed all judgment to the Son, that all should honor the Son just as they honor the Father. He who does not honor the Son does not honor the Father who sent Him" (NKJV). There is no contradiction between Jesus' statement that "the Father judges no one" and Peter's statement that "the Father . . . judges according to each one's work" (NKJV).

The mystery of the Incarnation is in view here (I Timothy 3:16). Jesus Christ Himself is fully God (Colossians 2:9; John 5:18), but He is God manifest in an authentic and complete human existence. Whenever the Bible speaks of "the Son" and of "Jesus Christ," it refers to the Incarnation. Romans 2:16 declares that "God will judge the secrets of men by Jesus Christ" (NKJV). God has determined to perform judgment by means of the Incarnation. At the Great White Throne, people will not stand before an invisible Spirit but before the visible manifestation of God, now in glorified humanity. (See Revelation 20:11 and comments on I Peter 1:2-3.) (For further discussion of the Incarnation, see the endnote.[68])

Properly speaking, "Father" describes God above and beyond the Incarnation, invisible and transcendent. (See John 16:10.) But Jesus is in some way the Father; He is the Father made known in human existence. (See Isaiah 9:6; John 1:18; I John 2:23-24; 3:1-2.) The revelation of Jesus Christ (I Peter 1:7, 13) is the revelation of the Father Himself (I John 2:28; 3:1-2).

God will judge believers on the basis of their work. This judgment will not be to determine salvation; believers are saved. Rather, it is a judgment to determine rewards. (See I Corinthians 3:12-15; II Corinthians 5:10; Romans 14:10; Colossians 3:24-25; II Timothy 4:8; Revelation 22:12.)

The word translated "work" (*ergon*) is singular, as it is consistently in all such contexts. It is not so much that believers will be judged for their works, but that "God judges according to every man's work as a whole, according to the whole scope and meaning of his life as issuing from the one governing principle, whether faith or selfishness."[69]

The translation "pass the time of your sojourning here in fear" (KJV) may obscure the connection between this verse and verse 15. The word translated "pass" (*anastraphete*) corresponds to the word translated "conversation" (*anastrophe*, which means "conduct") in verse 15. The translation offered by the NKJV is helpful to show the connection: "conduct yourselves throughout the time of your stay here in fear." In other words, the conduct to which verse 17 calls believers is the holy conduct of verse 15.

The word translated "sojourning" appears again in noun form in 2:11. It correlates with the idea in verse 1 of the readers being "strangers" (KJV) or "pilgrims" (NKJV). This word again underscores the theme of Jewish dispersion among the Gentiles. (See 2:12.) There is a larger sense, of course, in which all believers, Jewish and Gentile, are sojourners in this earth. They are aliens in a strange country. (See comments on verse 1.)

The "fear" to which believers are called is not cowardly fear or stark terror. I Peter has already pointed out that believers live in peace (verse 2.) (See also 2:17; 3:2, 15.)[70] This fear, often described as "reverential awe," involves the manner in which God's children know that whatever they "think or do is subject to the scrutiny of God's penetrating holiness and love."[71] This fear is "neither dread nor anxiety; rather, it is the healthy response of a human being before an altogether different kind of being, God, and is a sign of spiritual health and gratitude."[72]

Verse 18. The infinite value of Christ's death demonstrates the reasonableness of Peter's call to a holy, reverent lifestyle. Peter based his appeal on "the holiness and justice of God with the added thought of the high cost of redemption."[73] In view of the supreme sacrifice Christ made to redeem us, no sacrifice should be too great for us to make for Him.

Redemption is a metaphor based on the commerce of the times. Slaves could be set free from their masters by payment of a ransom, a sum of money (i.e., "silver and gold"). We should not press any biblical metaphor to every detail; it is a literary device to communicate a general theme or idea. The idea of the redemption metaphor is that people are slaves to sin, but Christ has done what is necessary to free them from that bondage. The redemption motif does not specify to whom the redemption price was paid.[74]

The word used in various forms to describe redemption is *lutron*, which was the ransom money paid for the release of slaves in ancient Rome. Jesus declared that He came to "give His life a ransom [*lutron*] for many" (Matthew 20:28; Mark 10:45). Paul affirmed that Christ "gave Himself a ransom for all" (I Timothy 2:6) and redeemed "us from all iniquity" (Titus 2:14). The disappointed disciples on the road to Emmaus told Jesus—whom they did not recognize—that they had hoped Christ would have "redeemed Israel" (Luke 24:21). We see a related idea in I Corinthians 6:20 and II Peter 2:1, where a form of the word *agora* ("marketplace") describes how the Lord has purchased believers.

All of this discussion reflects the prophecy of Isaiah: "You shall be redeemed without money" (Isaiah 52:3, NKJV). The Old Testament concept of redemption is built around the word *goel*, which describes a person who redeemed a relative. Under the law of Moses, a person or his inheritance could be redeemed by a relative. (See Leviticus 25:25, 48; Galatians 4:5; Ephesians 1:7, 11, 14.) The law required the redeemer to be a relative. (See Leviticus 25:48-49; Ruth 3:12-13; Galatians 4:4-5; Hebrews 2:14-15.) The relative had to be capable of redeeming without marring his own inheritance. (See Ruth 4:4-6; Jeremiah 50:34; John 10:11, 18.) Finally, the redeeming relative had to pay the full price that the law demanded. (See Leviticus 25:27; Galatians 3:13; I Peter 1:18-19.)[75]

The law of Moses in many ways prefigures the coming Messiah and His ministry. (See Hebrews 10:1; Colossians 2:16-17.) One area where Jesus fulfilled the law (Matthew 5:17-18) was by becoming our redeeming relative ("kinsman redeemer," KJV). In the Incarnation, He became one of us, thus fulfilling the requirement of being a relative. (See Galatians 4:4; Hebrews 2:14-15, 17.) By the redemption, He has restored to us an inheritance. (See Ephesians 1:7, 11, 14; I Peter 1:4.) For Christ to redeem us does not endanger His own inheritance. (See Romans 8:17.) He paid in full the price demanded for our redemption. (See Galatians 3:13; I Peter 1:18-19; Hebrews 9:11-15, 22; 10:10-14.)

The redemption that believers enjoy was not made possible by corruptible silver and gold. Silver and gold were used to redeem slaves in the marketplace, but the corruptible nature of the redemption price shows the imperfect nature of their redemption. That is, slaves were set free physically, but not spiritually. Their redemption affected only their corruptible existence: the human body. (See I Corinthians 15:44, 53.) The incorruptible price that Jesus Christ paid provides an incorruptible inheritance (verse 4).

I Peter is not the only place where Peter declared silver and gold to be powerless to procure spiritual benefit. (See Acts 3:6; 8:20.) In view of his role as the apostle to the Jews (Galatians 2:7-8), Peter's intent in these negative references to silver and gold may have been to contrast the focus of the old covenant with the focus of the new covenant. Wealth was central to the establishment of the old covenant (Deuteronomy 8:18). Since the covenant included promises of financial prosperity (Deuteronomy 28), it could not be separated from silver and gold. Indeed, people were redeemed by silver and gold. (See Leviticus 25:25-27, 47-52.) But the new covenant has no materialistic focus; it focuses rather on the atoning work of Christ, which provides a redemption and inheritance far surpassing that of the old covenant.

When viewed from the perspective of the Hebrew Scriptures, Peter's use of silver and gold in the context of redemption further suggests the original Jewish audience of this letter.

Believers are redeemed from their "aimless conduct received by tradition from [their] fathers" (NKJV). Some think this statement indicates that Peter wrote the book to a Gentile audience since he would not characterize Hebrew heritage as vain or aimless.[76] The reference here could be to paganism, but it could also be to Judaism.[77] (See Galatians 1:13-14; Philippians 3:4-9.) The ultimate aimless life is the life that is not lived by faith in God. Many of the Jewish people in the first century perpetuated their heritage of traditions, but without faith. (See Romans 9:30-33; 10:1-3.) Christ has redeemed believers from such aimless conduct. The central element of the new covenant is not tradition, but faith.

Verse 19. The redemption price that Christ paid is His "precious blood." The word translated "precious" means "costly." In Scripture, to speak of the blood of someone is to speak of his death. (See Psalm 115:16; Matthew

23:35.) "Blood" and "death" are often used as virtual synonyms.[78] It certainly is the blood of Christ that has redeemed us, but it is His blood as shed in His death.

Just as the redemption motif finds its roots in the Hebrew Scriptures, so does the picture of Christ as "a lamb without blemish and without spot." The analogy is obviously to the Passover lamb. (See Exodus 12:5; Leviticus 22:19-21.) Early in the ministry of Jesus, John the Baptist identified Him as the Lamb of God. (See John 1:29, 36.) Paul declared that "Christ, our Passover, was sacrificed for us" (I Corinthians 5:7, NKJV). An angel directed Philip to minister to an Ethiopian eunuch who was reading from Isaiah 53, including these words: "He was led as a sheep to the slaughter; and like a lamb silent before its shearer, so He opened not His mouth" (Acts 8:32, NKJV). Beginning at this passage of Scripture, Philip preached Jesus to the eunuch (Acts 8:35). Jesus is characterized in Revelation 5:6 as "a Lamb as though it had been slain" (NKJV, see also verse 12) and in Revelation 13:8 as "the Lamb slain from the foundation of the world" (NKJV).

To say that Christ is "without blemish and without spot" means that He is sinless. (See Hebrews 4:15.) As the last Adam (I Corinthians 15:45), Jesus was the perfect, flawless human being. He was so human as to be tempted, but so fully led by the Holy Spirit as to resist all temptation (Matthew 4:1-11).

As sinners, human beings deserve death. (See Romans 6:23.) Since Jesus Christ was a human being who had no sin, He could die in our place, fully satisfying the righteous judgment of God against sin. His death paid the price to redeem us from the consequences of our sins

Exhortations in View of Salvation

and to restore our inheritance to us.

Verse 20. The coming of Christ to provide redemption was "foreordained before the foundation of the world." The word *prognosis*, which appears in verse 2, translated "foreknowledge," appears here in the form of a participle. It is commonly translated "foreordained" but is sometimes rendered "predestined" (NEB) or "chosen" (NIV). Although the word technically means simply "to know beforehand," its translation as "foreordained," which implies some kind of predestination, is justified on the basis that "the foreknowledge of God implies the exercise of his will."[79] It is, however, a theological rather than a literal translation. Peter's second letter uses a form of *prognosis* to indicate human foreknowledge. (See II Peter 3:17.) There is, of course, no idea of predestination when the word is used in a purely human context.

It is true, however, that when God knows something in advance, what He knows will in fact come to pass.[80] If He is the only one involved in bringing something to pass, we can say that His foreknowledge equals predestination. But if human beings are involved in any way in bringing something to pass, and if God has granted human beings genuine freedom of choice, foreknowledge retains its simple meaning of knowing something in advance.[81]

For example, to say that believers are "elect according to the foreknowledge of God the Father" (verse 2) means that on the basis of His foreknowledge as to how individuals will exercise their freedom of choice, God has elected to save those He knows will come to Him. But to say that Christ "was foreordained [foreknown] before the foundation of the world" indicates something beyond the foreknowledge associated with human choices, for God

75

alone was involved in the decision to provide redemption.

Here is a literal translation of this verse: "having been foreknown before the foundation of the world, but manifested in the last of the times for you." The word translated "having been foreknown" (*proegnosmenou*) is in apposition to "Christ" in verse 19. That is, it is Christ who was foreknown before the foundation of the world. The point is not simply that God knew from all eternity that "Jesus Christ should come into the world, but that he should fulfill a certain role, the role intimated already in v 19."[82]

The focus of this verse is the Incarnation, when God was manifest in the flesh, not so much on the preexistence of the one who was incarnate. Jesus certainly did preexist the Incarnation; He is God Himself. (See Isaiah 9:6; John 1:1.) But the point here is that God planned the redemptive work of the Messiah even before He created the heavens and the earth. As Grudem has pointed out, "it is *as a suffering saviour* that God 'foreknew' or thought of the Son before the foundation of the world."[83]

One cannot use this verse to teach that Jesus is eternally a second person in the Godhead. If this were Peter's point, the statement "He indeed was foreordained before the foundation of the world" (NKJV) would be inappropriate, for the following reasons:

1. The verse refers to the redemptive work associated with the Incarnation, not the Messiah's preexistence.

2. What was "foreordained" or foreknown was not His eternal state but His redemptive work.

3. If Jesus did exist throughout eternity as a second person in the Godhead, the verse would not say that God the Father, as the first person in the Godhead, foreknew

Exhortations in View of Salvation

Him, for the second person's existence would be completely concurrent with the first person's existence. In other words, there would never be a point at which one existed and the other did not, so it would be a contradiction in terms to speak of one person's having foreknowledge of the other in any sense. It would be just as problematic to say that one person had foreknowledge of the actions of another person, or predestined the actions of another person, for if both persons are equally God, both would have participated fully in the plans for redemption. One would not be the initiator of the plan and the other the executor. That would imply a fragmentation or division within God that is incompatible with the scriptural emphasis on His wholeness and oneness. As Frank Stagg pointed out, "The oneness of God as a single, integral person is not to be compromised as pagans did with Baal and other gods; nor is it to be shattered by splitting God up into 'three persons of the Godhead.'"[84] John did not declare the Word to be the second person in the Godhead; he declared the Word to be God (John 1:1).

"The foundation of the world" means "the creation of the world."[85] (See Matthew 25:34; Luke 11:50; John 17:24; Ephesians 1:4; Hebrews 4:3; 9:26; Revelation 13:8; 17:8.) The word translated "foundation" (from *kataballo*) means literally "to throw down," but it is used idiomatically of sowing seed or laying the foundation of a building.[86] Here it describes the creation of the world as having been completed.

Here is the biblical answer to those who suggest it was unjust of God to create human beings if He knew in advance they would sin. Since God knows all things, He certainly knew what Adam and Eve would do, but He cannot be faulted. Since God knew they would fail even though He equipped them and commanded them to resist temptation, He provided for their redemption even before He created them. The only way anyone might fault God would be if He knew in advance that people would sin and created them anyway but with no provision for redemption.

If God had created humans without the ability to fail, we would have to redefine human existence. Without complete freedom of choice, people would be animals, robots, or puppets. There is certainly a risk in having freedom of choice, but in Christ God made every provision for humanity to choose freely to come to Him.

Though God planned the redemptive work of Christ even before He created the world, Christ was not manifest until "these last times." The present age is "these last times"; the second coming of Christ will usher in "the last time."[87]

Christ's being "manifest" refers specifically to the Incarnation, wherein "God was manifest in the flesh" (I Timothy 3:16). (See also John 1:14; I John 3:5.) God took on genuine human nature. (See Philippians 2:5-8; Hebrews 2:14, 17.) By virtue of His identification with us Christ was able to redeem us, dying on the cross in our place.

This manifestation occurred "in these last times," indicating that there was no comparable manifestation of Christ prior to these times. Some have suggested that various appearances of the "angel of the LORD" in the Old Testament era were manifestations of the preincarnate Christ. But when the New Testament speaks of the manifestation of God, it does so with exclusive reference to the Incarnation.

Exhortations in View of Salvation

Throughout the Hebrew Scriptures, the invisible God used appearances discernible to human senses in His communication with people, but none of them were a permanent, incarnational manifestation. Theologians often use word *theophany* to describe these appearances. These appearances of the invisible God were varied. Some were discerned by the human sense of hearing (Genesis 3:8). Some were discerned by the human sense of sight (Exodus 13:21). Some had the appearance of a human being (Genesis 18:2). Some had the appearance of a fiery flame (Exodus 3:2). Some had the appearance of a cloud (Exodus 13:21). In some cases, the people of God had visions (Isaiah 6:1). In visions, one does not see a literal reality, but a representation of a literal reality. These manifestations explain how various persons could testify to having seen God, when Scripture declares that He is invisible and that He cannot be seen. (See John 1:18; Colossians 1:15; I Timothy 1:17; Hebrews 11:27.)

Jacob said he saw God "face to face" (Genesis 32:30), but Hosea indicated that Jacob's struggle was actually with an angel (Hosea 12:4). Seeing God "face to face" means something other than physically confronting God. The Lord spoke to Moses "face to face" (Exodus 33:11; Deuteronomy 34:10), but when Moses asked to see God's glory, God replied, "You cannot see My face; for no man shall see Me, and live" (Exodus 33:20, NKJV). When Moses pleaded with God to forgive the people of Israel, he said the Egyptians had heard that the people of Israel saw the Lord "face to face" (Numbers 14:14). What Moses meant was that the Lord went before Israel in a pillar of cloud by day and in a pillar of fire by night (Numbers 14:14). Moses declared to the people of Israel that the Lord talked with them "face to face" on the mountain in the giving of the law (Deuteronomy 5:4). (See also Ezekiel 20:35-36.)

We must understand the phrase "face to face" (Hebrew, *paniym 'el-paniym*) according to the idiomatic use of "face" in the Hebrew language. When used of God, and often of people, places or things, "face" signified "presence." For example, in Genesis 3:8, *paniym* is translated "presence," in the statement, "Adam and his wife hid themselves from the presence of the LORD God." It is also translated "presence" in Genesis 4:16, where Cain "went out from the presence of the LORD." *Paniym* is translated "before" in many cases to indicate the presence of God. (See Genesis 6:11, 13; 7:1; 10:9.) Hagar fled from the "face" (*paniym*) of Sarah (Genesis 16:6). Obviously, she fled from her presence.

We should not understand "face to face" in the Hebrew Scriptures to mean people had direct, visible encounters with God. At most, it means they encountered a visible representation of the invisible God. At least, it means they were in the presence of God.

As wonderful as all of these Old Testament experiences were, they pale in comparison with the manifestation of God in Christ in "these last times." Jesus Christ is not merely a theophany. He is not a temporary appearance, which may go through a metamorphosis. In the Incarnation, God permanently added genuine, authentic, and complete human existence to His existence as God. Now, to see Jesus is to see God. (See John 12:45; 14:7-9; Colossians 1:15; II Corinthians 4:4; Hebrews 1:3.) To believe on Jesus is to believe on God (John 12:45). To acknowledge the Son is to acknowledge the Father (I John

2:23). To abide in the Son is to abide in the Father (I John 2:24). To know Jesus is to know the Father (John 8:19).

Those who saw Jesus as He walked on this earth did not see the essence of the divine nature; they saw His human existence. But the human being they saw was nevertheless God manifest in the flesh, "manifest in these last times" to provide redemption for the human race with His "precious blood."

Peter wrote that Christ was manifest "for you." God did not come among us with an impersonal, generic interest in "humanity." He came for individuals, like those to whom this letter was originally written, and like those of us who read this letter today.

Verse 21. Through Jesus Christ we believe in God. It is impossible to reject Christ and to believe in God. Since the Incarnation (verse 20), knowing and believing in God is bound up with knowing and believing in Jesus Christ, God manifest in the flesh. (See John 8:19; 14:1, 6; I John 2:23.) Elsewhere, Peter indicated that faith comes through Jesus Christ (Acts 3:16). It is the Son who reveals the Father (John 1:18). Not only do we believe in God through Christ, but "God . . . has reconciled us to Himself through Jesus Christ" (II Corinthians 5:18, NKJV). "God was in Christ reconciling the world to Himself" (II Corinthians 5:19, NKJV).

These statements underscore the mediatorial ministry of Jesus. "For there is one God and one Mediator between God and men, the Man Christ Jesus" (I Timothy 2:5, NKJV). The Incarnation mediates God to humans and humans to God. God is the unique Being existing in the category of deity. Genesis 1:1 establishes the radical distinction between the Creator and the created. Humans could not span the vast gap between God and humanity; humans could not attain to deity. But in the marvelous mystery of the Incarnation, God spanned the gap by becoming one of us. Since He has become one of us, we can identify with Him, communicate with Him, and believe in Him. And by believing in Him, we believe in God.

This is not to say that it was impossible for people to believe in God before Christ came. Clearly, people of faith came to God before the Incarnation. (See Hebrews 11.) But though they were justified by faith, there was a dimension of blessing they never enjoyed. (See Hebrews 11:39-40.) The ultimate revelation of God, and thus the ultimate intimacy that people could have with God, awaited the Incarnation. (See John 1:18; Acts 2:17.)

God raised Jesus from the dead and gave Him glory. For Peter and all the apostles, the resurrection of Christ was central to the gospel message.[88] It was His resurrection from the dead that Christ offered as a sign of the genuineness of His person and mission. (See Matthew 12:38-40; 16:4.) The resurrection was a divine declaration of the deity of Christ (Romans 1:4).

Elsewhere, the Bible says the resurrection was accomplished by the Holy Spirit (Romans 1:4; 8:11) and by Jesus Himself (John 2:19-21). There is no contradiction between these statements and the idea that Jesus was raised by God the Father (Galatians 1:1). God is Spirit (John 4:24), and Jesus is God manifest in the flesh.

In conjunction with the resurrection, God gave Jesus glory. Ordinarily, the Bible says Jesus was "glorified" in conjunction with His resurrection. (See Acts 3:13, 15; John 7:39; 12:16, 23.) It also calls His resurrection body

His "glorious" body (Philippians 3:21). Jesus Himself indicated that following His suffering He would enter "into his glory" (Luke 24:26). Entering into glory here is synonymous with being raised from the dead (Luke 24:46). Michaels pointed out that the phrase "gave him glory" defines "the significance of 'raised him from the dead.' The 'glory' (i.e., the vindication, or demonstration of divine favor) given to Jesus at his resurrection is the glory they are waiting to see revealed (4:13; 5:1, 4) even as they suffer ridicule for the sake of his name (4:14)."[89]

We should note that the word translated "glory" (*doxan*) is singular in verse 21 and plural (*doxas*) in verse 11 (even though the KJV translates it as singular in verse 11). Although the resurrection of Jesus is certainly a glorious event, it does not exhaust the glories into which He will enter. (See comments on verse 11; see also Philippians 2:9-11.)

For God to give Jesus glory does not suggest a radical distinction between Jesus and God. Jesus is God manifest in the flesh. All statements like this in Scripture underscore the genuineness and fullness of the Incarnation; indeed, they would not be possible apart from the Incarnation. In John 17:5, Jesus prayed, "And now, O Father, glorify Me together with Yourself, with the glory which I had with You before the world was" (NKJV). Some may think that such a prayer indicates Jesus' existence as a person distinct from the Father prior to the Incarnation, but even this prayer arose from the Incarnation (Hebrews 5:7). The Incarnation did not pre-exist the womb of Mary, so this prayer cannot refer to some preincarnate state of existence identical to Jesus' identity when He offered this prayer.

In other words, Jesus was both God and man in the Incarnation, but He was not God and man prior to the Incarnation. Before the Incarnation, He was God alone. In the Incarnation, Jesus was one integrated person who was at once both God and man. Once God added an authentic human nature to His deity, the divine nature and human nature could not be separated. They could not function independently of one another, or the Incarnation could not be real. Thus, when Jesus prayed in John 17:5, He prayed as a man who was simultaneously God. The prayer indicated the genuineness of His humanity (Hebrews 5:7). Somehow, in the miracle of the Incarnation, Jesus limited Himself to the experiences, knowledge, and ministry of a man completely yielded to and anointed by the Holy Spirit. (See Mark 13:32; Luke 2:52; 4:16-18; John 5:19-20, 30; 14:12; Philippians 2:5-8; Hebrews 2:14, 17-18; 4:15.)

Since the identity of Jesus included His human nature, since He could not disregard His humanity any more than He could His deity, and since His prayers arose from His humanity, the glory He had with the Father "before the world was" cannot mean the state in which He actually existed before the world was and thus before the Incarnation. His existence before creation was not the same as His existence when He uttered this prayer; it did not include the full-orbed humanity He assumed in the Incarnation.

We should understand the glory that Jesus had with the Father "before the world was" in the same sense as believers being chosen before the foundation of the world (Ephesians 1:4), even though they did not exist at that time. God "calls those things which do not exist as though they

Exhortations in View of Salvation

did" (Romans 4:17, NKJV). If the incarnate Christ could be "foreordained" (foreknown) by God before the foundation of the world (verse 20) even though the Incarnation had not yet occurred, He could at the same time have glory with the Father. If the Lamb, the incarnate God, could be "slain from the foundation of the world" (Revelation 13:8), even though the crucifixion had not yet occurred in time, He could have glory with the Father from before the world was without having concurrent existence as a person distinct from the Father. "What was foreknown to and ordained by God is spoken of as having taken place."[90]

The phrase "that your faith and hope might be in God" indicates the purpose of the resurrection.[91] Faith, hope, and love are common themes in the Epistles. (See comments on verse 3.) The reference to hope here forms the closing bracket on the section that begins with a call to hope in verse 13. To have faith in God is to trust Him. To place one's hope in God is to have the assurance that He will keep His promises.

The final phrase of the verse points out clearly that to be valid, faith must have God as its object. Some have misunderstood faith to be a force in and of itself. Some have even suggested that we must have "faith in our faith." This idea is as meaningless as suggesting that we should "trust in trust." In this view, the word "faith" has lost its meaning. If we do not trust in God, our faith is misplaced and it will not be rewarded.

Likewise, hope that is not in God is merely empty, wishful thinking. To be valid, hope must have God as its object.

Our faith and hope in God is caused and made legitimate by the resurrection of Jesus Christ. If God has protected the integrity of His promises in the face of

His greatest challenge—the rejection of Jesus Christ—we can be sure He will keep all other promises He has made. (See Romans 8:32; II Corinthians 1:20; I Peter 1:11.)

D. Call to Love (1:22-25)

(22) Seeing ye have purified your souls in obeying the truth through the Spirit unto unfeigned love of the brethren, see that ye love one another with a pure heart fervently: (23) being born again, not of corruptible seed, but of incorruptible, by the word of God, which liveth and abideth for ever. (24) For all flesh is as grass, and all the glory of man as the flower of grass. The grass withereth, and the flower thereof falleth away: (25) but the word of the Lord endureth for ever. And this is the word which by the gospel is preached unto you.

I Peter has previously called the readers to hope (1:13), to holiness (1:14-16), and to reverence (1:17-21). Here it calls them to love. It bases the call to love upon the new birth. Believers are now members of a new family, and it is appropriate for the members of this family to love one another.

The new birth occurs through the influence of the incorruptible and permanent Word of God, which Peter connected with the gospel message.

In order to emphasize the permanence of the Word of God, Peter quoted a variation of the Septuagint.

Verse 22. The purification of the soul is connected with sincere love for one's brothers (and, of course, sisters) in Christ. That is, sincere love is possible only when the soul is purified.

This emphasis on love complements the treatment of the other two enduring virtues: faith and hope. (See verse 21 and comments on verse 3.) Where genuine and mature Christianity exists, it is characterized by faith, hope, and love.

Grudem points out that the purification in view "could refer to initial conversion as a completed event in the past with continuing effects," but he considers more persuasive the "arguments in favour of the view that Peter has post-conversion growth in moral purity in mind."[92] These arguments include the following: (1) obedience "never clearly means initial saving faith"; (2) the previous references to obedience in verses 2 and 14 speak of conduct as opposed to initial salvation; (3) figurative references to purification elsewhere refer to moral cleansing subsequent to conversion; (4) the context of the call to obedience is the call to holiness in verse 15; and (5) the reference here to purification as something the readers have themselves done conflicts with the consistent New Testament witness that "Christians are never . . . said to be active agents in God's initial cleansing of their souls at conversion" whereas they are said to be "active in the progressive work of sanctification."[93]

There seems to be good reason, however, to understand the purification in this verse as occurring in conjunction with initial salvation.

First, the New Testament does connect obedience to initial saving faith. In Hebrew thought, one could not separate faith from behavioral response. (See Hebrews 11.) In a very real sense, to believe is to obey, and to obey is

First Peter

to believe. The Western mindset may allow us to think that it is theoretically possible for a person to believe without obeying, or to obey without believing, but such an idea was foreign to the Hebrew audience to which much of Scripture was addressed. (See James's letter, which was apparently addressed to an audience much like that of I Peter [James 1:1; I Peter 1:1].) Western anthropology tends to fragment the human being in a dualistic way; biblical anthropology had a much more holistic view.

For example, Jesus indicated that people would receive the Holy Spirit based on faith in Him (John 7:37-39). Peter, however, said that the Holy Spirit was "given to them that obey him" (Acts 5:32). Indeed, the first obedient response to the hearing of the gospel is to place one's faith in Christ. Romans 1:5 and 16:26 discuss the "obedience which springs from faith."[94]

It is true that the New Testament sometimes speaks of obedience with reference to the obedient lifestyle of a believer growing toward maturity. (See Romans 6:16, II Corinthians 7:15; 10:6; Philemon 21; I Peter 1:14.) But other references to obedience have to do with the initial salvation experience. In addition to Romans 1:5 and 16:26, Romans 15:18 refers to the initial obedient faith response of Gentiles. II Thessalonians 1:8 equates knowing God to obeying the gospel. It pronounces the vengeance of God on those who neither know Him nor obey the gospel, apparently referring to those who have never been saved.

Second, though the reference to obedience in verse 14 is to conduct, the reference to obedience in verse 2 seems to be to the initial faith response to the gospel message. (See comments on verse 2.) If that is not the meaning of obedience in verse 2, we are left with a discussion of salvation apart from faith. Moreover, if we separate faith from obedience, then verse 2 promises the cleansing effects of Christ's blood on the basis of obedience rather than on the basis of faith. This would be an unbiblical fragmentation of the elements leading to salvation. (See Ephesians 2:8-9.) Context is a powerful determinant of the meaning of any word, but immediate context takes precedence over more remote contexts.

Third, though figurative references to purification elsewhere refer to moral cleansing subsequent to conversion (James 4:8; I John 3:3), that need not be the case here. Context determines meaning. If the contexts of this verse, James 4:8, and I John 3:3 were the same, obedience would have the same meaning in each case. But neither the grammar nor the context of this verse require the meaning of "progressive moral cleansing."

Fourth, though Grudem suggests that the context of the call to obedience is the call to holiness in verse 15, the more immediate context is verse 23, which is grammatically still in the same sentence as this reference to obedience. Thus, grammatically and contextually, the reference in verse 23 to being born again informs the meaning of the purification of verse 22. That is, when believers obey the gospel, they are born again and thus purified. (See I Corinthians 6:11.)

Finally, Grudem asserts that "Christians are never . . . said to be active agents in God's initial cleansing of their souls at conversion" but they are said to be "active in the progressive work of sanctification." The New Testament teaches, however, that the believer cannot effect his own cleansing, independent of the effect of Christ's blood, under any circumstances or at any point in his Christian life. The question is not whether the believer has any responsibility for being cleansed; the question is how the believer receives the cleansing that only the blood of Jesus provides. The only way a person can be cleansed, whether at initial salvation or during his Christian life, is to appropriate Christ's blood by faith. Any suggestion that salvation comes by works apart from faith is abhorrent to the Scriptures and offensive to the Cross of Christ. There is no biblical evidence that Christians are at any point "passive agents" in receiving God's cleansing, however. There is no idea of "passive" faith. For faith to be real, it must be active. (See James 2:14-26.)

In summary, the grammar of verse 22 permits the phrase "seeing ye have purified your souls in obeying the truth through the Spirit" to refer to the initial purification at the point of salvation. The immediate context suggests that this phrase is a reference to the new birth (verse 23), which occurred in response to the preaching of the gospel (verse 25). There is no compelling reason to reject this meaning, so it is best to let this meaning stand.

Those who obey the truth (the gospel message [verse 25]) have purified their souls. (Of course, this purification was accomplished by Christ's blood [verse 2].) If the phrase simply read "ye have purified your souls," it would be problematic, for it would imply salvation by one's own efforts. But the means of purification is the response to the gospel. To suggest that there is some difference between how cleansing occurs at the initial point of salvation and afterward is untenable. As Caffin pointed out, "Obedience is the condition of purification."[95]

The use of the word "souls" (*psychas*) provides an

example of how words are defined by their contexts. In some contexts, the word refers to the whole person. (See 3:20; II Peter 2:14.) In other contexts, it refers to the inner person. (See Matthew 10:28; II Peter 2:8.) The latter is the case here. (One of the most common causes of misinterpreting Scripture is to suppose that a specific word always means the same thing in every context.)

The phrase "your souls" appears only twice in the Gospels. (See Matthew 11:29; Luke 21:19.) It is, however, common in the Septuagint, where it means "your lives." Besides his direct quote from the Septuagint in verses 23-24, Peter's familiarity with and respect for the Septuagint may be reflected in his repeated use of this phrase. (See also 2:25; 4:19, in addition to 1:9 and 3:20.)[96] The phrase also appears in the letter that Jewish leaders wrote to Gentile believers (Acts 15:24), in the letter to Hebrew believers (Hebrews 13:17), and in James's letter to Jewish Christians of the diaspora (James 1:21). These examples demonstrate that the Septuagint was the translation of choice in the first century. Toward the end of the first century, in his discussion of purification, John used the more direct *heauton* ("himself") of the object of purification. (See I John 3:3.)

We see the use of the Septuagint in the phrase "ye have purified your souls." In Jeremiah 6:16, the Septuagint translates the literal Hebrew phrase "you will find rest for your souls" as "you will find purification for your souls."[97] Jesus alluded to a portion of this verse in Matthew 11:29 but quoted it directly from the Hebrew text. In the final analysis, the soul rests when it is purified or cleansed from sin. There can be no rest when the soul is marred by sin. (See Isaiah 57:20.)

First Peter

The obedience to the truth that resulted in the purification of the soul occurred "through the Spirit." This phrase is absent from the critical text because of its absence from some early manuscripts, but it appears in the majority of manuscripts.[98] If original, it demonstrates "the Spirit's divine working in regeneration-conversion."[99] The new birth, which is the topic here (see verse 23), is the work of the Holy Spirit. (See John 3:5; 7:37-39; Acts 2:38.)

As a result of the purification that occurs with the new birth, believers become part of a new family, which is characterized by "sincere love of the brethren" (NKJV). (The "unfeigned" of the KJV is translated from the Greek *anupokriton*, which means "sincere" or "not hypocritical.")

The first word translated "love" in this verse is *philadelphian*, which has to do with brotherly affection. It is natural for those who have been born again to have an affection for the members of their new family. (See 2:17; 3:8.) But the letter urges its readers to move beyond this level of love to *agape*: "See that ye love one another with a pure heart fervently." *Agape* is more than affection; it is "a self-sacrificing desire to meet the needs of others that finds expression in concrete acts."[100] Although there is an overlapping range of meaning between *philadelphia* and *agape*, each also has a distinctive range of meaning.[101] Here, the distinction must be in view, for it would seem strange to affirm the readers' love and then to command it.

A "pure heart" is doubtless synonymous with the sincerity already mentioned, but the *agape* is to be "fervent" (*ektenos*). The word means "'intensely,' with all the energies strained to the utmost."[102]

Exhortations in View of Salvation

The Christian life begins with the purification of the soul, which occurs in conjunction with the new birth. The new birth results from obedience to the truth, the gospel message. The result of this new birth is identification with a new family and a sincere love for the members of that family. But the natural family affection that one has for his brothers and sisters is not the extent of one's love. Rather, believers must press beyond this affection to a fervent love that demonstrates itself in caring actions.

Verse 23. This verse begins with a participle (*anagegennemenoi*, translated "being born again"). Thus it a continuation of the sentence that begins in verse 22, and it gives the ground or reason for the statements in the previous verse.[103] That is, on the basis of having been born again believers have purified their souls, resulting in sincere brotherly love. Where there is no new birth, there can be no purification of the soul and no brotherly love comparable to what is seen in the family of God.

A form of the word translated "being born again" appears also in verse 3, where it is translated "hath begotten [us] again." Life in Christ begins with a new birth, by which believers become "newborn babes" (2:2). Jesus and various New Testament writers used the same terminology. (See John 1:12-13; 3:3-5; Titus 3:5; James 1:18; I John 3:9.) The new birth is necessary because of the state of spiritual death in which all people exist as a consequence of Adam's sin. (See Ephesians 2:1, 5; Colossians 2:13; Romans 5:12, 17, 19, 21; I Corinthians 15:21-22.)

This beginning participle is in the perfect tense, which indicates the continuing effects of the new birth. It is not just something that has happened in the past; it is something that continues to influence the life of the believer. Among other things, the new birth continues to influence the believer to love his brother sincerely, and it continues to enable him to move beyond brotherly affection to fervent love. (See comments on verse 22.)

The agent of the new birth is not "corruptible seed, but . . . incorruptible." The letter emphasizes the incorruptibility of the seed by which believers are born again, the incorruptibility of the blood of Christ by which we are redeemed (as opposed to the corruptibility of silver and gold) (verses 18-19), and the incorruptibility of the inheritance we receive on the basis of the new birth (verses 3-4).

To be incorruptible means not subject to decay and incapable of wearing out with the passage of time. The New Testament uses this word only of eternal heavenly realities (Romans 1:23; I Timothy 1:17; I Corinthians 9:25; 15:52). Everything else will decay (Luke 12:33; Romans 1:23; II Corinthians 4:16; Colossians 2:22). Even the creation is in the "bondage of corruption" (Romans 8:21).[104]

The word translated "seed" here is *spora*. This is the only place the word occurs in the New Testament. The word commonly translated "seed" is *sperma*. Apparently *spora* here emphasizes the process of sowing rather than the seed itself.[105] Though the new birth occurs "by the word of God," it occurs specifically as the gospel is preached (verse 25).

There is a grammatical uncertainty here as to whether the seed by which we are born again is the Word of God or the Holy Spirit. In the phrase "not of corruptible seed," the preposition "of" is translated from *ek*, which means "out of" or "from." In the phrase "by the word of God," the preposition "by" is translated from

Exhortations in View of Salvation

dia, which means "through" or "by means of."

If the seed is the Spirit, then the Holy Spirit works by means of the Word of God to bring about the new birth. This would be another way of expressing what the Majority Text says in verse 22: "You have purified your souls in obeying the truth through [*dia*] the Spirit" (NKJV). In other words, verse 22 indicates that believers obey the truth (the Word of God) by means of the Spirit. Verse 23 would then indicate that the Holy Spirit, the incorruptible seed, brings about the new birth by means of the Word of God. In any case, the "distinction is not of great significance theologically, for . . . the Holy Spirit is active in causing regeneration . . . and the word of God is the means God uses to awaken new life in an unbeliever."[106]

Caffin has pointed out that "God's elect are begotten again *through* the Word, the Word preached, heard, read, pronounced in holy baptism. The Word preached by St. Peter on the great Day of Pentecost was the means by which three thousand souls were led to be baptized in the Name of Jesus Christ for the remission of sins, and to receive the gift of the Holy Ghost."[107]

The new birth occurs by means of the Word (*logos*) of God. In verse 25, *rhema* is translated "word." An attempt to make radical distinctions between these words may be ill informed. Though it is true that *logos* refers primarily to the idea while *rhema* refers primarily to the spoken word,[108] the words also have a common range of meaning, and the context strongly influences their meaning. (See Acts 10:36-37, where Peter used the words as synonyms.) Here, *logos* seems to refer both to God's written and spoken message.[109] The focus is on the written Word of God,

First Peter

which is spoken in gospel proclamation.

It is certainly an error to make a sharp distinction between *logos* and *rhema* in an attempt to attribute magical powers to the vocalization of the written Scriptures. The Word of God has the same power whether we read it silently with a heart of faith or whether we read or speak it aloud. The authority of the Word of God does not depend upon physical or mental gymnastics, but upon the character of the One who has given His Word. The virtue that appropriates the authority of the Word of God is faith, not the vibration of vocal cords. When people misuse the Word of God in a shamanistic way apart from faith, they deny its genuine authority.

The Word of God lives and abides forever. That the Word of God is alive (see Hebrews 4:12) indicates its ability to impart life in the new-birth experience. That the Word of God abides forever (see Mark 13:31) indicates that it continues to impart life to those who are born again.[110]

Verses 24-25 quote a variation of the Septuagint translation of Isaiah 40:6-8. James also makes use of this Isaiah passage but in a much looser fashion. (See James 1:10-11.) The word "flesh" in this context seems to refer to all unregenerate human existence.[111] (See Psalm 103:15.) The idea is to contrast the temporary, corruptible nature of human existence with the permanence of the Word of God. Compared to Jesus' glory (verse 21), the glory of humans is like a fading flower. The inheritance given to believers on the basis of their new birth does not fade away (verse 4), but like the grass, unregenerate people wither.

The Hebrew text of Isaiah 40:8 refers to "the word of our God." So does the Septuagint. By rendering the phrase "the word of the Lord," Peter either quoted from a version of the Septuagint no longer extant or he provided his own free translation to suit the new context in which he used the passage.[112] Regardless, he thus equated the word of the Lord Jesus (verse 3) with the word of God (verse 23). Grammatically, the reference is to the word spoken by the Lord. Peter may have had in mind specific words spoken by Jesus, such as those found in Matthew 11:29 and John 3:3-5.[113]

The Word of the Lord is the content of the gospel message. Believers receive new life as they hear His Word proclaimed. (See Romans 10:17; James 1:18.)

E. Call to Spiritual Growth (2:1-10)

(2:1) Wherefore laying aside all malice, and all guile, and hypocrisies, and envies, and all evil speakings, (2) as newborn babes, desire the sincere milk of the word, that ye may grow thereby: (3) if so be ye have tasted that the Lord is gracious. (4) To whom coming, as unto a living stone, disallowed indeed of men, but chosen of God, and precious, (5) ye also, as lively stones, are built up a spiritual house, an holy priesthood, to offer up spiritual sacrifices, acceptable to God by Jesus Christ. (6) Wherefore also it is contained in the scripture, Behold I lay in Sion a chief corner stone, elect, precious: and he that believeth on him shall not be confounded. (7) Unto you therefore which believe he is precious: but unto them which be disobedient, the stone which the builders disallowed, the same is made the head of the corner; (8) and a stone of stumbling, and a rock of offence, even to them

First Peter

which stumble at the word, being disobedient: whereunto also they were appointed. (9) But ye are a chosen generation, a royal priesthood, an holy nation, a peculiar people; that ye should shew forth the praises of him who hath called you out of darkness into his marvellous light: (10) which in time past were not a people, but are now the people of God: which had not obtained mercy, but now have obtained mercy.

In conjunction with its emphasis on the new birth (1:3, 23), the letter gives specific instructions regarding the steps toward spiritual maturity. It hints at these disciplines in 1:13-17, 22 but begins to develop them more fully in 2:1. Spiritual growth involves radical changes in one's relationships with others (2:1), the development of a healthy appetite for the Word of God (2:2), and the offering of spiritual sacrifices (2:5). Beyond the immediate context of 2:1-10, spiritual growth involves abstinence from fleshly lusts (2:11), honorable conduct among unbelievers (2:12), submission to civil authority (2:13-15), restraint of freedom (2:16), extending honor to all people including civil authorities (2:17), loving the brotherhood (2:17), fearing God (2:17), honoring social structures (2:18-25; 3:1-7), empathy and courtesy (3:8-12), readiness to answer those with questions about the faith (3:15), and a clear conscience (3:16).

Verse 1. The word "wherefore" refers back to the command to practice fervent and sincere love for the brethren (1:22).[114] Grammatically, the discussion of the new birth in 1:23-25 is parenthetical; 2:1 resumes the discussion of the appropriate treatment of one's brothers and sisters in Christ.

Exhortations in View of Salvation

The word translated "laying aside" (*apotithemi*) is used literally of removing clothing (Acts 7:58). Here, as in a number of other references, it is a metaphor for the kinds of behavior that believers must discard.[115] Believers can fulfill this command only by positive action.

The first behavior that we must lay aside is malice (*kakia*). In a broad sense, the word means something like "badness." Here, it refers to ill will, a desire to harm others in some way or to see them harmed.[116] This attitude is incompatible with the love commended in 1:22. There is something about human nature as it is marred by sin that tends to rejoice in the misfortune of others and to gloat in one's own well-being. This is reprehensible to God. (See Proverbs 24:17-18.)

We must also discard guile ("deceit," NKJV). The word (*dolos*) has to do with cunning or treachery by which harm is done to another person.[117] There is no place in the fellowship of believers for clever manipulation of people for any reason, and certainly not for personal advantage. The Christian life thrives in openness and light, not in dim smoke and mirrors.

Hypocrisy is incompatible with love. This word, transliterated from the Greek *hypokrisis*, has to do with "playing a part."[118] To act hypocritically is to make a pretense to something that is not true. The word's antonym appears in 1:22, where it is translated "unfeigned" ("sincere," NKJV). Contextually, the reference here is apparently to a pretended love that actually masks ill will. Christianity is about reality. Therefore, hypocrisy is excluded. (See Matthew 23:28; Mark 12:15; Galatians 2:13.)

Envy (*phthonos*) has no place in the believer's life. The word suggests jealousy over the good that others experience.[119] Genuine love rejoices with those who rejoice. (See Romans 12:15.)

Finally, we must discard evil speaking (*katalalias*). Specifically, this evil speaking is slander or defamation.[120] The verb form appears in 2:12 and 3:16 to indicate that unbelievers may slander believers, but believers must not defame others. This command excludes gossip, rumor-mongering and evil speculations. (See James 4:11.)

Verse 2. Just as a newborn baby has a natural desire for the milk of the mother, a desire that results in physical growth, so believers, having been born again (1:23) and thus being in a very real sense "newborn babes," will experience spiritual growth as they develop a desire for the pure (*adolon*, the antonym of *dolon*, translated "guile" in verse 1) milk of the Word.

Paul and the writer of Hebrews both used the image of milk to rebuke believers for their spiritual immaturity. (See I Corinthians 3:1-2; Hebrews 5:13.) When those to whom they wrote should have matured enough to be eating solid food, they were still drinking milk exclusively. But the purpose here is not to rebuke the readers for immaturity, but to encourage them to do the things that would lead to maturity.

It is doubtful that Peter intended to characterize all his readers as new believers. Given the date of this letter, it is possible that some of his readers had been believers for at least thirty years.[121] The focus here is not on how recently the believers were born again, but on the intensity of the desire they were to have for the pure milk. The word translated "desire" appears frequently in the New Testament.[122] It also appears in the Septuagint. (See Psalm 42:1; 84:2.)

The letter commands its readers to strongly desire the pure milk. *Epipothesate* is an imperative. Spiritual growth is not an option; it is as much an imperative as any other command in the New Testament. Those who do not grow are subject to rebuke, as noted earlier in Paul and the Book of Hebrews.

The word translated "of the word" is the Greek *logikon*. Because of its relationship to *logos*, many translators and commentators take it to be a reference to the Word of God, the Scriptures. The meaning of *logikon* is problematic, however, because it appears only in one other place in the New Testament. Romans 12:1 translates it as "reasonable." The use of the word in its two New Testament occurrences and in Greek literature suggests that its meaning is "spiritual" as contrasted to "literal." It seems to mean "metaphorical."[123]

Romans 12:1 uses the word to describe metaphorically the way believers are to make their bodies a "living sacrifice." I Peter uses it in the extended metaphor of "newborn babes" and "pure milk." In other words, just as babies grow as they drink literal milk, so believers grow as they drink figurative milk.

Nevertheless, Grudem makes a strong case that this figurative milk is the written Scriptures.[124] The context is most convincing. In 1:23, Peter pointed out that believers are born again "through the word of God." He then proceeded to quote from the written Scriptures (1:24-25) and to refer to the Word by which the gospel was preached (1:25). In 2:6-8, he again quoted from the Scriptures and pointed out that those who are disobedient to the Word stumble.

By listening to the preached word and studying and

First Peter

meditating on the Scriptures, believers experience spiritual growth. (See II Timothy 2:15.) It is true, as McKnight points out, that first-century Christians did not have copies of the Bible to study, and for that reason he thinks that the spiritual milk does not include Bible study.[125] If Peter wrote this book to Jewish Christians, however, they had many centuries of rich tradition of communicating the written Hebrew Scriptures orally. Indeed, the very next verse (verse 3) is a reference to Psalm 34:8.

Verses 1-2 are part of the same sentence. Spiritual growth requires not only the figurative drinking of pure milk; it also requires the discarding of the vices listed in verse 1, figuratively described as taking off undesirable clothing.

This verse is one of the few places where the Greek text upon which the KJV is based preserves a shorter reading. The critical Greek text, which is based on a few ancient manuscripts, reads, "That you may grow thereby to salvation." In the strictest sense, however, we do not "grow" to salvation. Salvation occurs instantaneously at the point of being born again. If the longer reading is original here, the reference to salvation is the same as in 1:5, 9. (See also comments on 1:13.) That is, it refers to the ultimate outworking of our present salvation, which we will experience at the revelation of Jesus Christ.

Verse 3. Continuing the metaphorical language of the previous two verses, this verse uses the language of Psalm 34:8 to describe the experience of believers as "tasting" the graciousness of the Lord. The condition is first class ("if" is translated from *ei*), indicating the reality of the condition. That is, they have indeed tasted. A suitable translation would be, "Since indeed you have

Exhortations in View of Salvation

tasted. . . ." Believers begin to taste of the graciousness of the Lord when they come to Him in faith. (See 1:21.) The experience continues into the new birth (1:23) and throughout the Christian life.

"Tasting" has to do with "learning by experience." (See Matthew 16:28; John 8:52; Hebrews 2:9; 6:4.) The connection between "tasting" the graciousness of the Lord and desiring the pure milk of the Word (verse 2) indicates that by means of His Word believers experience His graciousness. The souls of believers are purified as they "obey the truth" (1:22), they are born again "through the word of God" (1:23), and by the gospel the Word is preached (1:25). Since it is the Lord Himself who has spoken the words of Scripture, they are His words, and to experience them is to experience Him. Though it is possible to experience the Lord in some way through general revelation (e.g., creation, conscience, history [Psalm 19:1-6; 89:37; Romans 1:19-20; 2:14-16; Acts 17:26]), this experience pales in comparison to the experience we obtain through special revelation (e.g., the written Scriptures and the Incarnation [I Timothy 3:16; II Timothy 3:16]).

The word translated "gracious" (Greek, *chrestos*) is the same word used to translate the Hebrew *tov* ("good") in the Septuagint rendering of Psalm 34:8. Like *tov*, *chrestos* has a range of meaning that embraces usefulness, suitability, worthiness, goodness, moral goodness, good repute, kindness, love, and benevolence.[126] The specific meaning here is indicated by the context of Psalm 34. That psalm praises the Lord because He delivers from their fears those who seek Him, He saves the poor from their troubles, His angels encamp around those who fear Him to deliver them, and those who fear Him do not lack

First Peter

any good thing. Thus, the goodness of the Lord is the wide range of benevolent acts by which the Lord delivers those who trust Him from fear, trouble, and want.

Psalm 34 is uniquely appropriate for this letter, for the undergirding theme of the psalm is much like that of this letter: In the face of the troubles and afflictions of the righteous, some of which arise from mistreatment by unbelievers, they can still trust God. (Compare Psalm 34:4, 6, 17-20, 22 with I Peter 1:6-7; 2:19-23; 3:9, 17; 4:1, 12-13, 19 and Psalm 34:16, 21 with I Peter 2:12; 3:13-16; 4:14, 16.)

The word translated "gracious" (*chrestos*) was sometimes used in Greek literature to mean "delicious" when applied to foods.[127] Peter's appeal to his readers to grow spiritually by laying aside the sins of verse 1 and by fervently desiring the pure milk of verse 2 was based on their experience of the Lord as a God who had only their good in mind. The goodness they had already experienced provided them with every motivation to come to know Him more intimately.

In the immediate context of I Peter 2:3, the Lord is Jesus Christ. Thus, the LORD (Hebrew, *Yahweh*) of Psalm 34:8 is also a reference to Him. That is, the LORD of Psalm 34:8 is the Lord of I Peter 2:3. As Grudem pointed out, "The Lord who is the source of spiritual delight for Old Testament saints is now in the new covenant seen to be the Lord Jesus Christ, in whom our soul delights."[128]

Verse 4 quotes the Septuagint translation of Isaiah 28:16. The letter borrows from those words and from the words of Psalm 118:22, quoted in verse 7, to describe Jesus Christ as "a living stone," rejected by unbelieving people, but chosen by God and precious to Him. In verse

6, He is "a chief cornerstone." In verse 7, He is "the head of the corner." In verse 8, He is "a stone of stumbling, and a rock of offense."

The word translated "coming" (*proserchomenoi*) is a present participle, which indicates that believers are continually coming to Christ. They initially come when they first believe (1:21), but they continue to come as they obey the truth (1:22), experience the new birth (1:23), partake of the pure milk of the Word (2:2), and offer spiritual sacrifices (verse 5.) The Septuagint and the Book of Hebrews frequently use the same Greek word (*proserchomai*) to describe coming to God in acts of worship.[129]

This is not the first time Peter referred to Christ as the stone that people rejected. (See Acts 4:11.) Jesus likewise applied the stone prophecies of the Hebrews Scriptures to Himself. (See Matthew 21:42-44.)

Just as Peter confessed Jesus to be the Son of the "living" God (Matthew 16:16) in contrast to the dead gods commonly worshiped by the Gentiles in the area of Caesarea Philippi, so he now confessed Jesus to be a "living" stone in obvious contrast to the lifeless stones of which the Jewish Temple was built. Verses 5-9 contrast the life inherent in the new covenant with the shame, rejection, and offense of those who rejected Christ and who continue to associate with lifeless stones, the carnal priesthood (Hebrews 7:16), and the animal sacrifices. The reason these unbelievers stumble is because they have disobeyed the Word (verse 8).

Those who rejected Christ included the unbelieving Jews (Jesus focussed on this group in Matthew 21:42-45), but apparently this context also includes unbelieving Gentiles (verse 12). Though people reject Christ, He is chosen of God and precious. The word translated "chosen" also appears in the Greek text of 1:1, although it is ordinarily translated with 1:2 as "elect." Since the choice concerning the identity of the Messiah was God's alone, we can correlate the Messiah's being "chosen" with the Messiah's being "foreordained before the foundation of the world" (1:20).[130]

The Messiah is "precious" (Greek, *entimos*), a word used of stones in Greek literature to mean "valuable."[131] This is a fitting translation of the Hebrew *yaqar*, which appears in Isaiah 28:16 and which carries the same meaning. If God esteems the Messiah to be precious, those who reject Him as worthless make a fatal error.

Verse 5. Because of their association with Jesus Christ, the living stone, through faith (1:21), the new birth (1:23), and tasting his graciousness (2:2-3), believers are living stones. The Greek word translated "stones" is from *lithos*, not *petros*. It indicates that believers are not just rocks existing in their natural state, but stones that a craftsman has carefully worked, shaped, and prepared to fit into a structure. Thus, each stone fits perfectly in its place.

In a similar metaphor, Paul indicates that believers are stones resting upon the foundation (Ephesians 2:20-22). This is a reference to actual contact with the foundation. They are "fitly framed together," indicating the care with which they are prepared for their precise place.

As living stones, believers form a spiritual house. In the context of priesthood, this house is a temple, for it is in a temple that priests offer sacrifices. Indeed, the Bible often refers to the Temple in Jerusalem as a house. (See I Kings 5:5; Isaiah 56:7; Matthew 12:4; 21:13; Mark 2:26;

Exhortations in View of Salvation

Luke 11:51; John 2:16.) Elsewhere, Paul described believers as the temple of God. (See II Corinthians 6:16.)

Because of the difficulty in visualizing believers as both the stones and as the priesthood offering sacrifices, Grudem suggests a change of analogy:

> It is better to change our visual image of a temple, so that we no longer think of a rectangular building made of stones but of an amorphous "building" that continually takes on the changing dimensions of God's assembled people. The beauty of this new and living "temple made of people" should no longer be expensive gold and precious jewels, but the imperishable beauty of holiness and faith in Christians' lives, qualities which much more effectively reflect the glory of God (cf. 1 Pet. 3:4; 2 Cor. 3:18).[132]

That believers form a "spiritual" house indicates that they are "influenced or dominated by the Holy Spirit."[133] The "spiritual" sacrifices they offer are sacrifices prompted by and made possible by the work of the Holy Spirit in the lives of believers.

The temple is constantly growing, as the members mature and as new believers are added (Ephesians 2:21). The word translated "are built up" by the KJV is a present passive indicative, more precisely translated "are being built up" by the NKJV. The building is ongoing.

The temple is to be holy (I Corinthians 3:16-17), for it is the habitation of God (II Corinthians 6:16). Just as God dwelt in the Tabernacle and Temple under the Mosaic economy, He now dwells in the church (Exodus

First Peter

25:8; 29:42-43; I Corinthians 6:19; 3:16-17; Ephesians 2:21-22).

For the concept of the priesthood of the believers, Peter drew on the language of Exodus 19:6. (See also verse 9.) Since all believers are priests, each believer has direct access to God without going through another person, and each is to witness to those outside the body of Christ. (See Hebrews 10:19-21.)

There is no longer any need for priests to offer sacrifices for sin; Christ finished that work once and for all (Hebrews 9:26; 10:12, 18). Instead, the New Testament priests offer the following spiritual sacrifices: praise and thanksgiving (Hebrews 13:15; Philippians 4:18; I Peter 2:9), doing good and giving to those in need (Hebrews 13:16), reasonable service (Romans 12:1), their lives (Philippians 2:17), and the results of evangelistic efforts, new believers (Romans 15:16). Even the Old Testament speaks metaphorically of the sacrifices of prayer, thanksgiving, and a repentant heart.[134] (See Psalms 50:13-14, 23; 51:17; 141:2.)

Through Christ we believe in God (1:21), and through Christ our spiritual sacrifices are acceptable to God. (See comments on 1:21.) As acts of worship, we must offer spiritual sacrifices to God through Jesus, for Jesus is God made known to us. (See John 1:18; 8:19; 12:45; 14:9; I Timothy 3:16; I John 2:23.) Any attempt to approach God while ignoring or denying the fullness of Christ's deity is vain.

Verse 6 and the following two verses quote from the Septuagint to support verses 4-5. The passage introduces the first quote, from Isaiah 28:16, as a saying "contained in the scripture." The New Testament consistently uses

Exhortations in View of Salvation

the Greek word translated "scripture" (*graphe*) to refer to the inspired writings of the Bible. It ordinarily refers to the Hebrew Scriptures, as they existed in the time of Jesus, but on occasion the word reaches out to include portions of the New Testament that were complete at the time. (See John 19:37; Romans 1:2; 16:26; I Timothy 5:18; II Timothy 3:16; II Peter 1:20; 3:16.) The New Testament never uses *graphe* to describe the Apocrypha or any other nonbiblical writings.[135]

In its context in the Old Testament, this quote is a warning to the spiritual rulers in Jerusalem, located in the southern kingdom of Judah, to learn from the lesson of the judgment of God upon the northern kingdom, Israel. Since Jerusalem (Zion) already had the Temple with its cornerstone, the statement that God would lay a "chief corner stone" in Zion indicated that God would do a new and different work that would supersede and replace the work He had done through the Temple. Since the Temple and its priesthood represented the entire function of the law of Moses, this was a prophecy of the termination of the law. The Temple in Jerusalem was in some way a prophetic picture of the Messiah, who would Himself be a far greater temple. (See John 2:13-22; Matthew 24:1-2; Revelation 21:22.) Jesus fulfilled all the Messianic prophetic implications of the law of Moses. (See Matthew 5:17-18; Luke 24:27, 44.)

As opposed to cornerstones in today's buildings, which are largely decorative or commemorative and are often the last to be added to the building, the cornerstone in the buildings of ancient Israel were the first to be laid and were functional in that every other stone had to line up with the cornerstone. The cornerstone was, in other words, critical to the foundation and design of the building.

This chief cornerstone is Jesus Christ (verse 4.) Indeed, this translation of Isaiah 28:16 includes two significant words not in the Hebrew text: "He that believeth *on him* shall not be confounded." The Hebrew text reads, "Whoever believes will not act hastily" (NKJV). The Hebrew text does not specify the object of faith, but Peter, under the inspiration of the Holy Spirit, declared faith's object to be the person of Jesus Christ. The chief cornerstone is a person in whom we can place faith. Here we see the superiority of the new covenant, with its living stone foundation, over the old covenant, with its lifeless cornerstone.

Jesus Christ is elect and precious. (See comments on verse 4 and 1:20.) The promise that those who believe on him shall "not be confounded" means they will not be "put to shame" (NKJV). Their faith is well placed; they will never be ashamed that they trusted in Jesus. (See also Romans 9:33.)

The faith of this verse is not a one-time profession. The Greek present active participle describes the believing as ongoing. That is, whoever continues to believe on Him will not be ashamed.

Verses 7-8. Those who place their faith in Jesus Christ find Him to be precious.[136] (See comments on verse 4.) In contrast, those who disobey find that the stone they reject has become not only the "head of the corner" but also "a stone of stumbling and a rock of offence." These words come from Psalm 118:22 and Isaiah 8:14.

This passage contrasts disobedience with believing. It may at first seem that the contrast should be between believing and disbelieving. But the choice of words here reflects the Jewish equation of faith with obedience and

Exhortations in View of Salvation

the lack of faith with disobedience. There was no idea in the Jewish mind of "faith" that did not produce a behavioral result. To believe is to obey. (See James 2:14-26; II Thessalonians 1:8; Acts 6:7; Romans 10:16; I John 2:4-6, 9; 3:6-10; 4:8, 20-21; 5:18.) By their rejection of Jesus Christ, people indicate their lack of faith. They indicate the same lack of faith by disobedience to the Word of God. In the context, the specific word that unbelievers disobey is in verse 6; it is the command to believe on Jesus.

The first identification of those who rejected Christ was the unbelieving Jewish religious leaders. (See Matthew 21:42-45.) The present context, however, also includes unbelieving Gentiles (verse 12).

The stone that God intended to be the chief cornerstone becomes a stumbling stone and an offense to the builders who reject it. The image here is of a stone that builders reject and put aside. As time passes, grass grows up around it, obscuring the stone, and as the building progresses, the builders continually trip over this stone they have rejected. Their frustration over this stone grows; it is continually a source of irritation. How much better it would have been if they had placed it in the building, where God intended it to be! (See Romans 9:30-33.)

Verse 8 provides another example of ascribing to Jesus an Old Testament statement about Yahweh ("Jehovah"). Isaiah 8:14 identifies Yahweh as the stone of stumbling and rock of offense. I Peter identifies the stone as Jesus.

Those who through lack of faith in Jesus Christ are disobedient to the Word "were appointed" to stumble. Grudem argues that God predestined these people to disbelieve and to disobey the Word.[137] He admits, however, that the word translated "whereunto" (*ho*) could refer to the stumbling, the disobedience, or both. The idea that God predestines some to be saved while passing over others arises from a simple error. That error is the assumption that God appointed these unbelievers to their unbelief. The text does not say who appointed them, nor does it indicate the time of the appointing.

The text indicates that those who reject Jesus Christ are appointed to stumble. Though it could perhaps grammatically mean that those who reject Jesus Christ were appointed to reject Him, this meaning is not required, and it would fly in the face of the many passages of Scripture that declare the freedom of the human will. (See John 3:16; 7:37; Revelation 22:17.) Though God has determined that those who reject Jesus Christ will not be saved, this does not mean that He predestined them to reject Jesus.

Verse 9. By means of a somewhat free rendering of a series of quotations from the Septuagint, Peter elaborated on the idea established in verse 5. (See Exodus 19:5-6; Deuteronomy 4:20; 7:6; Isaiah 43:20-21.) There, believers are a holy priesthood who offer spiritual sacrifices. Here, they are, among other things, a royal priesthood and, by implication, the sacrifices they offer are praises to God.

The idea of being "chosen" appears here, as in 1:2, where the same Greek word is translated "elect." (See comments on 1:2.) The focus here is on the collective choosing of believers as a whole rather than the choosing of individuals. The KJV uses "ye" to represent the second person plural *humeis*, and those who are chosen are collectively identified as a "generation" (*genos*, which could be translated "race" or "people"). Nothing in the text requires this choosing to be based on predestination without regard to individual choice. In its original context in Deuteronomy, under the auspices of the old covenant, the idea of chosenness did refer to the entire nation of Israel on the basis of God's initiative without regard to individual choice, but the idea here is in the context of the new covenant, under which individuals come to God by the free exercise of their will in response to the universal effect of the grace of God. (See Titus 2:11.) Those who respond to the grace of God obtain mercy (verse 10) and enter into the company of the "chosen generation."

Believers also make up a "royal priesthood." Here, I Peter follows precisely the Septuagint version of Exodus 19:6. The Hebrew text describes Israel as a "kingdom of priests." The idea is the same—a kingdom represents royalty—although the Hebrew text focuses on Israel as a kingdom, while the Greek translation focuses on the priesthood of the people. (See Revelation 1:6; 5:10; 20:6.) The priesthood of believers is "royal" because it belongs to the King, just as the members of a king's house are part of the "royal household."[138]

Next, believers are a "holy nation." To be holy means to be separated in some way unto God and from the nations of the world. Israel was a "holy nation" (Exodus 19:6) because God chose Israel out of all the nations of the world to be His special treasure (Deuteronomy 7:6, NKJV). The church is special, not because of the ethnic identity of its members, but because of their identification with Jesus Christ. (See Ephesians 2:11-22; Galatians 3:28; Colossians 3:11.) Caffin has pointed out that the "Israelites were a holy nation as separated from the heathen and consecrated to God's service by circumcision.

Christians of all nations, and kindreds, and people, and tongues, are one nation under one King, separated to his service, dedicated to him in holy baptism."[139] (See Colossians 2:11-12.) As a holy, or separated, nation, the church is expected to exhibit specific behaviors, and verse 11 begins to explain them.

The words translated "a peculiar people" by the KJV (*laos eis peripoiesin*) do not follow precisely the Septuagint translation of Deuteronomy 7:6, which has *laon periousion*, does not include the preposition *eis*, and which would translate into "a special people." Neither does the phrase follow exactly the Septuagint of Exodus 19:5, which has *laos periousios*. Rather, the words here are apparently influenced by the Septuagint version of Isaiah 43:21, *laon mou hon periepoiesamen*, which translates into "my people whom I have preserved." Isaiah 43:21 reads in its entirety, "My people whom I have preserved to tell forth my praises." It appears that Peter had this passage in mind, for he used the word translated "praises" (*aretas*) in his statement "that ye should shew forth the praises of him."

Peripoiesin is from *peripoiesis*, and it means "possessing." *Periousion*, as in Titus 2:14 and the Septuagint version of Deuteronomy 7:6 and Exodus 19:5, is from *periousios*, which means "chosen" or "special." Though both words have as a prefix the preposition *peri*, they are quite different words. *Peripoiesin* is formed from *peri* and *poieo*. *Periousios* is formed from *peri* and *eimi*.

Thus the Greek text here indicates that believers are more than special, although they certainly are special. They are a people whom God has destined for His possession. Michaels points out that Peter characteristically used *eis* eschatalogically (1:3-5, "unto a lively hope, "to an inheritance," "unto salvation") and that in three out of four occurrences of *peripoiesis* in the New Testament it is the object of *eis* with a future reference (I Thessalonians 5:9; II Thessalonians 2:14; Hebrews 10:39).[140] The focus is not so much on the unique character of the people of God at this time, but on the certainty that God will ultimately own them. That believers are "a chosen generation, a royal priesthood, an holy nation" indicates their present uniqueness. That they are "a people for possession" indicates that their uniqueness is not limited to the present; it extends into the future.

The priesthood of believers finds expression in proclaiming the praises of God. The word translated "praises" (*aretos*) appears only four times in the New Testament (Philippians 4:8; II Peter 1:3, 5, and here). It usually means something like "virtues" or "excellencies." By their lives and words, believers are to proclaim the virtuous excellence of God. They are to model His character and testify to His excellence. The word translated "shew forth" by the KJV and "proclaim" by the NKJV (Greek, *exangeilete*) occurs nowhere else in the New Testament, but the Septuagint uses it several times for praising God. (See Psalm 9:14; 71:15; 73:28; 79:13; 107:22; 119:13, 26.)

Blum points out that "light-darkness is a common dualism in the Bible to describe God-evil, good-bad, revelation-ignorance, new age–old age (e.g., Isa 8:21-9:2; John 1:4, 8-9; Eph 5:8; I John 1:5-2:2).[141] The Dead Sea Scrolls present this theme by the image of the Sons of Light versus the Sons of Darkness.

The darkness out of which God has called His people is the darkness of sin and ignorance (1:14, 18). The light

First Peter

into which He calls believers is the light of the gospel of Jesus Christ.

Verse 10 draws from Hosea 1:6, 9-10 and 2:23 words that in their original context described the consequence of Israel's unfaithfulness to God. Because Israel, the northern kingdom, was unfaithful, God told Hosea that He would no longer have mercy on Israel (Hosea 1:6). God would no longer claim Israel as His people; He would not be their God (Hosea 1:9). But then, the Lord also promised that one day He would restore Israel to fellowship with Him (1:10; 2:23).

Romans 9:25-26 refers to the same idea, also using Hosea's words, to show that Gentiles would become the people of God. This use demonstrates how that Old Testament passages sometimes take on a new dimension of meaning in the New Testament. It does not mean, however, that we can extract passages from their Old Testament context and give them a meaning different from what the original authors intended. The Holy Spirit inspired the writers of the New Testament in their use of the Old Testament. If the Holy Spirit wished to invest new meaning in old words, He could do that; they are His words. But inspiration ceased with the completion of the New Testament. Our task today is to discover the meaning of all Scripture in the context in which it presently exists, whether in the Old Testament or New.

Nothing requires the words in this verse to refer exclusively to Gentile believers. In their original context, they referred to Israel, and unless something in their New Testament context requires otherwise—as in Romans 9:25-26—there is no reason they could not refer to

Exhortations in View of Salvation

Jewish believers. Here they can refer to Jewish believers who at one time were not the people of God because of their unfaithfulness to the old covenant or because of their rejection of the Messiah.

IV

Exhortations in View of Social Groupings
2:11-3:12

I Peter 2:9 identifies believers as "an holy nation." To be holy means to be separated in some way unto God and from all that is unlike God. Ancient Israel was also to be a holy nation (see comments on 2:9). The law of Moses spelled out their separation by 613 commandments, of which 248 were positive and 365 were negative. If believers also form a holy nation, we would expect that the context which so identifies them would also specify the terms of their separation. That is just the case here. I Peter specifies the conduct that God expects of believers in their relationships with unbelievers, with civil government, toward masters, in marriage, and in the family of God at large.

A. Responsible Conduct among Unbelievers (2:11-12)

(11) Dearly beloved, I beseech you as strangers and pilgrims, abstain from fleshly lusts, which war against the soul; (12) having your conversation honest among the Gentiles: that, whereas they speak against you as evildoers, they may by your good works, which they shall behold, glorify God in the day of visitation.

Verse 11. Peter began his appeal by identifying his readers as "beloved" (*agapetoi*). He intended to deal with real problems, and his words would sometimes sting, but he wanted his readers to have no doubt about his affection for them.

The word translated "beseech" by the KJV (*parakalo*) is rendered "beg" by the NKJV. "Beseech" is not a wrong translation, but it is an archaic word that for many today may have lost the force Peter intended. The word "beg" expresses the forcefulness of Peter's appeal.

On "strangers" (*parepidemous*), see comments on 1:1, where the same word appears. Here, Peter also identified his readers as "pilgrims" (*paroikous*), a word that means "one who lives in a place that is not his true home."[142] (See 1:17, where the KJV translates *paroikias* as "sojourning.") We see the Jewish flavor of this letter in the use of these two terms, both of which appear in the Septuagint translation of Genesis 23:4 and Psalm 39:12. Peter did not intend to limit their significance to Jewish believers, of course. All believers are strangers and pilgrims in this world, much as Abraham was in the land of Canaan.

I Peter appeals to believers to abstain from fleshly lusts on the basis that they are not at home in this world. When sinful passions pull us, we must remember that this present world, with its focus almost exclusively on self-gratification, is not our identity. Our citizenship is elsewhere (Philippians 3:20, NKJV).

The word translated "abstain" (*apechesthai*) is a present infinitive that carries the force of an imperative.[143] To abstain from fleshly lusts is not a one-time challenge, but an ongoing responsibility. We do not face temptation and get it over with once and for all. The fall in the Garden of Eden marred every aspect of human existence, including the mind. Even though the new birth makes our spirit alive to God, we retain the sin principle and find it necessary to resist temptation continually. (See Galatians 5:17; Romans 6:12-19; I John 1:8.) I Peter offers no formulaic approach to abstinence from sin, but this command indicates that one can refuse to yield to fleshly lusts. The classic example of successful resistance of temptation is Jesus' victory over Satan. (See Matthew 4:1-11.) Essentially, we win victory in the arena of the mind as we bring every thought into obedience to Christ. (See II Corinthians 10:4-5.)

For a discussion of the nature of lust (*epithumion*), see the comments on 1:14, where the same word appears.

In this context, the reference to the flesh (*sarkikon*) is to human nature as it is marred by sin. The reference is not to the human body, but to the human mind, will and emotions. The battle here is not for the human body, but for the soul, against which fleshly lusts wage war. The soul here is a reference to the immaterial part of man. Essentially, the message is the same as that of Galatians 5:17: Sinful human nature attempts to block the influence of the regenerate spirit or soul, just as the regenerate spirit or soul attempts to limit the influence of the sin principle. The spirit achieves victory in this war only as the individual makes the choice to be led by the Spirit (Galatians 5:18).

Verse 12. The word translated "conversation" by the KJV is *anastrophen*, which is better translated into modern English by "conduct" (NKJV). This was the original meaning of the English word "conversation." Peter used the word frequently. (See I Peter 1:15, 18; 3:1-2, 16; II Peter

2:7; 3:11.) Indeed, eight of its thirteen appearances in the New Testament are in Peter's letters. (See also James 3:13; Hebrews 13:7; I Timothy 4:12; Ephesians 4:22; Galatians 1:13.) Peter used the related word *anastrepho* twice (I Peter 1:17; II Peter 2:18). *Anastrepho* appears in five other references, where it has something to do with conduct (II Corinthians 1:12; Ephesians 2:3; I Timothy 3:15; Hebrews 10:33; 13:18).

The frequency of the appeals to good conduct underscores the relationship between genuine Christianity and lifestyle. Every aspect of the believer's conduct is to be holy (1:15). The knowledge that God is a completely impartial judge should motivate believers to proper conduct; He will show no favoritism (1:17). The non-Christian life is characterized by "aimless conduct" (1:18, NKJV). Wives of unsaved husbands have hope of influencing them to have faith in Christ by their "chaste conduct" (3:1-2, NKJV). By their good conduct believers will silence false accusations (here and 3:16). The certainty of the dissolution of the created realm should motivate believers to holy conduct (II Peter 3:10-11).

The word translated "honest" by the KJV (*kalen*) means "good" or "honorable." Believers are to conduct themselves in a good, honorable way. Though this will certainly include honesty, the implications extend beyond what we normally associate with honesty. Specifically, this honorable lifestyle encompasses the believer's attitude toward civil government (2:13-17), the believing slave's attitude toward his master (2:18-21), the believing wife's attitude toward her unbelieving husband (3:1-6), the believing husband's attitude toward his wife (3:7), the believers' attitude toward other believers (3:8; 4:8-11), the believers' attitude toward unbelievers who persecute them (3:9-17; 4:12-19), the elders' attitude toward those they are responsible to shepherd (5:1-4), and the attitude of younger believers toward their elders (5:5).

Peter urged his readers to conduct themselves honorably "among the Gentiles." As with all words, this one (*ethnesin*, from *ethnos*) is defined by its context. It is translated in a variety of ways in the New Testament: as "Gentiles," "nations," "heathen," and "people." Paul used it to describe Gentile Christians (Romans 11:13; 15:27; 16:4; Galatians 2:12). Here, as in 4:3, it clearly refers to unbelievers. If the letter is written primarily to Jewish believers, the contrast between them and the unbelieving Gentiles is even more pronounced. If the letter is written primarily to Gentile believers, it is somewhat difficult to understand why Peter would refer to unbelievers as "Gentiles."[144] This difficulty would vanish only if Peter characterized Gentile Christians as "spiritual" Israel, as some commentators suggest, but this idea lacks clear support either in this letter or in other writings.[145]

The problem addressed here was not hypothetical. In the first century, unbelievers accused Christians of a variety of perversions and actions offensive to society at large. I Peter addresses this problem again in 3:16 and 4:14-16. Some of these accusations were disloyalty to the civil government (John 19:12), teaching unlawful customs (Acts 16:20-21), overturning the economy (Acts 19:23-27), teaching that slaves were free from their masters, refusal to participate in various festivals because of a hatred for humanity, holding values contrary to the society at large, and being atheists.[146] It was said that they turned the world upside down and acted contrary to

Caesar's decrees (Acts 17:6-7). At least by the second century unbelievers accused Christians of cannibalism, because the celebration of the Lord's Supper was associated with eating the flesh and drinking the blood of Christ (I Corinthians 11:24-27), and of incestuous relationships, because of the early practice of referring to fellow believers as brothers and sisters. It could be that some unbelievers in the first century accused Christians of being murderers, thieves, evildoers, and busybodies (4:15).

I Peter urges its readers to live in such an honorable way that their accusers will see their good works and "glorify God in the day of visitation." Some commentators think that the day of visitation is the day of judgment upon unbelievers. Others hold that it is the day when unbelievers are converted and salvation comes to them. Keener suggests that there is an allusion here to Isaiah 10:3, where the day of visitation is definitely a day of judgment.[147] In Luke 19:44, however, the day of visitation is a day of potential salvation.

In view of the close proximity of this verse to 3:1-2, which instructs the wives of unbelieving husbands as to how they could see their husbands "won by the conduct of their wives, when they observe [their] chaste conduct" (NKJV), it seems better to understand the day of visitation as a day of salvation. This day comes to unbelievers as they are convinced by the behavior of believers of the reality of the Christian faith and make the decision to place their faith in Jesus Christ as well. The view that the day of visitation is a day of salvation receives support from the statement that, after observing the good works of believers, those who have been unbelievers will "glorify God." This is the language of true worship, not of coerced acknowledgement of God's supremacy. (See 4:16, where the same language appears.) This view receives further support in that the same word (*epopteuo*) appears both in this verse and in 3:2, translated "behold" ("observe," NKJV). The idea is to bring unbelievers to faith by demonstrating faithful Christianity before them.

B. Responsible Conduct toward Civil Authority (2:13-17)

(13) Submit yourselves to every ordinance of man for the Lord's sake: whether it be to the king, as supreme; (14) or unto governors, as unto them that are sent by him for the punishment of evildoers, and for the praise of them that do well. (15) For so is the will of God, that with well doing ye may put to silence the ignorance of foolish men: (16) as free, and not using your liberty for a cloke of maliciousness, but as the servants of God. (17) Honour all men. Love the brotherhood. Fear God. Honour the king.

The call for believers to submit to civil government is not unique to Peter. The issue was also addressed by Jesus (Matthew 22:15-22) and Paul (Romans 13:1-7; Titus 3:1-2). Jesus placed His call for submission in the context that certain things rightfully belong to God and certain things rightfully belong to the civil authority. Paul placed his call for submission in the context that civil government is of God. Peter placed his call for submission in the context of witnessing to unbelievers.

First Peter

Beginning at this point, Peter's letter takes on the flavor of the ancient house codes that occur with some frequency in secular Greek literature. The literary form in 2:18-3:7, Ephesians 5:21-6:9, and Colossians 3:18-4:1 reflects the house codes common in secular literature in the first century. The house codes addressed the proper deportment of citizens in relation to the state, wives in relation to their husbands, children in relation to their fathers, and slaves in relation to their masters. The idea was that "the household mirrored the government of a city-state, so public obligations and obligations within the household . . . were commonly treated together."[148] The house codes of Scripture are, of course, inspired, which lifts them into another realm.

Much of the New Testament literature addressed to specific problems in the first-century church, and the house codes are no different. Nonbelievers accused early Christians of destroying society by their emphasis on freedom, love, and following Christ, an emphasis that placed new value on children,[149] servants (Mark 10:44), and women.

With the ethnic, gender, and social boundaries that divided people in the first century, nothing could have been more shocking than Paul's declaration that "there is neither Jew nor Greek, there is neither slave nor free, there is neither male nor female; for you are all one in Christ Jesus" (Galatians 3:28, NKJV). Critics of Christianity concluded that it was a subversive religion that relieved Christians of their duty to submit to the state, wives of their duty to submit to their husbands, children of their duty to submit to fathers, and slaves of their duty to submit to their masters.[150]

Paul's advice to Titus, which followed to some degree the pattern of the house codes, establishes a pattern of behavior among Christians that would remove any possibility of criticism from the non-Christian community. Wives were to love their husbands and children, to be discreet, chaste, homemakers, good, and obedient to their own husbands for a specific purpose: "that the word of God may not be blasphemed" (Titus 2:4-5, NKJV). To blaspheme is to speak evil against something. The behavior of Christian wives was to be such that unbelievers would have no ground to speak evil against the gospel as if it were a movement subversive to the stability of the family. Young men were to be sober minded, to show a lifestyle of good works, to be persons of integrity, reverence, incorruptibility, and sound speech so that "one who is an opponent may be ashamed, having nothing evil to say" (Titus 2:6-8, NKJV). Slaves were to be obedient to their masters and well pleasing, not engaging in back talk or pilfering, but showing good faithfulness "that they may adorn the doctrine of God our Savior in all things" (Titus 2:9-10, NKJV). All of this was to be done so the early believers would not be despised (Titus 2:15). The close connection of these instructions with the command to "be subject to rulers and authorities, to obey" (Titus 3:1, NKJV) seems to extend the idea of submission as Christian witness to the relationship of a Christian citizen to the government.

Rather than viewing the house codes as focusing on the submission of citizens, wives, children and slaves—which was already the norm in society at large—we should understand them as introducing a new dimension and purpose to the citizen-government, wife-husband, child-father, and slave-master relationships. It was nothing new to call on citizens to submit, but there was a new dimension in viewing this submission as voluntary, in view of the true freedom of believers and as a part of their Christian witness (2:15-16). It was nothing new to call on wives to submit, but it was something new to call on husbands to love their wives in a self-sacrificing way. There was nothing novel in the appeal for children to obey their parents, but there was something innovative in calling on fathers not to provoke their children but to bring them up in the nurture and admonition of the Lord. There was nothing strange about the call for slaves to be obedient to their masters, but it was a radically new idea to call on masters to reciprocate by giving up threats and treating them with goodwill.

In other words, Christianity did not seek to overthrow the established ethics of society. It sought to lift those ethics to new heights by infusing love, kindness, and thoughtfulness into human relationships.

Verse 13. The word translated "submit" (*hypotagete*) is the imperative form of *hypotassein*, which I Peter uses of the submission required of believing citizens to the civil rulers, of believing slaves to their masters (2:18), of believing wives to their unbelieving husbands (3:1, 5) and of younger believers to their elders (5:5). In the midst of this discussion there is a reference to Sarah's obedience (*hypakouein*) to Abraham (3:6). In his treatment of the house codes, Paul used *hypotassein* in the call for mutual submission and the submission of wives to husbands (Ephesians 5:21, 22, 24; Colossians 3:18), but he used *hypakouein* to describe the obedience of children to their parents and of slaves to their masters

(Colossians 3:20, 22; Ephesians 6:1, 5).

The two words are not synonyms. *Hypakoe* (from which *hypakouein* derives) calls for a "primary and radical commitment while *hypotassein* represents a secondary and more limited one."[151] Other than the brief reference to Sarah, Peter used *hypakoe* exclusively to describe the believer's obedience to the gospel (1:2, 14, 22). The point is that the submission that Christians are to give to civil government, masters, and unbelieving husbands is not identical to the obedience they are to give to Christ. Michaels makes a strong case that the contextual idea behind *hypotassein* is more an idea of deference or respect than of radical obedience.

Indeed, it is evident that God does not call believers to unquestioning obedience to civil authority. Examples of civil disobedience approved by God are not uncommon in Scripture. (See Exodus 1:17; I Kings 21:1-3; Daniel 3:13-18; 6:10-24; Acts 4:18-20; 5:27-29; Hebrews 11:23.) By definition, then, the submission given to human beings cannot be in the same category as the unquestioning and total obedience given to God. When obedience to civil authority would at the same time be disobedience to God, believers must obey God regardless of the temporal consequences.

The word translated "ordinance" is the Greek *ktisis*, which in this context describes the result of the establishment of an "authoritative or governmental body."[152] We might infer from the English word "ordinance" that it is the believer's responsibility to be fully obedient to every humanly established law, but that is not the point. It is the institution of human authority itself that is due the believer's respect and deference. The idea is that believers are

First Peter

to submit to established human authority. These authority structures include civil government (verses 13-14), the master-slave relationship (verses 18-20), and the marriage relationship (3:1-7). There may be specific laws of human government that the believer cannot endorse or obey. There may be specific demands made by a master that a believing slave cannot obey. There may be specific wishes of an unbelieving husband that a believing wife cannot obey. The call to submit to "every ordinance of man" is not a call to unquestioning obedience to all that those in any structure of human authority may demand; it is a call to respect and defer to every structure of human authority.

The reason believers are to show respect to human authority is "for the Lord's sake." The motivation for believers is not the fear of man, but the fear of God (verse 17). The believer's conduct in his relationship with other people, regardless of the social structure, is a part of his Christian witness (verses 12, 15; 3:16)

That we should understand "every ordinance of man" to mean every established human authority rather than every specific law is indicated not only by the meaning of *ktisis* but also by the first "ordinance" to which I Peter refers, namely, "the king, as supreme." In other words, the call is for deference and respect to a person rather than to an impersonal code of laws.

The word *basileus*, translated "king," referred to "world monarchs (like Alexander the Great or the Roman emperors) and to kings and princes of more limited domain (like Alexander's successors or the Herods)."[153] In this case, Peter referred to the Roman emperor Nero, who reigned A.D. 54-68, and who was responsible for the per-

130

secution that would later take Peter's life.[154] By qualifying the king as "supreme," Peter distinguished Nero from various representatives of the Roman Empire who ruled under Nero's authority.

In no reference to the believer's responsibility to submit to human authorities is there any suggestion that he should submit only to those authorities who are themselves believers. Instead, the indication is that those in authority will ordinarily be unbelievers, for the believer's submission is designed to "put to silence the ignorance of foolish men" (verse 15), an apparent reference to those unbelievers who are in authority.

Verse 14. Not only must believers respect and show deference to the supreme human authority; they must have the same attitude toward those to whom the supreme king has delegated authority.[155] The word translated "governor" (*hegemon*) describes Pilate (Matthew 27:2) and Felix (Acts 23:24).[156] To submit to those whom the king has appointed is to submit to the king himself.

Ideally, the purpose for civil government is to punish those who do evil and to reward those who do good. Romans 13:3-4 expresses the same idea. It is a responsibility of civil government to punish (*ekdikesis*) wrongdoers. The word "punish" is not a mild word; it indicates actually taking revenge. (See its use in Luke 18:7-8, 21:22; Acts 7:27; Romans 12:19; II Thessalonians 1:8; Hebrews 10:30.) The biblical idea of civil government's role in dealing with evildoers is not rehabilitation. Capital punishment as a function of civil government is first indicated in Genesis 9:6, but it is reiterated as late as Romans 13, where the representative of civil government is a minister of God who does not bear the sword for nothing.[157]

First Peter

Instead, he is "God's minister, an avenger to execute wrath on him who practices evil" (Romans 13:4).

Contextually, this statement informs Romans 12:19, which indicates that believers are not to seek their own vengeance against those who do evil to them. The reason is that vengeance belongs to God. The way God takes vengeance in the temporal realm is by civil government. The sword was the most common instrument of capital punishment in the Roman Empire in the first century. Though many were crucified, crucifixion was reserved for those considered to be the dregs of society, the most hardened and disgusting criminals. For this reason, Philippians 2:8 points out that not only did Jesus humble Himself to become obedient to the point of death, but that it was "even the death of the cross."

One difficulty here is that those whom God has raised up to exercise civil authority may themselves disobey God in the exercise of their authority. Theoretically, a civil ruler could punish those who do good and reward those who do evil. In such a case, civil government abdicates its responsibility and thus compromises to a large degree its claim on the people for submission. In the area of spiritual leadership, a leader can legitimately call on people to follow him only if he is faithful in following Christ (I Corinthians 11:1; Hebrews 13:7). Likewise, the civil ruler who is not fulfilling his God-given role has little claim on the obedience and loyalty of the people.

Some oppressive governments in today's world forbid people to have faith in Christ, to worship the true God, or to share their faith. Obviously, governments that make such decrees are rebelling against God. There is little room to respect and defer to those who rebel against

God, whether their rebellion is in the area of the spiritual life, in civil government, in marriage, or in the family. This does not mean that a man must be a believer before his wife should submit to him (3:1-6), but it does mean that if he exercises his prerogatives as a husband in rebellion against God, contrary to the responsibilities God gives to husbands, then he has abdicated his right to the respect and deference of his wife. For example, if he abuses his wife physically, mentally, or morally, he is due no respect or deference. If a father abuses his children, he is not due their respect or deference.

Insofar as those in authority exercise their authority in a way that reflects their God-given purpose, they are due the submission discussed by Peter and Paul.

It is true that servants should submit not only to good and gentle masters, but also to those who are harsh (verse 18), but this does not mean believing servants are to respect and defer to masters who abuse them in their own rebellion against God. The point is simply that the servant's duty to submit is not conditioned upon the master's personality. In submitting to a harsh master, a servant may be falsely accused and even beaten (verses 19-20). This possibility is inherent in the master-slave relationship, and the slave should take such treatment patiently, viewing his submission to his master as his duty to God. But a slave is not obliged to submit to every conceivable kind of abusive behavior imaginable at the hands of his master. There comes a time when the master's ill treatment of the slave is not a simple, though painful, matter of the master exercising poor judgment, in the same sense that a father may mistakenly discipline a child for something the child did not do. When the treatment goes beyond human error or poor judgment into the realm of unreasonable abuse resulting from the master's (or a father's) rebellion against God, the person being injured is under no obligation to submit to that injury.

Some people interpret the passage from 2:13-3:6 as suggesting that believers must submit unquestioningly and without reservation to ungodly civil rulers, masters, and husbands. They suggest that just as Jesus died for our sins, resulting in the Atonement (verse 24), so we can suffer for the sins of others, thus in some way bringing them to faith in Christ. Such interpretations are usually rich in anecdotes to "prove" the effectiveness of this approach.

But this view reads into the passage a meaning not there, and it fails to take into consideration the broad evidence in Scripture for reasoned disobedience by believers when to obey an authority figure who is in rebellion against God would be to sin against God Himself.

It is true that the passage draws upon the example of Christ, who suffered for us, leaving us an example that we should follow (verse 21). It is true that He suffered unjustly to the point of death (verses 22-24). But His example does not mean that believers must die at the hands of an unbelieving husband or of an unbelieving master. I Peter carefully defines the extent of submission expected of believers in these relationships, and it nowhere mentions death as a possible outcome. The servant is to be submissive to the point of accepting unjust punishment. The wife is to be submissive to the point of being gentle and quiet (3:4). The example of Christ simply shows that submission to those in authority sometimes results in unjust treatment. In Jesus' case, this treatment concluded with death. But, of course, it had been the plan of God from the foundation of the world that the Messiah would die for the sins of the people (1:18-20). It may be the will of God for others to die (4:19), but this does not mean it is the will of God for all believers to die at the hands of unbelievers. Neither does the death of any believer atone in any way for the sins of others. There was only one atoning death.

When civil government strays from its God-ordained responsibilities—punishing evildoers and rewarding those who do good—into other areas, it is out of its depth. Generally speaking, the efforts of civil government in education, health care, child care, and other social agendas will be more costly than necessary and less effective than desired. Ideally, families, churches, and private charitable organizations should take care of social concerns. We do not live in an ideal world, however.

It is the responsibility of believers to pray for those who are in authority, so that they "may lead a quiet and peaceable life" (I Timothy 2:2, NKJV). Believers should pray that those in civil government would fulfill their God-ordained responsibilities of punishing evildoers and rewarding those who do good. In addition, believers should pray for the salvation of those who are in authority (I Timothy 2:4).

Verse 15. Submission to civil government is the will of God. The idea of the "will of God" is a characteristic of Peter's letter. (See 3:17; 4:2, 19.) The intent of this submission is to silence the criticism that ignorant, foolish people direct against believers. The word "ignorance" (*agnoisia*) is not derogatory. It simply indicates that these people are unable to understand Christian beliefs, values, and behavior because of their lack of Christian experience.[158] The word "foolish" (*aphron*) is a derogatory term. It describes the same group identified as "Gentiles" in verse 12. (See also verse 12 and 3:16.) It may be that these critics claimed that Christianity was subversive to civil government. If so, the submission of believers to civil government would silence that claim.

Verse 16. Although I Peter calls on believers to submit to every institution of human authority, it acknowledges that they are "free." This discussion recalls Peter's encounter with Jesus concerning the payment of religious taxes. (See Matthew 17:24-27.) Even though the sons of God were by virtue of their identity exempt from paying the Temple tax, Jesus said that they should pay it to avoid offending those who were in authority at the Temple.

The law of Moses told Israelite males who were twenty years of age and up to pay the Temple tax annually (Exodus 30:11-16).[159] Jesus' statement that He and His disciples were really free from any obligation to pay the tax was a significant statement concerning the termination of the law. After the coming of Jesus, and even before the establishment of the church, people of true faith in God were free from obligation to the Temple rituals in Jerusalem. Although the law of Moses was still in effect (Galatians 4:4), the religious authorities in Jerusalem did not accurately represent the law themselves. The high priesthood had degenerated into a political appointment. Although some people of faith were still involved (Luke 1:5-25), those in authority were not faithful to God. Twice Jesus found it necessary to cleanse the Temple, which had become a house of merchandise. The Holy of Holies was an empty chamber; the ark of the covenant had not been seen since the invading Babylonians had destroyed Jerusalem and the Temple.

The true sons of God were those who had faith in Jesus (John 3:16-18). Their faith in Jesus made them exempt from the empty ceremonies surrounding Herod's Temple. They thus had no obligation to pay the Temple tax. But Jesus based the payment of the tax not upon obligation but upon the need to avoid offending those who perpetuated the Temple rituals. To refuse to pay the tax because of their freedom would have further alienated the Jewish leaders, who were among those Jesus wished to win.

Likewise, believers are free from obligation to civil government since they are the children of the heavenly King. But they are to show respect and deference to civil government because of their larger concern of winning those in civil government to Christ. (See I Timothy 2:2-4.)

The word "as," which begins this verse, refers back to verse 13 (verse 15 is grammatically parenthetical), indicating that believers are to submit as those who are free.[160] In other words, their submission is voluntary. Believers are not servants of civil government; they are servants of God.

> This theme emerged from a Jewish strand of thought that developed . . . when the people of the Land found themselves in subjection to foreign powers. . . . True members of the covenant knew that their ultimate allegiance was only to the God of the covenant. Consequently, while submission was required, it was not the relationship that sustained and protected them. They were servants of God alone. This theme became a natural setting for

understanding early Christian persecution, and Peter's words here are to be interpreted in that setting.[161]

Although believers are free in the sense that civil government is not their master, they are to submit voluntarily rather than "using liberty as a cloak for vice" (NKJV). They are the servants of God, and their complete obedience to Him entails voluntary submission to civil government. Rather than engaging in anarchy, they are to use voluntary submission as a witness to their faith in Christ and to eliminate a potential stumbling block to faith from the path of unbelievers.

Verse 17. Here, four statements define the believer's duty to all people, to the brotherhood, to God, and to the king. The first statement, "Honour all men," is an aorist imperative. The following three statements are present imperatives, indicating the ongoing nature of the responsibility specified. The use of the aorist here does not indicate that honoring all people is merely a one-time duty; it is the tense to use when commanding an action without specifying any more about it.[162]

The word "men" is not in the Greek text. A literal translation would be "honor all," with the understanding that Christians are to honor all people. The word translated "honor" (*time*) means to show respect based on the value one perceives others to have.[163] In a practical sense, it is a simple demonstration of common courtesy. Later, I Peter urges readers to "be courteous" (3:8). There is no place for rudeness in the Christian life.

Though believers are to honor all people, whether these people are themselves believers or not, they are to love the brotherhood. Encouragement to love one another is common in the New Testament.[164] The word translated "love" here is from *agapao*, the highest form of love in the Greek language. It is love that involves intelligence, reason, and comprehension rather than merely feelings. We see its practical demonstration in I Corinthians 13:4-8. It is the kind of love that proves Christian discipleship (John 13:35).

Believers are to fear God. The word translated fear (*phobeo*) is from *phobos*, which Peter used in 1:17, 2:18, 3:2, and 3:15. Although the word can have to do with terror, it also can denote reverence, veneration, or deference. (See comments on 1:17.) Believers are not to fear any human being in the same sense that they are to fear God. (See 3:14.) The immediate context of this command contrasts the attitude that believers are to have toward God with the attitude they are to have toward others. They are to honor all people, to love the brotherhood, and to honor the king. But they are to fear God. (See also Acts 5:5, 11; 9:31; Romans 3:18; II Corinthians 7:1, 11; Philippians 2:12; Colossians 3:22; I Timothy 5:20.) The fear to which servants are called in 2:18 is evidently still the fear of God, not the fear of their masters. (See Colossians 3:22.) The fear exercised by the believing wife in 3:2 is thus also the fear of God, not a terror of her unbelieving husband. The fear with which believers are to answer their questioners in 3:15 is also the fear of God.

Believers are to have the same attitude toward the king as they are to have toward all people: they are to honor him. Thus the relationship of the believer with civil government is underscored. It does not consist of servitude, nor is it characterized by terror. (See Romans 13:8.)

First Peter

It is a voluntary showing of respect or deference. The first-century readers may have read between the lines that even though the emperor claimed to be divine, he was merely a human being worthy of respect by virtue of his humanity and office. He was not worthy of the kind of fear reserved for God alone.[165]

C. Responsible Conduct of Slaves toward Their Masters (2:18-25)

(18) Servants, be subject to your masters with all fear; not only to the good and gentle, but also to the froward. (19) For this is thankworthy, if a man for conscience toward God endure grief, suffering wrongfully. (20) For what glory is it, if, when ye be buffeted for your faults, ye shall take it patiently? but if, when ye do well, and suffer for it, ye take it patiently, this is acceptable with God. (21) For even hereunto were ye called: because Christ also suffered for us, leaving us an example, that ye should follow his steps: (22) who did no sin, neither was guile found in his mouth: (23) who, when he was reviled, reviled not again; when he suffered, he threatened not; but committed himself to him that judgeth righteously: (24) who his own self bare our sins in his own body on the tree, that we, being dead to sins, should live unto righteousness: by whose stripes ye were healed. (25) For ye were as sheep going astray; but are now returned unto the Shepherd and Bishop of your souls.

In view of the obvious repulsiveness of slavery to cultures that have been influenced by the Christian ethic of the equal value of all people (Galatians 3:28; Colossians 3:11), it may seem strange that New Testament writers urged believing slaves to submit to their masters. (In addition to 2:18-25, see Colossians 3:22-25; Ephesians 6:5-8.)

By Roman law, "the head of a household could legally execute his slaves, and they would all be executed if the head of the household was murdered."[166] Although Roman law did recognize slaves as persons, it also declared them to be property.[167] As property, they were abused by some owners and treated as socially inferior by nearly all owners.[168] During the expansion of the Roman empire, many of the conquered people were taken as slaves; some people had simply been kidnapped and forced into slavery. By the time of the first century, many slaves were the descendants of such victims. These first-century slaves were born in the household of their masters.

There were three basic categories of slaves during the first century. The first, discussed in this passage, consisted of household slaves. A second category was the field slaves, who did much of the agricultural work. A third category consisted of mine slaves; they were abused most harshly and often died after only brief service in the mines.[169]

But slaves could be found in all professions. They were paid for their work and could entertain the possibility of eventually being able to purchase their freedom.[170] In many ways, household slaves found themselves in a situation superior to free peasants, most of whom worked "as tenant farmers on the vast estates of wealthy landowners."[171]

It would have been pointless for New Testament writers to lash out against the institution of slavery. They did

First Peter

not address their letters to political movers and shakers who perhaps could, if they would, do something about the problem. They wrote to believers who found themselves living in the full range of social relationships of the first century, including slavery. These believers needed to know how to live out their Christian faith where they were.

Though a few people in the first century apparently declared that slavery was "against nature," their views were not popularly accepted.[172] Peter's letter offers practical advice, not hopeless rhetoric intended to incite social upheaval. "No ancient slave war was successful, and abolition was virtually impossible in [Peter's] day except through a probably doomed bloody revolution."[173]

In view of the prohibition of the law of Moses on returning a runaway slave to his master (Deuteronomy 23:15-16), it is significant that Paul sent Onesimus back to his believing master, Philemon. First, his action signals the termination of the law of Moses; Paul did not view it as binding. Second, it demonstrates how first-century believers functioned, so far as possible, within the social structure of the day. Paul did not endorse Onesimus's escape. Neither did he command Philemon to release all his slaves. Instead, he appealed to him to treat Onesimus as a beloved brother. (See Philemon 16; Ephesians 6:9; Colossians 4:1.)

Verse 18. The servants in view here are household servants. The Greek word for "house" or "household" is *oikos*, and the word translated "servants" is *oiketes*. The more common Greek word for slaves of all kinds in the New Testament is *doulos*.

Some have suggested that the nearest relationship to this in the modern world is the employer-employee relationship.[174] On this basis, some use the master-slave passages of the Epistles to teach employers and employees how to relate. But this use overlooks the fact that the slave served involuntarily. Employees, on the other hand, choose where they wish to work, and they are free to terminate their employment at any time. In a sense, all employees are really self-employed. To draw too heavily on these passages in applying them to the employer-employee relationship might result in some employees unnecessarily submitting to ruthless treatment and passing up excellent opportunities for advancement with other employers. We can draw greater insight for employer-employee relationships from passages of Scripture that address voluntary relationships between equals, such as the command to honor all people (2:17) and the command to show courtesy (3:8). The Book of Proverbs is rich in wisdom affecting the complete spectrum of human relationships.

The word translated "be subject" is from the same word that is translated "submit yourselves" in verse 13. In contrast with the word translated "obeyed" in 2:6, this word has to do with deference and respect. Though it implies obedience, it is not unquestioning, unqualified obedience. (See comments on verse 13.) Indeed, as in the relationship of believers to civil government, it is voluntary submission. (See comments on verse 16.)

One might think that the command for servants to submit to their masters "with all fear" means that the servants are to fear their masters. But the influence of the context indicates that this is still the fear of God. In the immediately previous verse, it is God alone who is to be feared. (See comments on verse 17.) Believers are

First Peter

not to fear human beings (3:6, 14). In Paul's letters, it is clearly God whom slaves are to fear (Colossians 3:22). When Paul called on slaves to relate to their masters with "fear and trembling," it was because the masters in some way represented Christ (Ephesians 6:5).[175] From a Jewish perspective, any other view would at least tend toward idolatry, because only God deserves unquestioning obedience; He alone is to be feared. Where Scripture commands people to fear a human king, it is in conjunction with the fear of God. That is, the king in some way represents God. (See Matthew 4:10; Proverbs 24:21.) Doing good is a way to avoid the fear of civil government (Romans 13:3). The only people who need to fear civil government are those who do evil (Romans 13:4).

Servants are to "be submissive" to their masters, whether they are good and gentle or "harsh" (NKJV). The word translated "froward" by the KJV is *skolios*, which means "crooked, unscrupulous, dishonest."[176] Here, unbelieving masters are in view, whereas Ephesians 6:9 and Colossians 4:1 have believing masters in view. Even the "good and gentle" masters were apparently unbelievers, or I Peter would have addressed believing masters to inform them of their Christian duties, as did Paul. Therefore, although I Peter does not repeat its earlier reasoning for submission, it describes the believing slave's submission to the unbelieving master as "the will of God, that by doing good you may put to silence the ignorance of foolish men" (verse 15, NKJV). This is an extension of the idea introduced in verse 13, where "Gentiles" are obviously unbelievers who may come to glorify God by observing the good works of believers.

Exhortations in View of Social Groupings

Unfortunately, the passages in the house codes sections of the Epistles were sometimes used to justify slavery in the early history of the United States of America. Whereas these passages were written to instruct believers on how to relate in a social milieu that predated Christianity, an environment in which they lived when they came to Christ, the meaning was twisted to condone slavery as an institution that so-called Christians could impose on free people. Contrary to this notion, Paul encouraged those who came to the Lord while they were slaves to obtain their freedom, if possible. Even if it was impossible, believing slaves were not to view themselves as the slaves of people, but of Christ. (See I Corinthians 7:21-23.) Paul told Philemon that he should no longer treat Onesimus as a slave but as a brother. Overall, the New Testament's message of equality and freedom was so powerful that many slaveholders in the United States did not want their slaves to be exposed to Christianity.[177]

Verses 19-20 call believing slaves to suffer wrongfully and to endure grief because of their "conscience toward God." In other words, Peter did not base his appeal on a divine mandate for slavery but on the possibility of turning a painful but unavoidable social requirement into an opportunity for Christian witness. God counts the willing endurance of wrongful suffering as "commendable" (NKJV). The word translated "thankworthy" by the KJV and "commendable" by the NKJV is *charis*, which is ordinarily translated "grace." In this context, it refers to "that which counts with God or that with which God is pleased."[178] It is repeated in verse 20, where the KJV translates it as "acceptable."

It is not suffering in and of itself that counts with God;

this passage does not endorse asceticism or Stoicism. The suffering that counts with God is wrongful suffering "for conscience toward God." It is undeserved suffering for the sake of one's Christian testimony. (See 3:14, 17; 4:14-16.)

There is, of course, nothing worthy of praise in patiently submitting to being beaten if one deserves the beating. No unbelieving slaveholder would have considered it remarkable for a slave to submit to deserved punishment. There would have been nothing in this to impress him with the slave's Christian testimony. But if a slave did the right thing and yet patiently submitted to suffering just as if he had done the wrong thing, that was remarkable, and the potential for witness was there.

The word translated "glory" is *kleos*, which carries the idea of "praise." The word translated "buffeted" is *kolaphizo*, which means "to mistreat" or "to treat roughly."[179] It is translated "beaten" by the NKJV. It was not uncommon for masters in the first century to beat their slaves. But I Peter introduces the possibility that an unbelieving master might beat his slave for doing good. This beating might occur even at the hands of a "good and gentle" master who exercised poor judgment in executing his legal rights. Or it could occur at the hands of a crooked master who knew his slave did not deserve a beating. In any event, the believing slave who patiently submitted as a Christian testimony would please God.

We should not read into this text more than is actually here. Although it cites Christ as an example of unjust suffering that led to death (verses 21-24), it does not follow that believing slaves must willingly die at the hands of unscrupulous masters. Even the law of Moses recognized a slave's right to escape from his master (Deuteronomy

Exhortations in View of Social Groupings

23:15-16). There is no reason to think that if a slave's life was in danger it would be dishonorable for him to flee for his life. The limits of the slave's duty is to submit willingly to unjust suffering. If there are circumstances that justify a wife in departing from her husband (I Corinthians 7:11), there must be circumstances that would justify a slave in fleeing from a master.

Verse 21. As an example to believing slaves who suffered at the hands of their masters, I Peter turns to the suffering of Christ. No doubt, as we shall see, it also applies the example of Christ to all believers in any relationship where they are subject to authority.

When believers encounter unjust suffering, they are to accept it as their calling. If Christ willingly suffered, so should those who profess to be followers of Christ. (See John 13:14-16 for another instance of following Jesus' example in servanthood.) I Peter uses the calling motif several times. Believers are called to holy conduct (1:15); they are called out of darkness into the marvelous light of Christ (2:9); they are called to return blessing to those who revile them or do evil to them (3:9); they are called ultimately to enjoy eternal glory (5:10); and they are called to patiently endure unjust suffering (2:20). The word "this" refers back to the immediately previous discussion of believing slaves who suffer for doing good.[180]

Christ was a completely innocent sufferer (verse 22). Believers, at best, are not completely innocent. That is, even if they are suffering for good they have done, they still retain the sin principle and are not flawless in attitude, words, or behavior. If the completely innocent Christ willingly suffered, it is only reasonable that believers willingly accept the suffering that sometimes comes with doing good. (See John 15:18-20; 16:33; Acts 14:22; I Thessalonians 3:3-4; II Timothy 3:12.)

The reference in this verse is to the sufferings of Christ rather than to His death. That is, it cites the ongoing sufferings that led up to His death. The passage connects the sufferings in verse 21 with the reviling and suffering in verse 23. In that verse, the imperfect tense of the words translated "threatened" and "committed" indicates that it was ongoing activity in the past. (See Luke 24:26; Philippians 3:10; Hebrews 2:10; 12:2-3; I Peter 1:11.) Although Jesus suffered once for sins (3:18), His suffering was not limited to His atoning work on the cross. It was in a very real sense characteristic of His entire life.

This ongoing suffering is an appropriate example, because to some degree it characterizes the experience of believers. Believers may suffer at various points throughout their Christian life, as they experience the rejection of unbelievers. This rejection is always uncomfortable; it sometimes blossoms into full-blown persecution. Ultimately, suffering may result in martyrdom.

One may think that the phrase "Christ also suffered for us" refers specifically to the atoning work of Christ, but though the Atonement is definitely the subject of verse 24, the idea of Christ suffering "for us" here is contextually defined in terms of the example He has provided for us. In other words, He suffered "for our benefit" in the sense of leaving us an example to follow.[181]

This is the only place the word translated "example" (Greek, *hypogrammon*) appears in the New Testament. It has to do with a "model" or "pattern to be copied in writing or drawing."[182] Clement of Alexandria used the word for the patterns of letters impressed upon wax tablets so children could learn to shape the letters properly.[183] In conjunction with the metaphorical phrase "that ye should follow in his steps," it indicates that to follow Christ's example is not to "reproduce all the details" of His suffering but "to move in the direction he is going."[184] The idea is not that the suffering of believers will in any way be redemptive or atoning; the example is limited to the ongoing suffering itself.

I Peter characteristically uses "Christ" to refer to the Messiah in "his suffering and redemptive death (1:11, 19; 3:18; 4:1, 13, 14; 5:1) and in the daily life of the Christian community (3:15,[185] 16; 4:14; 5:14), while 'Jesus Christ' (in the genitive) is used in connection with his resurrection from the dead (1:3; 3:21), his place at the center of Christian worship (2:5; 4:11), and in his final revelation in glory (1:7, 13)."[186] "Christ" is transliterated from the Greek *Christos*, which is the equivalent of the Hebrew *Messiach*, and both words mean "anointed." "Christ" focuses on the genuineness and fullness of the Messiah's humanity as anointed by the Holy Spirit (e.g., Luke 4:18), whereas "Jesus" (transliterated from the Greek *Iesous*, which means "Yahweh will save") focuses on the genuineness and fullness of His deity. It is by means of the Incarnation, in which He added true human existence to His prior existence as God, that Jesus suffered, died redemptively, and identifies with the day-to-day existence of human beings. On the other hand, it is because of His deity that He rose from the dead, deserves worship, and will ultimately be revealed in glory. II Peter uses "Jesus Christ" exclusively, always with an emphasis on His deity. (See II Peter 1:1, 8, 11, 14, 16; 2:20; 3:18.)

Verse 22. Beginning here and extending through verse 25 there is a series of rather free quotes from the Septuagint version of Isaiah 53. Here, Peter referred to Isaiah 53:9b. The Hebrew text is translated, "Because He had done no violence, nor was any deceit in His mouth" (NKJV). The Septuagint reads, "For he practiced no iniquity [literally "lawlessness" (Greek, *anomian*)], nor craft with his mouth." I Peter renders the statement, "Who committed no sin, nor was deceit found in His mouth" (NKJV). It is possible that I Peter uses "sin" rather than "lawlessness" or "violence" because thematically it deals with the issue of suffering even when one is not guilty of sin. Verse 20 contrasts "faults" with doing well. The word translated "faults" is *hamartanontes*, from *hamartano*, which means "to sin." Verse 24 declares that Jesus bore our sins in His own body on the tree. Thus, verse 22 is framed by a reference to sin before and after it. This focus on innocent suffering may influence the meaning of verse 22, prompting the use of "sin" in the place of the Septuagint "lawlessness" and the Hebrew "violence." In any event, the Septuagint rendering of Isaiah 53:9 poetically equates sin (*hamartias*) and lawlessness (*anomias*), as did the apostle John. (See I John 3:4.)[187]

The emphasis at this point is not so much on the inherent sinlessness of Christ, as described elsewhere (e.g., Matthew 27:4; John 8:29, 46; John 18:38; II Corinthians 5:21; Hebrews 4:15; 7:26; I John 3:5), but that His sufferings were unprovoked. Although He had done nothing and said nothing to merit the suffering He experienced, He willingly suffered at the hands of His critics.

Likewise, it was possible that first-century believers

would find themselves in situations where they would face unprovoked suffering. They could certainly expect this to occur in any relationship where they were called on to submit to authority. If this happened, they were to follow Christ's example and suffer patiently. Their submission would be a testimony to the genuineness of their faith; it would serve to defuse the criticisms that claimed Christianity was subversive of the established order.[188]

Verse 23. There may be an allusion here to Isaiah 53:7, although the connection is not as clear as the obvious relationship of verses 22, 24, and 25 with Isaiah's great Messianic passage describing the suffering substitutionary work of the Redeemer. Although He had done nothing to deserve being reviled, Christ did not respond in kind or threaten those who reviled Him.

The word translated "reviled" (*loidoroumenos*, from *loidoreo*) means "to reproach" or "to heap abuse upon." Jesus was frequently reviled. This included, but was not limited to, the verbal abuse to which He was subjected in conjunction with His capture, trial, and crucifixion. (See Matthew 11:19; 26:67-68; 27:12-14, 28-31, 39-44; Mark 3:22; Luke 22:63-65; 23:9-11; John 7:20; 8:41, 48, 52.) Modeling His own counsel from Matthew 5:10-12, Jesus refused to allow His persecutors to set an agenda for Him. (See also Romans 12:14, 17-21; I Peter 3:9.)

Not only did Christ not respond in kind to those who reviled Him, neither did He threaten them. That is, He not only refused to seek immediate vengeance, He also refused to threaten future vengeance. In many cases, those who are unable to exact immediate revenge will threaten future revenge "to give their enemies at least the anxiety that revenge may be taken sometime in the future."[189]

First Peter

It may be that I Peter focuses on sins of speech because that was the primary sort of persecution the readers had experienced up to this point. (See 2:12, 15; 3:16; 4:4, 14.)[190] Believers would immediately set themselves apart from the unbelieving world around them if they refused retaliation. (See 2:1; 3:9.)

Instead of responding in kind or threatening to do so later, Christ "committed himself to him that judgeth righteously." The word "himself" is supplied by the translators; there is no equivalent in the Greek text. The context, however, suggests that the implied object of "committed" is Christ's enemies, just as they are the object of the verbs translated "reviled not again" and "threatened not." In other words, Christ entrusted to God those who reviled Him. He knew that God was a righteous judge who would make precisely the right decision in every situation.[191] (See 1:17; 4:5.)

The words translated "reviled not again" (*antiloidoreo*), "threatened not" (*apeileo*), and "committed" (*paradidomi*) are all in the imperfect tense. It indicates ongoing activity in the past. The verbal abuse heaped upon Jesus was not a one-time phenomenon. But He was completely consistent in responding to the ongoing abuse by entrusting to God those who abused Him. He did not take the situation into His own hands to seek vengeance.

Believers are to follow the example of Christ's response to unjust suffering. They are never to resort to responding in kind to verbal abuse, nor are they to threaten future reprisals. Instead, they must commit the situation and those who abuse them to God. (See 3:15-17.)

Verse 24 clearly indicates the substitutionary and aton-

Exhortations in View of Social Groupings

ing nature of Christ's death. The reference here is apparently to Isaiah 53:12: "He hath poured out his soul unto death: and he was numbered with the transgressors; and he bare the sin of many, and made intercession for the transgressors." There could also be a reference to the Septuagint translation of Isaiah 53:4: "He bears our sins, and is pained for us." Peter was not the only writer to see the prophecies of Isaiah 53 fulfilled in the sufferings of Christ. Luke 22:37 records Jesus applying Isaiah 53:12 to Himself; Acts 8:32-35 has Philip preaching Jesus to the Ethiopian eunuch with a Septuagint form of Isaiah 53:7-8 as his text.

God is absolutely holy and sinless. By virtue of His very nature, He cannot countenance sin. Sin carries the death penalty (Genesis 2:15-17; Ezekiel 18:20; Romans 6:23).

Sinners are unable to do anything to help themselves. No one is righteous, no one understands, and no one seeks after God in and of himself (Romans 3:10-11). Therefore, if there is to be an atonement, someone else has to make it on behalf of humanity. The only one who could make such an atonement would be one who, while human, was not merely human. Only God could offer a sufficient price, since a sacrifice of infinite value would be necessary to atone for a world of sin.

In the person of Christ, God added humanity to His deity in order to atone for the sins of humanity. Since Jesus was a man who had never sinned, He could die in place of people who had; since He was God His life was of infinite value.

We must understand the Atonement in the context of the Old Testament sacrificial system, which was a foreshadowing of Christ's sacrifice. (See Hebrews 9:22, 28;

10:1-14.) The word "atonement" means "to cover." In the Old Testament era, a sacrifice was offered as a substitute for the sinner, providing a covering for his sin by interposing a sacrifice between the sin and God. The sacrificial animal had to be perfect in every way. The one for whom the atonement was being made was to present the sacrificial animal to the priest and lay his hands upon it as a confession of guilt and as a symbolic transfer of that guilt to the animal. (See Leviticus 1:3-4.)

Jesus saw His primary purpose for coming into this world as the death of the cross, by means of which He would provide a ransom by being a substitute. (See Luke 22:37; Mark 8:31; Matthew 20:28; John 15:13.) Jesus said, "And for their sakes I sanctify myself" (John 17:19). The word translated "sanctify" (*hagiadzo*) is a common term in sacrificial contexts in the Septuagint.

John the Baptist declared the substitutionary and sacrificial roles of the Messiah. (See John 1:29.) Even Caiaphas, the unbelieving high priest, was an instrument in the hands of the sovereign God in declaring the substitutionary work of Christ. (See John 11:49-52; 18:14.)

The Atonement was the work of God Himself in Christ. (See II Corinthians 5:19.) It was a demonstration of the love of God and was substitutionary in nature. (See Romans 5:8-11; II Corinthians 5:14-15; I Thessalonians 5:10.) Christ fulfilled the symbolism of the Passover lamb. (See I Corinthians 5:7.) The death of Christ was propitiatory. It actually appeased the wrath of God against sin. (See Romans 3:24-26; 5:9; Ephesians 1:7; 2:13; Colossians 1:20-22; Galatians 3:13-14.)

The Atonement was such a supreme price that it guaranteed all lesser gifts. (See Romans 8:32.)

I Peter personalizes the prophecy of Isaiah 53:12. The Hebrew text reads, "He bore the sin of many," as does the Septuagint. I Peter, however, declares that Christ bore "our sins." In some wonderful, miraculous, incomprehensible way, "the LORD has laid on Him the iniquity of us all" (Isaiah 53:6, NKJV). The death of Jesus on the cross fully and finally satisfied the righteous judgment of God against sin. As a result, no one can bring a legitimate charge against God's elect. On the basis of the death of Christ, God has justified us. (See Romans 8:33-34.)

The Atonement occurred as Christ bore our sins in His own body. (See Hebrews 10:5, 10.) The Incarnation was essential to redemption. Christ was able to bear the sins of the human race because He was a human being. (See Hebrews 2:9-18; 4:15; 5:7.) It was on the "tree" that He bore our sins in His body. The word translated "tree" (*xylon*) is used in a variety of contexts to mean wood, objects made of wood, a pole, a club, a cudgel, gallows, a cross, and a tree.[192] It is significant that Peter did not use the Greek *dendron*, which specifically has reference to trees.[193] Peter did not use *xylon* in an attempt to indicate that Jesus did not, after all, die on a cross. His use of *xylon* rather than *stauros* ("cross") connects the death of Christ with the Septuagint rendering of Deuteronomy 21:22-23, a passage linked to the death of Christ in a variety of New Testament references. (See Acts 5:30; 10:39; 13:29; Galatians 3:13.)

That Jesus bore our sins in His body on the tree indicates that His death was the specific means by which He atoned for the sins of the world. In other words, the Atonement was not an ongoing process during the life of Jesus. The Atonement occurred at a specific point in time;

the cataclysmic events that transpired at the time of Christ's death testify to the uniqueness of that moment.

The purpose for which Christ bore our sins in His own body was that "we, being dead to sins, should live unto righteousness."

The believer's death to sin is addressed in Romans 6:2-11; II Corinthians 5:14-15; Galatians 2:20; 6:14. The death-to-sin metaphor expresses freedom from the ruling power of sin. (See Romans 6:6-7, 11-14, 16-18, 20, 22.) The believer obtains this freedom as he identifies with Jesus Christ in His death. (See II Corinthians 5:14-15; Galatians 2:20; 6:14.) The specific point in time at which this occurs is water baptism. (See Romans 6:3-5.)

Romans 6 indicates that the believer's sanctification—his separation unto God and from sin—occurs as a consequence of the believer's identification with Jesus Christ in His death and burial. Because the believer has identified with Jesus in His death and burial, he is also identified with Him in His resurrection, and thus in life, or in freedom from the domination of the sin nature. (See Romans 6:2-5. For further discussion of this passage, see the endnote.[194])

In Romans 6:6-7, Paul wrote, "Knowing this, that our old man is crucified with him, that the body of sin might be destroyed, that henceforth we should not serve sin. For he that is dead is freed from sin."

The "old man" is the sin nature or sin principle that dwells in everyone as a consequence of Adam's sin. (See Romans 5:12; Ephesians 4:22; Colossians 3:9.) It is not necessary for believers to experience physical crucifixion as Jesus did; His death was on our behalf. It *is* necessary for the believer to identify with Jesus in His crucifixion or death, which occurs at water baptism. Thus baptism, when received in faith, is much more than a mere public profession of one's desire to follow Christ. It actually accomplishes the crucifixion or death of the sin nature, or, in other words, it does away with the "body of sin." (See Colossians 2:11-12.)

The death of "the old man" does not mean the believer no longer has the sin nature indwelling him (I John 1:8) or can no longer be tempted, for death does not mean extinction. It means separation. The point is that when we identify with Jesus Christ in His death, the ruling power of sin over us is broken, so that "we should no longer be slaves to sin" (NKJV). The human body without the human spirit is dead (James 1:26), but the human body is not extinct simply because of its separation from the human spirit. It still exists and can be acted upon, although it cannot act. In a similar way, the sin nature, the "body of sin," is not extinct because it is dead. And although it is incapable of dominating the believer's life, the believer can still act on it by choosing to yield his members as instruments of unrighteousness unto sin (Romans 6:12-13).

It may seem strange at first to think that anyone who is free from domination by the sin nature would yield to sin, but that is precisely what Adam and Eve did in the Garden of Eden. Temptation to sin does not arise from the sin nature, but from the power of choice inherent in being human. Certainly the sin nature enhances temptation and tilts a person more decidedly toward sin, but a person can be tempted based on the power of choice alone. Jesus was tempted, and He certainly did not possess a sin nature. (See Hebrews 4:15.)

First Peter

One primary difference between the unbeliever and the believer who has been united with Jesus Christ in His death, burial, and resurrection is that the unbeliever is a slave to sin; he has no power to break free from it. (See Romans 6:17-20.) The believer has been set free from sin's controlling power; he has the ability, by the power of the Holy Spirit, to resist temptation. (See Romans 6:12-14, 18.) As Paul put it, "He who has died has been freed from sin" (NKJV). Identification with Jesus Christ in His death frees the believer from sin's control.

In Romans 6:8, Paul wrote, "Now if we be dead with Christ, we believe that we shall also live with him." Identification with Jesus Christ in His death results in identification with Jesus Christ in His life. Exactly the same point appears in Galatians 2:20, I Peter 2:24, and Colossians 2:20. There may be an ultimate reference to the bodily resurrection of the believer and to eternal life in the presence of God, but the immediate and contextual concern is for the believer's life on earth, or, as Galatians 2:20 says, "in the flesh."

Peter and Paul agreed that the death of the believer to sin should result in living "unto righteousness." (See Romans 6:11-13.) Righteousness deals with what is right. It is the believer's death to sin, and thus his freedom from sin's dominating power, that enables him to make progress in sanctification.[195] Where there has been no death to sin, there can be no true sanctification, or holiness. There may be self-discipline, moderation in lifestyle, or even self-denial, but biblical sanctification results from and springs out of identification with Jesus Christ in His death.

The final phrase of I Peter 2:24 reflects the Septuagint

translation of Isaiah 53:5: "by whose stripes ye were healed." The immediate context refers to spiritual healing, or to the healing of one's relationship with God that sin has wounded. The earlier portion of verse 24 refers to Christ bearing our sins in His body on the tree that we might die to sins and live unto righteousness. The next verse carries through this theme of spiritual healing, under the metaphor of the straying sheep that has returned to the Shepherd of "souls."

The immediate context of Isaiah 53:5 also refers to spiritual healing. In the poetic parallel of Isaiah, to be "healed" with the stripes received by the Messiah is the same as saying that "the chastisement of our peace was upon him" (Isaiah 53:5). The "peace" in view is peace with God, a peace that sin has ruptured.

The New Testament uses the word translated "healed" (Greek, *iaomai*) for both physical[196] and spiritual[197] healing. The Gospels also use another Greek word, *therapeuo*, to refer to physical healing exclusively. The word translated "healed" in Isaiah 53:5 (Hebrew, *rapha'*) is used both of physical[198] and spiritual[199] healing. *Rapha'* is also used in a variety of other ways.[200] Elsewhere Isaiah used *rapha'* exclusively for spiritual healing.

None of this detracts from the power of God to heal those who are physically sick. Jesus applied the prophecy of Isaiah to physical healing (Matthew 8:16-17). He not only healed the sick, but He also gave authority to His disciples to do the same. (See Matthew 10:1, 8; Luke 10:9.) He promised that those who believe would have specific signs following them, including the ability to minister recovery to the sick (Mark 16:17-18). Physical healing accompanied the preaching of the gospel throughout

First Peter

the Book of Acts. (See, e.g., Acts 3:7-8; 8:6-7; 14:5-10; 19:11-12; 28:7-9.) It is promised to the church in James 5:14-16.[201]

Verse 25. The description of unbelievers as sheep going astray reflects the thought of Isaiah 53:6. Both testaments frequently use the sheep-shepherd imagery to represent the relationship between God and people.[202] The imagery is also used to describe the nature of Christian ministry. (See John 21:15-17; Acts 20:28; I Corinthians 9:7; Ephesians 4:11 [where "pastors" means "shepherds"]; I Peter 5:2-4.)

The word translated "going astray" (*planomenoi*) is in the imperfect tense, indicating ongoing action in the past. The word translated "returned" (*epestraphete*) is an aorist tense middle voice, which indicates that the readers had turned themselves from their habitual wanderings at a specific point in time. This occurred when they purified their souls in obeying the truth through the Spirit (1.22).

Christ is the "Shepherd and Bishop" of the souls of believers. (See Matthew 10:6; 15:24; 18:12-14; 26:31-32; 28:7; Mark 6:34; 14:27-28; 16:7; Luke 15:3-7; John 10:11-18; Hebrews 13:20; I Peter 5:4.) The word translated "bishop" (*episkopon*) means "overseer." An overseer, like a shepherd, was one who "watched over, protected and had authority."[203] "Shepherd and Bishop," used together this way, should probably be taken as a literary figure, a hendiadys, meaning "overseeing Shepherd."[204]

To say that Christ is the Shepherd and Bishop of souls does not mean that He limits His watchful care to the immaterial part of man. I Peter frequently uses the word translated "souls" (*psychai*) to refer to lives. (See 1:9, 22;

3:20; 4:19 and, in the singular, 2:11.) The Jewish view of human existence was holistic, not fragmented as in Western thought. Christ is the overseeing Shepherd of all that the believer is; His concern extends to the whole person, not just to the inner man.

D. Responsible Conduct in Marriage (3:1-7)

(1) Likewise, ye wives, be in subjection to your own husbands; that, if any obey not the word, they also may without the word be won by the conversation of the wives; (2) while they behold your chaste conversation coupled with fear. (3) Whose adorning let it not be that outward adorning of plaiting the hair, and of wearing of gold, or of putting on of apparel; (4) but let it be the hidden man of the heart, in that which is not corruptible, even the ornament of a meek and quiet spirit, which is in the sight of God of great price. (5) For after this manner in the old time the holy women also, who trusted in God, adorned themselves, being in subjection unto their own husbands: (6) even as Sara obeyed Abraham, calling him lord: whose daughters ye are, as long as ye do well, and are not afraid with any amazement. (7) Likewise, ye husbands, dwell with them according to knowledge, giving honour unto the wife as unto the weaker vessel, and as being heirs together of the grace of life; that your prayers be not hindered.

This section continues the house codes, which originated in 2:13. (See the discussion of house codes in the introductory section to 2:13-17.) Here, I Peter calls on believing wives to defer to their unbelieving husbands, with a view to leading their husbands to faith in Christ. (See the discussion of the Greek *hypotassein*, a form of which is translated "be in subjection" here. The word has to do with voluntary deference, as opposed to *hypekouein*, which is used in 3:6 of Sarah's "obedience.")

Verse 1. As Christianity swept through the Roman Empire, it was inevitable that there would be cases where one spouse came to faith in Christ before the other. It was expected in Roman society that a woman would take her husband's gods.[205] With the emphasis on male dominance, those wives who were converted to Christ could easily have been viewed as subversive as they cast off their husbands' gods. This would certainly have been counterproductive to the cause of Christ.

Thus, those women who have embraced Christianity are still responsible to submit to their husbands who have not. This is the only way these husbands can be expected to believe. If their wives became Christians and then overthrew all social conventions, rebelling against their husbands, few of those men would ever come to Christ, and other men would make sure their wives were never exposed to the gospel.

The saved wife is not to try to convince her unsaved husband to place his faith in Christ by talking him into it so much as by demonstrating genuine Christianity before him. The word translated "conversation" (*anastrophes*) means "conduct." Peter used the same word in 1:15, 18.

We should understand the word translated "likewise" (*homoios*) as a simple connective. It does not imply that the wife's submission to her husband is in the same category or to the same degree as the slave's submission to his master (2:18).[206] The same word appears in verse 7, where it certainly does not indicate that the husband's behavior finds its antecedent in the slave's submission to his master. Although the idea of submission originates in 2:13 and continues through 3:1, we must find the nature of each individual relationship in the immediate context of each (2:13-14, 18; 3:1).

In the social context of the Roman world, unqualified submission of a wife to her husband required her to embrace his gods. Obviously, I Peter has a specific limitation in mind when it calls on believing wives to submit to their unbelieving husbands. God does not expect believing wives to embrace their husbands' gods. God expects just the opposite.

This counsel is not based upon any perceived inferiority of women. Instead, wives should submit "*because of the influence* . . . they can exert on their non-Christian husbands."[207] Certainly submission is in view, but what a powerful submission! The point is not to subjugate women and to justify masculine domination, which was common in the Roman Empire, but to put in the hands of believing women their most potent and effective instrument for influencing their unbelieving husbands: submission.

It is not for women alone that submission serves as a tool of persuasion. Believers in general may "put to silence the ignorance of foolish men" by submitting to civil government (2:13-16). Slaves may influence their masters by submitting to them (2:18-20). Christ redeemed the human race by submitting to unjust suffering (2:21-25).[208] It is characteristic of unbelievers to seek to dominate others by the exercise of authority, but among believers the greatest

First Peter

trait is to serve. (See Matthew 20:25-28.) In the kingdom of God, the position of the servant is far more influential than the position of the ruler. Christianity is characterized by servant leadership.

Although the counsel in 3:1-7 applies to all aspects of the marriage relationship, it is possible that, like I Corinthians 7:2-5, it refers specifically the sexual aspects of married life. This idea is indicated in three ways. First, wives are to submit to their "own husbands." There is no supposed obligation of women in general to submit to men in general. Rather, the passage discusses the specific relationship of a married woman to her husband. One of the responsibilities of married life is the conjugal relationship. Second, the reference to Sarah's obedience to Abraham in verse 6 comes from the Septuagint translation of Genesis 18:12, which was Sarah's response when she overheard the angel declare to Abraham that she would bear Abraham a son. Third, the Greek *synoikountes*, translated "dwell with them" in verse 7, includes sexual relations between a husband and wife.[209]

If these verses indeed discuss the continued conjugal responsibility of a believing woman to her unbelieving husband, then they expose the error of sects throughout church history which have taught that marriage people are to avoid the sexual relationship. These groups, like the American Shakers of the nineteenth century, mistakenly perceived the sexual relationship in marriage to be a hindrance to spirituality.[210] This notion is at least in part a consequence of viewing human existence in a fragmented way, as the Western mind tends to do, rather than in the holistic perspective of Hebrew thought.

The word translated "obey not" (*apeithousin*) indi-

Exhortations in View of Social Groupings

cates more than passive disobedience. It is the same word as in 2:8, and it indicates a strong sense "of active disobedience to the standards of Scripture and even rebellion against them."[211] The larger context suggests that some of these unbelieving husbands may have been among those who slandered believers.[212] (See 2:12, 15; 3:9, 16.) If so, the meaning is that the Christian lifestyle is powerful enough to defuse this antagonism. A wife would accomplish little by attempting to persuade her husband of the legitimacy of her faith by verbal apologetics. But it would be difficult for an unbelieving husband to deny the legitimacy of a faith that had transformed his wife's life for the good.

The word translated "won" (*kerdethesontai*) "focuses on the actual process of conversion, or changing one's attitude."[213] This verse is not the only one to say that Christian conduct has such a powerful impact. (See 2:12.)

This text has been abused in societies where it is seen as normative for men to dominate women. The abuse of the text has in some cases led to the abuse of women.[214] This situation is regrettable, and it demonstrates the dangers of coming to Scripture with preconceived notions and imposing them on the text.

There is no claim here for female inferiority or male dominance. The purpose is rather to assure believing women that they can win their unbelieving husbands to the Lord in the same way that all unbelievers may be brought face-to-face with the claims of Christ: It happens not as a result of arguments, debate, or rhetoric, but by the demonstration of genuine Christianity.

Verse 2 describes the kind of conduct by which a

believing wife can influence her unbelieving husband to faith in Christ. The two words that describe this conduct are "chaste" and "fear."

The word translated "chaste" (*hagnen*) seems in this context to mean chastity or sexual purity.[215] Thus one of the remarkable things to an unbelieving husband is that there would never be a question about his wife's faithfulness to him. It may be that a man with an unbelieving wife would be concerned that she might betray him with another man. That a believing wife would never do so is something her husband would find comforting and attractive. If, as the comments on verse 1 suggest, this entire passage has to do with the sacredness of the sexual relationship in marriage, the chastity of the believing wife contributes to that sacredness.

The "fear" that should characterize the believing wife is not terror of her husband. (See comments on 1:17; 2:17-18; 3:14-15.) No wife should live in terror of her husband. (See comments on 3:6.) The "fear" in view here is the fear of God, the reverence every believer must give to Him. This attitude contrasted with those of the pagans of the first century who worshipped various gods. Their attitudes ranged from stark terror to mere duty to casual acknowledgement, but they would not be reverence. (See Acts 17:16-23.) A believer in the true God does not attempt to appease a vengeful god or to curry favor with a temperamental deity. Those who believe in the only true God know something about His character, and they know that their standing with Him is based on the sufficiency of Christ's atoning work (2:24). Thus their attitude toward Him is one of deeply reverent respect bathed in love.

For a believing wife to have this kind of attitude

toward God would at least pique the curiosity of her husband. At best, coupled with her uncompromising loyalty and faithfulness to her husband, it could bring him to a place of exploring and finally embracing the Christian faith.

The word translated "while they behold" (*epopteusantes*) is an aorist active participle, indicating action that is finished. The point is that once unbelieving husbands have observed the conduct of their believing wives, it is possible for them to be won to Christ. An undetermined period of time may elapse, as indicated by the future passive indicative form of *kerdethesontai*, translated "may . . . be won" in verse 1. (See comments on verse 1.) It may not happen quickly. But once unbelieving husbands have had the opportunity to observe the consistent Christian conduct of their believing wives, there is a strong possibility that they will come to Christ.

Though the passage does not specifically state, the implication is that a believing wife should not expect her unbelieving husband immediately to place His faith in Christ simply because she announces that she has done so, or even after a week or a month. No one can predict how quickly another person will believe. But the scenario Peter had in mind is one that would occur over a period of time long enough for the believing wife to demonstrate faithfulness to her husband and reverence to God.

Verse 3. Still describing the conduct that should characterize a believing wife, the passage states what it should not be. Her "adorning" should not be outward, by means of "plaiting the hair," "wearing of gold," and "putting on of apparel." The NKJV translates the verse, "Do not let your adornment be merely outward—arranging the hair, wearing gold, or putting on fine apparel."

In the first century, as at many other times, women's hair "was braided in elaborate manners, and well-to-do women strove to keep up with the latest expensive fashions. The gaudy adornments of women of wealth, meant to draw attention to themselves, were repeatedly condemned in ancient literature and speeches."[216] I Timothy 2:9-10 addresses the same issue: "In like manner also, that the women adorn themselves in modest apparel, with propriety and moderation, not with braided hair or gold or pearls or costly clothing, but, which is proper for women professing godliness, with good works" (NKJV).

Ancient Jewish writings warn of the sexual temptations caused by the kind of adornments that Peter and Paul described.[217] Since married women are to demonstrate genuine Christianity by being faithful to their husbands, they should certainly avoid outward adornment that could compromise this faithfulness. In other words, Christian women should not dress so as to draw the wrong kind of attention to themselves. Obviously, this does not mean they must be dowdy, but they must dress modestly, with propriety and moderation.

Some see here a complete ban on certain kinds of hair arrangement or on the wearing of anything gold. But if the ban is absolute, then it would also be a complete ban on adorning oneself with the wearing of clothing. To avoid this obviously erroneous interpretation, the NKJV translators supplied the word "fine" to describe "apparel," but the KJV translation is more literal at this point.

Some think that "plaiting the hair, and of wearing of gold" is a figure of speech, a hendiadys, "whereby one idea is expressed by two (or occasionally three) nouns linked by the simple 'and.' The first noun is treated as the main substantive, with the second (and third) taken adjectivally."[218] The meaning would then be "gold-braided hair."[219] The fashionable and extravagant hairstyles of wealthy women in the first century amounted to "submerging the hair in lavish gold spangles."[220]

The word "adorning" has to do with "the focus of attention for one's attractiveness, the thing one uses to make oneself beautiful to others."[221] The point, as the next verse shows, is that believing women are not to focus on external appearance but on internal character.

Verse 4. Instead of focusing on externals, believing women should focus on "the hidden person of the heart, with the incorruptible beauty of a gentle and quiet spirit, which is very precious in the sight of God" (NKJV). Referring to the inner person as the "hidden person of the heart" is a typical Hebraism, further suggesting that the primary recipients of this letter were Jewish.

The things used to adorn the outer person are "corruptible," but the godly qualities of character are incorruptible. The focus on incorruptibility is typical for I Peter. (See 1:4, 18, 23.) Although these character qualities certainly influence one's behavior in the visible, tangible realm, they are rooted in the invisible, intangible realm of the spirit. Specifically, believing women are to adorn themselves with "a meek and quiet spirit."

The word translated "meek" by the KJV (*praeos*) means gentleness. The word translated "quiet" (*hesychios*) means tranquility and calmness. In other words, believing women are not to be loud, abrasive, or harsh. Meekness and quietness do not imply weakness of character, but strength. Those with little depth of character find it easy to be hard and loud. Gentleness and quietness spring from self-control and maturity. (See Proverbs 9:13; 11:22; 12:4; 21:9, 19; 25:24; 27:15; 31:26.) To be gentle means not to insist on one's own rights, not to be pushy or selfishly assertive, and not to demand one's own way.[222]

In contrast to the value some human beings place on expensive temporal adornment, which will corrupt and pass away, the incorruptible adornment of the inner person with gentleness and quietness "is in the sight of God of great price." God's value system is in direct opposition to the value system of the world. (See Luke 16:15.) Gentleness and quietness of spirit cannot be contrived; if these qualities are not genuine, the pressures of life will expose the pretense. Specifically, one cannot long pretend to have them under the day-to-day pressures of marriage. Genuine gentleness and quietness spring from one's relationship with God, which is rooted in deep trust in Him. (See comments on verse 5.)

Verse 5. As an example of the kind of behavior (described as adornment) it commends to believing wives, this verse refers to "the holy women" of "former times" (NKJV). These were women who "trusted in God" and who were "submissive to their own husbands" (NKJV).

In Jewish thought, the submission of a woman to her husband did not place her in a position of weakness, but of strength. "A certain wise woman said to her daughter: 'My child, stand before your husband and minister to him. If you will act as his maiden, he will be your slave, and honor you as his mistress. But if you exalt yourself against him, he will be your master, and you will become vile in his eyes, like one of the maidservants.'"[223]

Exhortations in View of Social Groupings

This saying reflects the significance of the words God spoke to Eve: "Your desire shall be for your husband, and he shall rule over you" (Genesis 3:16, NKJV). In the Hebrew text, the idea is that the woman would desire to rule her husband, but that he would rule her. A similar idea appears in Genesis 4:7, where God said to Cain concerning the sin at his door, "And its desire is for you, but you should rule over it" (NKJV).

Prior to the sin of Adam and Eve, their relationship was one of equality and mutual respect. Adam was incomplete alone; God made Eve as a "help" (*'ezer*) to compensate for the deficiency of Adam's solitary existence. The Hebrew word *'ezer* indicates a significant help that is not an option. The word translated "meet" (*k'negdo*) means the woman is a match for man. The word may mean either "at his side," signifying "fit to associate with," or it may mean "as over against him," signifying "corresponding to him." Adam recognized Eve as bone of his bones and flesh of his flesh (Genesis 2:23). That is, he could no more do without her than he could do without his own flesh and bones. Because of her equality with Adam, the Bible uses the feminine form of the word "man" to describe Eve. The Hebrew word translated "man" is *'ish*. The word translated "woman" is the feminine form, *'ishah*.

The sin of Adam and Eve introduced a subtle change into the dynamics of their relationship. Now there was a tension that God never intended. This tension is lessened, however, when a husband loves his wife as Christ loved the church and when a wife views submission to her husband as her service to God (Ephesians 5:22, 25). Any service, or worship, offered to God with a sincere heart has powerful results; so does this kind of submission of a believing woman to her husband. By her submission, a wife can influence her husband in significant ways. The most important decision a man can ever make is to put his trust in Jesus Christ. If a believing wife's submission to her husband influences him to make this decision (3:1-2), how much more influential can she be in lesser decisions?

Even here in I Peter 3:5, the word translated "subjection" is *hypotassomenai*, which indicates deference, as in 2:13, 18; 3:1. It does not mean that the holy women exercised blind, unthinking obedience based on inferiority of value or some kind of misguided caste system, but that they exercised thoughtful, creative submission to honor God and to provide a wholesome influence on their husbands.

Hillyer points out that the association of married life with holiness is a genuinely Jewish idea. "As a divine institution, marriage is viewed in a twofold light. First, as the means intended for the propagation of the human race. Secondly, as an ideal state for the promotion of sanctity and purity of life."[224] Paul agreed with this sentiment. He wrote, "Nevertheless, to avoid fornication, let every man have his own wife, and let every woman have her own husband" (I Corinthians 7:2).

The submission that the "holy women" in Hebrew history gave to their husbands sprang from their trust in God. They knew God was personally involved in their lives, including their marriages, and they believed He would direct the steps of their husbands. Where even one spouse trusts in God, there is a powerful influence for good in the marriage and home. (See I Corinthians 7:12-14.) But where there is no trust in God in the home—and thus no awareness by the husband that he is

Exhortations in View of Social Groupings

to mirror Christ's love for the church in his love for his wife and no awareness by the wife that she is to submit to her husband as an act of service to God—the relationship tends to grow increasingly strained.

Verse 6 now offers a specific example of a holy woman who portrayed the kind of behavior Peter commended to believing wives in the first century. The example is Sarah, the wife of the great patriarch Abraham.

It is obvious that this passage is no longer limited to the believing wives of unbelieving husbands, because Abraham was not an unbeliever. Neither, for that matter, were the husbands of the "holy women" in verse 4. In the minds of Jewish readers, these women included not only Sarah, but also Rebekah, Rachel, and Leah.[225] On the other hand, the focus at this point is still on the wives; it does not turn to the husbands until verse 7. Even though I Peter mentions Abraham, the concern is not so much for any particular episode in Abraham's life. It certainly would be possible to find examples where Abraham's behavior was not exemplary. (See, e.g., Genesis 12:13, 19; 20:2, 5.)

Here is the first time in the context of submission that the word *hypekouein* (translated "obeyed") appears. It is a stronger word than the word translated "submit" (2:13), "be subject" (2:18), "be in subjection" (3:1), and "being in subjection" (3:5). "Other NT household codes use [*hypekouein*] of the obedience of children to parents (Col 3:20; Eph 6:1) and slaves to masters (Col 3:22; Eph 6:5), but not of wives in relation to husbands. [*Hypekouein*] occurs nowhere else in I Peter, but the three instances of the cognate [*hypekoe*] (1:2, 14, 22) all refer to Christian conversion or faith in God, not to social relationships."[226]

Another element in the relationship between Sarah and Abraham is that on occasion he obeyed her. The Septuagint used the same word here translated "obeyed" to describe how Abraham "hearkened" to the voice of Sarah when she said to him, "Go therefore in to my maid, that I may get children for myself through her" (Genesis 16:2, LXX). The Greek *hypekouein* is an accurate translation here of the Hebrew *shema'*, which is often translated "hear" (as in Deuteronomy 6:4), meaning "obey."

Genesis 18:12 records the specific event that is apparently in view here. When Sarah, who was inside the tent, heard the angel tell Abraham, "Thy wife shall have a son," she laughed, saying to herself, "After I am waxed old shall I have pleasure, my lord being old also?" (Genesis 18:10, 12). Grudem does not think the reference here is to Genesis 18:12, for he finds no mention of obedience to Abraham in that passage and because Sarah spoke to herself rather than to Abraham.[227] But I Peter does not say that Sarah spoke to Abraham when she called him "lord."

Any difficulty in finding the exact episode of Sarah's obedience may result from reading too much into I Peter's use of *hypekouein*. Although *hypekouein* is a stronger word than *hypotassein* (used of voluntary deference in 2:13, 18; 3:1, 5; 5:5), the use of it here may be more stylistic than substantial. In this case, the meaning of "obey" is influenced by the prior references to "deference."

If I Peter emphasizes Sarah's obedience,[228] the obedience in view is defined by the context in which she referred to Abraham as her "lord." That is, even though she was old and past the time of childbearing (Genesis 18:11), she submitted to Abraham in the sexual relationship that resulted in the conception of Isaac. If this is the case, once again we see that the husband is not an iron-fisted dictator who dominates his wife. Sarah's obedience was actually submission in which she shared Abraham's hope for a son. I Corinthians 7:4 makes clear that the sexual relationship between a husband and wife is an expression of mutual submission.

If, as several points indicate (see comments on verse 1), the underlying theme of this passage is the sacredness of the sexual relationship in marriage, Sarah's example is even more significant. Believing wives are not to use their husbands' lack of faith as an excuse to abstain from sexual relationships with them. A misguided believing woman might think she could apply pressure to her unbelieving husband by isolating herself from him and depriving him of his conjugal rights. But this is not the way to bring an unbelieving husband to faith. If Sarah, as an aged woman with no physical reason to hope their union would be productive, did not reject Abraham, neither should believing wives reject their husbands, even if they are unbelievers.

When Sarah called Abraham "lord," she used the Hebrew *'adon* which, like all words, is defined by its context. Although the Hebrew Scriptures often use it for the true God, they also use it in a wide variety of other contexts. When one human being used it to address another, its meaning is often something like the English "sir." It is a title of respect. There is no basis here for saying that women must address men as their masters or rulers. Wives are to respect their husbands, but as Peter pointed out in this verse, they are not to be afraid of them with "any terror" (NKJV).

Believing women can become Sarah's daughters. Just as Jesus explained to the unbelieving Jews that if they were genuinely the children of Abraham they would do the works of Abraham (John 8:39), so I Peter ties the matter of being Sarah's daughters together with a certain kind of behavior. This verse specifically identifies the behavior as doing "well" and not succumbing to "terror" (NKJV). Michaels points out that the "wives to whom Peter is writing have become Sarah's 'children' . . . through their faith in Christ expressed in baptism (cf. 3:21)."[229]

Contextually, to "do well" is for a wife to give deference to her husband. (See also 2:15.) It may seem strange that the behavior that qualifies believing wives as the daughters of Sarah includes not being "afraid with any terror" (NKJV). But there is always the possibility that the unbelieving husband will not tolerate his wife's strange religion "and that consequently her freedom or safety may be jeopardized. Hence the ominous word of 'comfort' with which Peter's advice to wives concludes."[230]

The encouragement not to fear seems to reflect Proverbs 3:25: "Do not be afraid of sudden terror, nor of trouble from the wicked when it comes" (NKJV). The word translated "amazement" in the KJV and "terror" in the NKJV is *ptoein*, which appears in the Septuagint translation of Proverbs 3:25 but nowhere else in the New Testament. In the first century, it was always possible that submission to authority could have painful consequences. Submission to civil government could result in martyrdom (2:13-14). It was possible that for a slave to submit to his master could result in cruel and unjustified suffering (2:18-20). And it was possible that a wife could be

Exhortations in View of Social Groupings

abused by her husband. But believers must not allow fear to control them. (See 3:14, 17.) They can avoid this fear by their unswerving focus on eternity. (See comments on 1:3-9, 13.)

Verse 7 turns our attention to the responsibilities of the husband toward the wife. Although the passage began with instruction to believing wives as to how to influence unbelieving husbands toward faith in Christ (verse 1), the focus has now shifted to believing husbands and what they should do to honor their wives. This shift began in verse 5, which holds up as examples holy women whose husbands were not unbelievers, and it developed further in verse 6, which singles out one of the holy women, Sarah, as an example to believing women. Sarah's husband, Abraham, was certainly not an unbeliever; he is the father of all who believe. (See Romans 4:11-12.)

The word "likewise" (*homoios*) "functions only to connect related sections of the household duty code, not to point out any real analogy."[231] In other words, there is no idea here of the husband submitting to the wife in the manner of citizens to civil government (2:13) or slaves to their masters (2:18). But in retrospect, since verse 1 uses the same word (*homoios*), it serves there as a connective also, not to indicate that the wife's submission to her husband is analogous to the citizen's or the slave's submission. (See comments on verse 1.) The nature of the wives' submission appears in the immediate context of verse 1 and the following verses, not in the prior context of citizens and slaves.

It would be wrong to describe the wife's submission to her husband as of the same kind or to the same degree as the slave's submission to his master or as the citizen's submission to civil government. The relationship between a husband and wife is a completely different kind of relationship from the government-citizen or master-slave relationship. The relationship that best describes marriage is the one between Christ and His church. (See Ephesians 5:21-33.) It is much more of an intimate, mutually reciprocal relationship than what characterizes the government with its citizens or masters with their slaves.

We can fully appreciate this verse's counsel only in the context of the culture of the first century. Women had few legal rights. As far as Jewish law was concerned, women were the property of their husbands, right along with his sheep and cattle. He could divorce her; she could not leave him.[232] Greek philosophers and even Jewish teachers declared that women were morally and intellectually weaker than men. Aristotle's legacy continued to influence thinkers in the first century, including his idea that women were by nature inferior to men in every way except sexually. As far as the Roman legal system was concerned, women were weak and unable to make sound decisions.[233]

The Greek word translated "dwell with them" (*synoikeo*) commonly refers to sexual relations, and the Septuagint uses it in that sense.[234] (See Deuteronomy 22:13; 24:1; 25:5.) The point Peter made is that a Christian man is neither "demanding nor selfish in his sexual and marital relations; he is instead considerate, sensitive, and serving."[235] (See also I Corinthians 7:3-5; Hebrews 13:4.)

The man must dwell with his wife "according to knowledge" or "with understanding" (NKJV). Where a wife is viewed as a "thing," as in Jewish law,[236] there is little incentive to give careful thought as to how to relate to her. Men who view their wives as possessions on the level of livestock or property will not generally be sensitive to developing a meaningful and mutually rewarding relationship. On the other hand, men who view their wives as individuals uniquely made in the image of God, worthy of honor and sharing equally in the gift of life, will tend to exercise great care in getting to know their wives as persons. They will want to learn as much as possible about their wives' ideas, opinions, and values. They will want to assess realistically their wives' gifts and talents so as to help them explore their interests and to exercise a fulfilling, meaningful ministry to others.

The husband is to give honor to his wife "as unto the weaker vessel." Peter did not declare the wife actually to *be* a weaker vessel. Rather, he used the analogy of a weaker vessel to give the husband a specific and understandable image, illustrating the manner in which he is to honor his wife. Unbelievers in the first century commonly held that women were morally and intellectually weaker than men, but Peter gave the idea of "weakness" new significance.[237] The weakness he had in view was to be honored, not despised. It may be that by "weakness," Peter had in mind the "common early Christian conviction that honor in God's sight belongs to those who are (or make themselves) 'last,' or 'least,' in the eyes of the world."[238]

In any event, I Peter does not imply that women are in any sense inferior to men. The word translated "honor" (*timen*) means "respect" that springs from value.[239] We typically give respect only to those we consider of equal value or in some way superior. This respect is not the insincere, demeaning flattery that one person sometimes gives to another for personal advantage. The honor I Peter has in view springs from the husband's careful assessment of his wife's value.

The husband is not to take advantage of his wife's submission to oppress her. He is to be considerate of his wife and to treat her not in a rough and thoughtless manner—as he might a stout, cheap vessel—but gently and thoughtfully, as he would a fragile, expensive vase.

The husband and wife are not merely one flesh, they are also "heirs together of the grace [or gift, Greek *charitos*] of life." That is, they are to develop oneness in all areas of the life that God has graciously granted them together. This oneness includes the spirit, as we see in the purpose clause: "that your prayers may not be hindered." Marriage partners who unite not only in flesh but also in spirit will find their prayers to have new power and effectiveness, whether the prayer is private or together. When a husband fails to honor his wife and neglects to invest the time and effort necessary to gain a thorough knowledge of her as an individual, his prayers will tend to be ineffectual. A married couple's relationship with each other is one of the most important factors in making their prayers effectual.

E. Responsible Conduct in the Family of God (3:8-12)

(8) Finally, be ye all of one mind, having compassion one of another; love as brethren, be pitiful, be courteous: (9) not rendering evil for evil, or railing for railing: but contrariwise blessing; knowing that ye are thereunto called, that ye should inherit a blessing. (10) For he that will love life, and see good days, let

him refrain his tongue from evil, and his lips that they speak no guile: (11) let him eschew evil, and do good; let him seek peace, and ensue it, (12) for the eyes of the Lord are over the righteous, and his ears are open unto their prayers: but the face of the Lord is against them that do evil.

After addressing the way believing citizens should conduct themselves in relationship to the civil government (2:13-17), the way believing slaves should conduct themselves in relationship to their unbelieving masters (2:18-21), the way believing wives should conduct themselves in relationship to their unbelieving husbands (3:1-4), and the way believing husbands should conduct themselves in relationship to their wives (3:7), I Peter discusses how all believers should conduct themselves in relationship to one another and to unbelievers at large (3:8-9). The lengthy quote from Psalm 34:12-15 in I Peter 3:8-12 brackets the larger section of this letter, which begins in 2:1-3 with a quote from Psalm 34:8.

Verse 8. The word "finally" (*telos*) indicates that the following instructions conclude a larger teaching section, which begins at some point in the letter before this. That point is 2:1-2, which encourages the readers to lay aside "all malice, all deceit, hypocrisy, envy, and all evil speaking" and, "as newborn babes," to "desire the pure milk of the word" in order to "grow thereby" (NKJV). Christians are unique among the peoples of the world and they are to express their uniqueness by proclaiming "the praises of Him who called [them] out of darkness into His marvelous light" (2:9, NKJV). At least a part of this proclamation includes honorable conduct among unbelievers

First Peter

and in specific social groupings (2:12-3:7).

At this point, the discussion is no longer limited to specific social groupings. Beginning with verse 8, the concern is for "all" to "be of one mind, having compassion for one another" (NKJV). Believers are to "love as brothers," to "be tenderhearted," and to "be courteous" (NKJV).

The words "be ye . . . of one mind" are translated from a single Greek word (*homophrones*). The word appears only here in the New Testament. It means to be "like-minded, united in spirit," and "harmonious."[240] Similar admonitions appear in Romans 12:16; 15:5 and Philippians 1:27; 2:2; 4:2. The point is that believers are to see things from the perspective of others. Paul understood the value of being "of one mind" with those to whom he ministered. (See I Corinthians 9:19-22.) Where believers look at life from the point of view of their brothers and sisters, there will be no cause for "malice, . . . deceit, . . . hypocrisy, . . . envy" or "evil-speaking" (2.1). Jesus demonstrated "like-mindedness" with human beings by entering fully into the human condition by the Incarnation (Philippians 2:2, 5-8). It is His like-mindedness with us that enables us to identify with Him and that encourages us to come to Him. It is also our like-mindedness, or our identification with one another by sharing the perspective of our brothers and sisters, that enables us to be compassionate, to love, to be tenderhearted, and to be courteous. Where there is no shared view of life, none of the virtues following in this verse can be genuinely present.

Believers are to have compassion for one another. The word translated "compassion" is the Greek *sympatheis*, from which comes the English "sympathy." The same idea appears in Romans 12:15 and I Corinthians 12:26. Believers are to share in one another's joys and sorrows. There is no place in the life of faith for narcissism. Jesus, the believer's example, identified so completely with us that He suffered for us (2:21). Although we cannot suffer redemptively on behalf of others, we can share in their experiences and thus bring strength and encouragement to them.

Believers are to "love as brethren" (*philadelphoi*). This theme is common in the New Testament. (See 1:22; John 13:35; I Thessalonians 4:9; I John 2:10; 3:16-18; 4:7-8, 11-12, 20-21.) It expresses the spirit of the commandment that Jesus identified as the second of all. (See Matthew 22:39.) When a person genuinely loves his brother, he will never do anything to harm him (Romans 13:10). Instead, he will limit his freedoms to please his brother (Romans 15:2).

The KJV translates the Greek *eusplanchnoi* as "pitiful." The NKJV translates the word as "tenderhearted." The only other place in the New Testament where the word appears is Ephesians 4:32, where even the KJV renders it "tenderhearted." The word is formed from *splanchna*, translated "bowels" in Philippians 2:1 and I John 3:17, and the prefix *eu*, which means "well" or "good."

In Jewish thought, the internal organs represented the inner person. The Hebrews were a visceral people; they tied mental activity and emotions to the inner organs of the body. The Hebrew word translated "reins" in the KJV literally means "kidneys."[241] The Jews considered the kidneys as the seat of character, affections, and emotions. They identified the liver with anger. (See Lamentations 2:11). They equated the heart with the will. (See, e.g.,

Deuteronomy 6:5; Psalm 119:2; Proverbs 3:5; Ecclesiastes 8:11.)

The verb corresponding to *eusplanchnoi* describes the actions of the Good Samaritan (Luke 10:33), the father of the Prodigal (Luke 15:20), and the compassion that motivated Jesus in His ministry to the suffering (e.g., Mark 1:41.).[242] The idea is that believers must be emotionally involved with their brothers and sisters for good.

The majority of Greek manuscripts indicate that the final virtue in this verse is courtesy (*philophron*), which has to do with friendliness and kindness. The critical Greek text has instead *tapeinophrones*, which means "humble-mindedness." If *philophron* is original here, this is the only time it appears in the New Testament. The virtue of humility is a frequent topic of New Testament writers. (See, e.g., 5:5-6; Matthew 11:29; Galatians 5:23; Ephesians 4:2; Philippians 2:3.) The Greeks considered humility a sign of weakness,[243] but the values of the kingdom of God are diametrically opposed to those of unbelievers.

Verse 9. Although it is possible that the concern in this verse is for nonretaliation within the Christian community (believers are certainly capable of speaking evil of one another [2:1; Ephesians 4:29; Galatians 5:15; James 5:9]), it seems more probable that the focus is on the conduct of believers in response to unbelievers. It is the unbelieving Gentiles who in their ignorance speak against believers as evildoers (2:12, 15). Unbelieving masters may be harsh with their believing slaves, subjecting them to undeserved suffering (2:18-20). Unbelievers reviled Jesus, though He did not retaliate (2:21-23). Unbelieving husbands could fail to understand and honor their wives

Exhortations in View of Social Groupings

(3:7). The face of the Lord is against those who do evil (3:12). Unbelievers may threaten those who do good (3:13-14). They may also defame and revile those who follow Christ (3:16).

This contextual evidence strongly indicates that the concern here is not for problems within the fellowship of believers. It is for how believers should respond to those outside the circle of Christian fellowship who attempt to discredit the Christian faith by speaking evil of believers.

Believers are not to return "evil for evil or reviling for reviling" (NKJV). (See Romans 12:17; I Thessalonians 5:15.) That is, they are not to retaliate in kind for evil done to them or spoken about them. The noun translated "railing" by the KJV and "reviling" by the NKJV (*loidoria*) is used elsewhere in the New Testament only in I Timothy 5:14. There, it also appears in a context connected with house codes. In both places the teaching is the same: unbelievers must find no legitimate reason to speak evil of believers. Peter used the verb form of the word in 2:23 to describe Jesus' refusal to retaliate against those who reviled Him, and Paul used the same word of himself in I Corinthians 4:12.

I Peter does not commend stoical silence as the proper response to evil or insult. Instead, believers should bless those who do or speak evil against them. (See Romans 12:14; I Corinthians 4:12.) The word translated "bless" (*eulogountes*) means "to speak well" as it is used in Greek literature, but when used in Scripture it carries the distinctive meaning of extending to a person the prospect of salvation or of God's favor.[244] Jesus connected it with praying for one's enemies (Matthew 5:44; Luke 6:27-28). As Michaels points out, the difference is that in

First Peter

prayer one speaks to God on behalf of one's enemies; in blessing, one speaks directly to his enemies.[245] In other words, though our enemies may wish us evil, we must wish them good, and the ultimate good is their salvation and God's favor.

Believers are called to unjust suffering and to refusal to retaliate (2:21-23). The phrase translated "ye are thereunto called" (*eis touto eklethete*) appears also in 2:21, where it refers back to the slave's duty to submit even to harsh masters. Here, it refers back to the believer's duty to not retaliate but to bless. Grammatically, the calling does not refer to what follows but to what precedes.[246] This point is theologically significant, for a believer does not earn a blessing by nonretaliation. The blessing instead flows out of the believer's life of faith, which he expresses by his Christ-like behavior.

That believers are called to unjust suffering does not mean they seek persecution; even Jesus did not do so. But it does mean that when they are persecuted because of their faith in Christ, they are not to return evil or insults. (See Matthew 5:10-12; James 5:10; Hebrews 12:3.) They are to want the best for their enemies. That is their calling in the context of suffering.

The result of faithfulness is to "inherit a blessing." The concept of inheritance is one of I Peter's themes. I Peter 1:4 describes the believer's salvation as an incorruptible, undefiled, and unfading inheritance. In 3:7, believing husbands and wives are "heirs together" of the gift of life. The following verses describe the blessing here.

Verses 10-12 quote from Psalm 34:12-15 in a Septuagint version. This is the second quote from Psalm 34, the first of which appears in 2:3. The quotes form a literary bracket for the discussion of Christian ethics in diverse social relationships, the chief of which has to do with their interaction with unbelievers. (See comments under "Responsible Conduct in the Family of God.") We see the appropriateness of this psalm here by the Jewish tradition that David composed it when he pretended madness before Abimelech and was driven away. (See I Samuel 21:10-15.) Achish, the king of Gath, is referred to as Abimelech, a dynastic title.[247] Just as Achish spoke evil of David, thinking him mad, so unbelievers would speak evil of Christians, perhaps even accusing them of madness.

In the old covenant, the "life" that believers could enjoy was long life in the land of promise.[248] We must understand this use of Psalm 34, however, in the context of the new covenant. I Peter focuses on the eschatological results of faith (1:3-10, 13). It does not reestablish the law of Moses with its temporal promises. As Michaels points out, "The language of the psalm is the language of this world, but Peter has made it metaphorical of the world to come."[249]

Verse 9 explains in the inspired words of Peter how believers are to respond to their critics. Verses 10-11 make the same point again, but in the words of the psalmist. The person who would "love life" and "see good days"—both blessings associated with eternal life under the new covenant—must "refrain his tongue from evil, and his lips from speaking deceit" (NKJV). He must "turn away from evil" (NKJV), but this is not a call to passivity, for he must also "do good." To do good is defined as actively seeking and pursuing peace. This is a call to seek peace with one's enemies, a common theme in I Peter. (See 2:14-15, 20; 3:6, 17; 4:19. See also Romans 12:18; 14:19; Hebrews 12:14.)

The reference to the Lord's "eyes" and "ears" and "face" is anthropomorphic (using human terms to describe what is not human). The point is that the Lord watches over the righteous for their good; He stands ready to hear their prayers. But He opposes evildoers. In Old Testament terms, the face of the Lord refers to "a relationship of God to people, either his gracious turning toward them or his disappointed turning away from them, the latter implying his withdrawal of grace and a refusal to hear any prayer they may offer."[250] I Peter describes the fate of evildoers in 4:5, 18.

V

Exhortations in View of Suffering
3:13-4:19

To this point, I Peter has alluded several times to the possibility of suffering for one's faith. (See 1:6; 2:12, 15, 19-21; 3:9.) Beginning here, it deals specifically and at length not only with the possibility of suffering for one's faith in Christ but also with the proper response a believer should have to suffering. This response would ideally lead the persecutor to faith in Christ. (See also 2:12.)

A. Call to Boldness in the Face of Persecution (3:13-4:6)

(13) And who is he that will harm you, if ye be followers of that which is good? (14) But and if ye suffer for righteousness' sake, happy are ye: and be not afraid of their terror, neither be troubled; (15) but sanctify the Lord God in your hearts: and be ready always to give an answer to every man that asketh you a reason of the hope that is in you with meekness and fear: (16) having a good conscience; that, whereas they speak evil of you, as of evildoers, they may be ashamed that falsely accuse your good conversation in Christ. (17) For it is better, if the will of God be so, that ye suffer for well doing, than for evil doing. (18) For Christ also hath once suffered for sins, the just for the unjust, that he might bring us to God, being put to

death in the flesh, but quickened by the Spirit: (19) by which also he went and preached unto the spirits in prison; (20) which sometime were disobedient, when once the longsuffering of God waited in the days of Noah, while the ark was a preparing, wherein few, that is, eight souls were saved by water. (21) The like figure whereunto even baptism doth also now save us (not the putting away of the filth of the flesh, but the answer of a good conscience toward God,) by the resurrection of Jesus Christ: (22) who is gone into heaven, and is on the right hand of God; angels and authorities and powers being made subject unto him. (4:1) Forasmuch then as Christ hath suffered for us in the flesh, arm yourselves likewise with the same mind: for he that hath suffered in the flesh hath ceased from sin; (2) that he no longer should live the rest of his time in the flesh to the lusts of men, but to the will of God. (3) For the time past of our life may suffice us to have wrought the will of the Gentiles, when we walked in lasciviousness, lusts, excess of wine, revelings, banquetings, and abominable idolatries: (4) wherein they think it strange that ye run not with them to the same excess of riot, speaking evil of you: (5) who shall give account to him that is ready to judge the quick and the dead. (6) For for this cause was the gospel preached also to them that are dead, that they might be judged according to men in the flesh, but live according to God in the spirit.

Believers can face persecution boldly (3:14), for the following reasons: (1) Those who persecute them will ultimately be ashamed (3:16). (2) It is better to suffer for doing good than for doing evil (3:17). (3) Christ offered an example of suffering (3:18; 4:1). (4) Their persecutors will answer to God (4:5).

Keener has pointed out that a chiasmus seems to appear in this section of Peter's letter. A chiasmus is a literary device that uses an inverted parallel structure to emphasize its points. The greatest emphasis is on the central point, which is immediately reiterated as the chiasmus begins its inversion. Keener's construction of Peter's chiasmus is as follows:

A Your slanderers will be ashamed (3:16)
  B Suffer, though innocent, in God's will (3:17)
    C For Christ suffered for the unjust (3:18)
      D He triumphed over hostile spirits (3:19)
        E Noah was saved through water (3:20)
        E' You are saved through water (3:21)
      D' Christ triumphed over hostile spirits (3:22)
    C' For Christ suffered (4:1a)
  B' Suffer in God's will (4:1b-2)
A' Your slanderers will be ashamed (4:3-5)[251]

In this literary structure, Peter focused on Christian baptism as evidence of the ultimate deliverance from the fate of the hostile opponents of faith. Noah's salvation through water is symbolic of this deliverance. Peter returned to this theme in his second letter. (See II Peter 2:5, 9-10.)

As believers declare the gospel and live out their life of faith before a hostile world, they can be as confident as Noah was when he built the ark and preached righteousness (II Peter 2:5). Noah had a divine commission and promise (Hebrews 11:7). So do those who have placed their faith in Christ Jesus (4:12-14, 19; 5:4, 10).

Verse 13. At this point, the letter suggests that if believers follow what is good, they have less likelihood of being harmed. Although the next verse acknowledges the possibility of persecution, this verse indicates that when Christians do good they reduce the probability of being abused because of their faith.

We see the reason for the lessened probability of persecution in the specific definition of the "good" here. Contextually, doing "good" is seeking and pursuing peace. Those who seek peace with others minimize the potential of conflict. (See Proverbs 15:1; Matthew 5:25-26, 38-41.)

Verse 14. Although a person may pursue peace in all relationships, there remains the possibility of suffering "for righteousness' sake." The optative mood for the word translated "suffer" (*paschoite*), indicates that though suffering is possible it is relatively unlikely. As it turned out historically, though, a period of persecution was just ahead.

Contrary to what might seem true to human senses, those who suffer for righteousness' sake are "happy." The word translated "happy" (*makarioi*) is elsewhere translated "blessed" (e.g., Matthew 5:10); the NKJV translates it as "blessed" here. The usual sense of *makarios* is that a person is the "privileged recipient of divine favor."[252] It is a privilege to suffer for one's faith, for those who suffer will receive a great reward in heaven. In addition, their suffering allows them to stand in solidarity with the great Hebrew prophets. (See Matthew 5:12.)

To suffer "for righteousness' sake" is to suffer for doing right. In the context of Peter's letter, this means to suffer for believing in Jesus Christ and for the lifestyle that arises out of faith in Him. (See 1:6-7.)

I Peter appeals to Isaiah 8:12 to encourage readers not to fear those who threaten them. In their original context, Isaiah's words are part of his warnings about the coming invasion of Samaria by Assyria. It may be that Isaiah's opponents declared his rejection of an alliance with Assyria to be a conspiracy: "Do not say, 'A conspiracy,' concerning all that this people call a conspiracy, nor be afraid of their threats, nor be troubled" (Isaiah 8:12, NKJV). Rather than advising his hearers to link up with Assyria, Isaiah said, "The LORD of hosts, Him you shall hallow; let Him be your fear, and let Him be your dread" (Isaiah 8:13, NKJV).

This passage is appropriate for the present purpose. Believers could be threatened by unbelievers—just as the people of Samaria were threatened by Assyria—but the proper response is not to link up with them or even to fear them. The proper response is to keep their confidence in God. The next verse describes this response more fully.

Verse 15 adapts Isaiah 8:13 to form instruction as to how believers should respond to persecution. First, they should "sanctify the Lord God" in their hearts. The word translated "sanctify" (*hagiasate*) ordinarily refers to setting something or someone apart as holy, but here it means to treat the Lord God as holy or regard Him reverently.[253] In view of their origin in Isaiah 8:13, these words indicate that those who face persecution should remember that it is God who is in control, not those who persecute them.

The critical Greek text at this point reads, "But sanctify Christ as Lord in your hearts." If this is the original reading, I Peter identifies Jesus Christ as the same LORD (Yahweh) whom both the ancient Israelites and the first-century church trusted.

Secondly, when believers face persecution they should "be ready always to give an answer to every man that asketh . . . a reason of the hope that is in" them. In the larger context of the letter, the believers' conduct toward unbelievers enhances the possibility that unbelievers would ask questions of them concerning the reason for their hope. (See 1:17-18; 2:11-21; 3:1-2, 9-11, 16.) Even in the midst of persecution, the believers' conduct can be winsome. In this way, persecution would inevitably lead to the further growth of the church.

The word translated "answer" (*apologian*) means a "defense." (See its use in Acts 22:1; 25:16; I Corinthians 9:3; Philippians 1:7.) From this word the academic discipline of apologetics is derived. Apologetics has to do with developing reasoned responses to challenges to the faith. It is sometimes said that "a man with an experience is never at the mercy of a man with an argument." But before people have had a personal, life-changing experience with God, they often have many questions which must be answered so they can work through their honest doubts and come to a place of faith. In many cases, Christian witness occurs as believers initiate conversations. But in other cases, as described here, the Christian witness occurs as a response to the curiosity of unbelievers. Their questions are golden opportunities to bring people to faith in Christ.

The thing that will develop curiosity in unbelievers is their observation of the hope that believers have. There is something unusual about the believers' life and values as

Exhortations in View of Suffering

compared to the unbelieving world at large. They have hope, which arises out of the efficacy of Christ's resurrection (1:3, 21) and the way that His resurrection guarantees their eternal reward (1:4-9). Their hope is based exclusively on the future appearing of Jesus Christ (1:13). This hope will always, in every age, clearly identify those who are believers, for apart from Christ there is no hope in this world. As we progress toward the fulfillment of the prophecies concerning the decay of human civilization, the hope we embrace will become even more vivid in contrast to the hopelessness of Christless society.

Believers must offer their defense of the gospel with "meekness and fear." There is no place for arrogance in Christian witness. A form of the word translated "meekness" appears in verse 4. Essentially, the word has to do with gentleness. Here, "fear" is reverence for God, not terror of people. (See comments on 2:17-18; 3:2, 6, 14.) As believers respond to the questions of unbelievers, their gentleness and reverence for God must be evident to those who hear them. These qualities alone are very persuasive in a society where arrogance and harshness are common and where people often disregard or mock God.

Verse 16. There must be no basis in truth for the evil that critics speak against believers. (See 4:15-16.) Believers must have a "good conscience," that is, they must know that the evil spoken against them is completely false. If believers are to be defamed, it must be for their "good conduct in Christ" (NKJV).

Verse 21 mentions a "good conscience" again. Someone who who comes to God in faith and who clears his conscience with God will then demonstrate his "good conscience" by being baptized.

The New Testament mentions the conscience thirty times. The word translated "conscience" (*syneidesin*) has to do with moral awareness. The conscience is formed by several sources of input, including the values learned as a child (II Timothy 1:5), the influence of one's peers (I Corinthians 15:33), and one's understanding of Scripture (I Timothy 1:5).[254]

The references to the conscience in the New Testament fall in five categories: (1) the weak conscience (I Corinthians 8:7, 9, 10, 12; Romans 14:2); (2) the wounded or defiled conscience (I Corinthians 8:7, 12); (3) the seared or burned-out conscience (I Timothy 4:1-2); (4) the evil conscience (Hebrews 10:22); and (5) the good conscience (I Timothy 1:5, 19; Hebrews 13:8; I Peter 3:16, 21). (For discussion of the first four categories, see the endnote.[255])

The goal of all who have a weak conscience, a wounded conscience, a seared conscience, or an evil conscience should be to have a good conscience. When Paul went into Macedonia, he commanded Timothy to stay in Ephesus and to guard the purity of the teaching there (I Timothy 1:3). Specifically, Timothy was to warn against teachings based on fables and genealogies (I Timothy 1:4). These were traits of Jewish teaching at the time. The fables were Jewish fables (Titus 1:14) found in the oral tradition. The teachings from genealogies were supposed "spiritual" meanings of the names in Jewish genealogical records. According to Paul, these kinds of teachings produced disputes. The goal of all teaching should be edification.

After giving Timothy these instructions, Paul explained why he was commanding Timothy to do this: in order that love might flow from a pure heart, from a good conscience, and from sincere faith (I Timothy 1:5).

In Hebrews, those who have an evil conscience are those who have rejected the finality and sufficiency of the blood of Jesus to return to the shadowy imperfections of Moses' law. (See Hebrews 10:22 and endnote 255.) In this light, it is interesting that I Timothy contrasts a good conscience with the teachings of those who specialized in Jewish fables and genealogies. It refers to these teachers as having turned aside to "idle talk" (I Timothy 1:6, NKJV). They wanted to be teachers of the law of Moses, but they did not understand what they were talking about (I Timothy 1:7).

A good conscience is one that pays no heed to the idle teaching of Jewish fables and traditions. It is a conscience that does not construe the law of Moses as binding on New Testament believers.

Later in the same chapter, Paul urged Timothy to have faith and a good conscience (I Timothy 1:19). Some who had rejected a good conscience had consequently suffered shipwreck with their faith. Here we see the unbreakable tie between faith and a good conscience; if one does not have a good conscience, he will inevitably experience the loss of his faith. Paul gave two examples of people to whom this had happened (I Timothy 1:20). (See also II Timothy 2:17-18; 4:14.)

Rigid adherence to the law of Moses is unable to produce a perfect conscience (Hebrews 9:9; 10:2). Only the blood of Jesus can cleanse the conscience from dead works (the works of the law of Moses) and enable a person to serve the living God (Hebrews 9:14). As the Book of Hebrews concludes its eloquent effort to prevent Jewish Christians from turning away from the new covenant to embrace the old covenant all over again (which was evidence of an evil conscience [Hebrews 10:22]), the writer declared, "We are confident that we have a good conscience" (Hebrews 13:18, NKJV). This "good conscience" is obviously opposed to the "evil conscience" discussed earlier in the book; it is a conscience that does not believe that the new covenant is in any way insufficient or inferior.

In I Peter, the first mention of a good conscience is in the context of answering those who inquire as to a reason for one's hope (I Peter 3:15-16). In the second mention of a good conscience, the letter declares that water baptism is a natural response for one who has obtained a good conscience (I Peter 3:21). Just as Noah's good conscience prompted him to obey God by building the ark to save his family, so a person who has a good conscience will obey God by identifying with Jesus Christ in water baptism.

Other references to a good conscience include Acts 23:1; 24:16; Romans 13:5; II Corinthians 1:12; I Timothy 3:9; II Timothy 1:3. I Peter also refers to believers who suffer "because of conscience toward God" (2:19, NKJV).

We can say that a good conscience is well informed by scriptural truths so that it has biblical instincts. It is not weighted down by unnecessary regulations like those of the law of Moses, nor is it subject to teachings based on fables. It is not seared by repeated violations. Instead, the good conscience wholeheartedly endorses and agrees with the biblical definition of behavior to avoid and behavior to engage in.

I Peter 2:12 anticipates that those who speak evil of believers will, because of the good works they observe,

Exhortations in View of Suffering

"glorify God in the day of visitation." That passage expresses hope that unbelievers will come to a place of faith. I Peter 3:16, however, anticipates that unbelievers who speak evil of believers will be ashamed. There is no way to guarantee how another person will respond to a Christian witness.

In Old Testament and Jewish literature, to be ashamed is to be utterly defeated and disgraced in battle or before God. It is to be overthrown and left at the mercies of one's enemies.[256] (See Psalm 6:10; 25:2-3; 35:4; 40:14-15; 44:7; Jeremiah 17:13, 18.) If this does not happen during this life to those who reject Jesus, it will certainly happen when they stand before Him in judgment (4:5).

Here again, I Peter returns to the theme of "good conduct." (See 1:15, 17-18; 2:12; 3:1-2.) The Christian life results in a distinctive lifestyle.

Verse 17. Although those who are "followers of that which is good" (i.e., seeking peace [see comments on verse 13]) minimize the probability of being persecuted, sometimes it may be the will of God for a believer to suffer for doing good. (See 4:19.) Spiritual benefits arise from suffering in the will of God when we accept that suffering and recognize it as God's instrument in working out some good thing. (See I Corinthians 12:7-20; I Peter 1:6-7; 4:12-14; and comments on verse 14.) Suffering tends to purify motives; it helps a person reorient his priorities and reassess his values.

Most commentators view this verse as essentially restating for all believers the point that 2:19-20 makes specifically for believing slaves. Michaels makes the point, however, that the meaning may be that it is better "to suffer in this life at the hands of persecutors for doing

First Peter

good, than at God's hand . . . for doing wrong."[257]

As in verse 14, verse 17 uses the optative mood (*theloi*, "will"), forming a literary bracket in the passage. It is not certain that believers will suffer severe persecution for righteousness' sake, but it is a possibility.

Verse 18. The phrase translated "for Christ also" (*hoti kai Christos*) appears in 2:21 as well, where it refers to Christ's suffering "for us." Here, too, it refers to the suffering of Christ, but the verse further specifies that the suffering was "for sins." The context of 2:21-24 indicates that the suffering of 2:21 is for the same purpose. This statement emphasizes the substitutionary nature of Christ's suffering. (See comments on 2:24.)

The precise phrase "suffered for sins" (*peri hamartion epathen*) occurs only here in the New Testament, although a portion of the phrase (*peri hamartion*, "for sins") occurs in Hebrews 5:3 and 10:26. A similar phrase (*huper harmartion*, "on behalf of sins" or "for sins") occurs in Hebrews 5:1 and 10:12. The phrase *peri hamartias* ("for sin") occurs in Romans 8:3; Hebrews 10:6, 8; 10:18; 13:11. All of these references have to do with a sacrifice for sin; the death of Jesus Christ on the cross was the final, ultimate fulfillment of what all previous sacrifices merely prefigured. (See Hebrews 10:1.)

The substitutionary sufferings of Christ occurred "once." The word translated "once" (*hapax*) expresses "sufficiency and completeness."[258] As Michaels points out, "Christ's suffering is over, its purpose fully accomplished."[259] Other passages of Scripture make the same point. (See Romans 6:10; Hebrews 7:27; 9:12, 26, 28; 10:10.) Since the death of Christ was of infinite value, it was God's final answer to the sin problem.

Christ suffered as "the just [*dikaios*] for the unjust [*adikon*]." The Septuagint translation of Isaiah 53:11 identifies the Messiah as the "just one" (*dikaion*) who bears the sins of many. The Septuagint uses *dikaion* to translate the Hebrew *tsadiq*, which means "righteous." Christ, the righteous one, suffered on behalf of (*huper*) the unrighteous ones. This statement underscores again the substitutionary nature of His suffering and points to the marvel of redemption: since Christ suffered for our sins in our place, there is no further eternal consequence for our sins. The only people who will yet answer to God for their sins are those who have not placed their faith in Christ Jesus in order to receive the benefits of the Atonement.

The purpose for Christ's suffering was "that he might bring us to God." Placed in the context of Christ's substitutionary suffering, this statement parallels 2:24-25, where those who have received the benefits of the Messiah's substitutionary work have "returned to the Shepherd and Bishop" of their souls. We should not infer that coming to God is one thing and returning to the Shepherd and Bishop of our souls is another.[260] Jesus is God Himself. (See comments on 1:17.)

In ten verses, I Peter uses the name "Jesus" in reference to the Messiah, and in each case it is accompanied by "Christ," either before or after "Jesus." (See 1:1, 2, 3, 7, 13; 2:5; 3:21; 4:11; 5:10, 14.) In nine verses, I Peter uses "Christ" without the name "Jesus." (See 1:11, 19; 2:21; 3:16, 18; 4:1, 13, 14; 5:1.) A general pattern seems to emerge.

When I Peter identifies the Messiah as "Jesus Christ" or "Christ Jesus," the emphasis is more on triumph than on suffering. In 1:1, Peter identified himself as an apostle of Jesus Christ. In 1:2, even though it uses "Jesus Christ" in connection to the "sprinkling of the blood," the emphasis is not on Christ's suffering but on the victorious effect of the Atonement. In 1:3, Peter blessed "the God and Father of our Lord Jesus Christ," focusing on the abundance of His mercy and on the "resurrection of Jesus Christ" by which we have been "begotten . . . again." In 1:7, the reference is to the "appearing" or "revelation of Jesus Christ." The same theme appears in 1:13. In 2:5, believers are "lively stones" whose spiritual sacrifices are "acceptable to God by Jesus Christ." In 3:21, the emphasis is again on the "resurrection of Jesus Christ." In 4:11, God is glorified "through Jesus Christ." In 5:10, God has called us unto his eternal glory "by Christ Jesus." In the final reference, 5:14, Peter greeted all those who are "in Christ Jesus."

On the other hand, when Peter used the word "Christ" alone, the emphasis is almost exclusively on suffering. In 1:11, the "Spirit of Christ" in the prophets testified first to the sufferings of Christ and then to the glories that would follow His suffering. In 1:19, the reference is to the "blood of Christ," with the focus on Christ as a sacrificial lamb. This is somewhat in contrast to 1:2 where, even though the reference is to the "blood of Jesus Christ," the focus is on the application of the blood to the believer's life. In 2:21, "Christ . . . suffered." There is a reference to "your good conduct in Christ" (NKJV) in 3:16, where contextually the emphasis is on identification with Christ in His suffering. Again 3:18 and 4:1 say, "Christ . . . suffered." The reference in 4:13 is to "Christ's sufferings." In 4:14, the believer is "reproached for the name of Christ";

again the context indicates identification with Christ in His suffering. Finally, in 5:1, the reference is again to the "sufferings of Christ."

Apparently, when I Peter limits its reference to "Christ" rather than "Jesus Christ" or "Christ Jesus," the focus is on the atoning sufferings of the Messiah. (The Greek *Christos* is the equivalent of the Hebrew *Messiach.*) The substitutionary sufferings were made possible by the Incarnation, or by the genuineness and fullness of His humanity. Thus, "Christ . . . suffered . . . that he might bring us to God" means that by His identification with us in our human condition, by His solidarity with the human race, the Messiah provided for our restoration to fellowship with God. It seems doubtful that I Peter makes any statement here about the nature of the Godhead, and it certainly does not imply that Christ and God are distinct "persons."

The sufferings of Christ involved Him "being put to death in the flesh." Flesh (*sarki*) is contrasted here with spirit (*pneumati*). He was "quickened" (made alive) "by the Spirit." This is, of course, a reference to His resurrection from the dead.

Michaels points out that flesh and spirit "are both datives of respect."[261] That is, Christ was put to death with respect to the flesh, but He was made alive with respect to the Spirit. The distinction intended by "flesh" and "spirit" is not "between the material and immaterial parts of Christ's person . . . but rather between his earthly existence and his risen state."[262] Flesh refers to the "sphere of human limitations, of suffering, and of death."[263] Spirit refers to the "sphere of power, vindication, and a new life."[264] There is no suggestion here of a bifurcation of

First Peter

Christ's person: "Both spheres affect Christ's . . . whole person; one cannot be assigned to the body and the other to the soul."[265]

In other words, there is no hint here that the resurrection of Jesus Christ was the resurrection of a "spirit" only. The biblical idea of resurrection is of bodily resurrection, in direct opposition to the Greek idea of the immortality of the soul as disembodied existence after death. To those who saw Him after His resurrection and who thought He was a spirit, Jesus said, "Behold my hands and my feet, that it is I myself: handle me, and see; for a spirit hath not flesh and bones, as ye see me have" (Luke 24:39). Although He had been "quickened by the Spirit," He still had flesh and bones. (See Romans 1:4; 8:11; I Corinthians 15:44-45.)

Verse 19. Few verses are more puzzling than this one. Martin Luther wrote, "A wonderful text is this, and a more obscure passage perhaps than any other in the New Testament, so that I do not know for a certainty just what Peter means."[266] Attempts to interpret verses 19-20 have given rise to five predominate views, with variations within each. Grudem summarizes them as follows:

> *View 1:* When Noah was building the ark, Christ 'in spirit' was in Noah preaching repentance and righteousness through him to *unbelievers who were on the earth then* but are now 'spirits in prison' (people in hell).
>
> *View 2:* After Christ died, he went and preached to *people in hell,* offering them a second chance of salvation.
>
> *View 3:* After Christ died, he went and preached

to *people in hell,* proclaiming to them that he had triumphed over them and their condemnation was final.

View 4: After Christ died, he proclaimed release to *people who had repented just before they died in the flood,* and led them out of their imprisonment (in Purgatory) into heaven.

View 5: After Christ died (or: after he rose but before he ascended into heaven), he travelled to hell and proclaimed triumph over the *fallen angels* who had sinned by marrying human women before the flood. [267]

Views 2-5 can be defended only on the basis of extra-biblical literature or speculation. Each of these views require the acceptance of difficulties that cannot be resolved. Concerning view 2, there is no biblical evidence that individuals already in hell can have a second chance at salvation under any circumstance. All that remains after death is the judgment (Hebrews 9:27). Abraham's response to the rich man in hell indicates that there is no possibility of changing one's destiny after death (Luke 16:26). In response to view 3, what would be the point for Christ to visit hell only to inform the captives that there was no hope for their release? View 4 lacks any biblical support. There is no evidence that anyone other than Noah's family repented in those days, and the doctrine of purgatory is of human invention. View 5 rests upon speculation about the identity of the "sons of God" in Genesis 6:2, but the view that they were angels does not have unqualified support even from Jewish tradition.

Views 2-5 rest on the assumption that Christ went to

hell at some point after His death. This view arises from Acts 2:27, 31, where Peter quoted from Psalm 16:10 to affirm the resurrection of Jesus from the dead: "For thou wilt not leave my soul in hell; neither wilt thou suffer thine Holy One to see corruption." Those who believe that Christ went to the place where the unrighteous dead are suffering base their view on the mistaken idea that "hell" always refers to the same thing. This is not true, as we clearly see from Bible references to hell in both the Old and New Testaments.

In the Old Testament, the Hebrew *sheol*, often translated "hell," is the place to which the dead go. In the New Testament, the Greek counterpart is *hades*. As with all words, it is important to remember that these words are defined by their contexts. In some contexts, *sheol* and *hades* refer to death or, as a symbol of death, the grave. In other contexts, the words refer to the place of literal and conscious torment to which the unredeemed go after death.

When Reuben tried to persuade his father, Jacob, to allow Benjamin to accompany his brothers on a return trip to Egypt, Jacob said, "My son shall not go down with you; for his brother is dead, and he is left alone: if mischief befall him by the way in which ye go, then shall ye bring down my gray hairs with sorrow to the grave [*sheol*]" (Genesis 42:38). Here, Jacob used *sheol* as a reference to death itself. The grave symbolizes death.

Job's expressed his wish for death in these words: "O, that thou wouldest hide me in the grave [*sheol*], that thou wouldest keep me secret, until thy wrath be past" (Job 14:13).

In both of these cases, *sheol* is simply a reference to

death, not to a place of conscious torment. Job would have had no desire to go to a place of torment. That certainly would not have been an escape from the painful circumstances he faced on earth.

When it seemed to Heman the Ezrahite that death loomed near, he wrote, "For my soul is full of troubles: and my life draweth nigh unto the grave [*sheol*]" (Psalm 88:3). For Heman, *sheol* was death itself. He equated *sheol* with "the pit," another word for the grave (Psalm 88:4).

Other contexts use *sheol* to describe the specific destiny of the wicked: "The wicked shall be turned into hell [*sheol*], and all the nations that forget God" (Psalm 9:17). Since all people, righteous and wicked, will die, *sheol* in this case has a more restrictive meaning.

In a description first of the fall of the king of Babylon, then of Lucifer himself, Isaiah described *sheol* as a place of conscious suffering in a community of sufferers where communication between individuals occurs. (See Isaiah 14:9-11, 16-17). In this context, where *sheol* describes not simply the grave as the destiny of the body but also the destiny of the spirit/soul, a completely different Hebrew word, *qeber*, is used to describe the grave itself (Isaiah 14:19).

In a lament over Pharaoh and Egypt, *sheol* describes the destiny of those destroyed as a place of consciousness. (See Ezekiel 32:21). Here again, when *sheol* refers to something other than the grave, *qeber* is used to refer to the grave itself (Ezekiel 32:22).

Jonah used *sheol* to describe his experience in the fish's belly (Jonah 2:2). If *sheol* referred only to the grave, it would have been inappropriate for Jonah to describe his experience with the word. And if the idea of *sheol* excludes consciousness, the word would have been inappropriate, for Jonah was conscious and praying. But Jonah could use *sheol* in a poetic sense, for the belly of the fish was to him what *sheol* is to those who are there.

The New Testament uses *hades* in the same way that the Old Testament uses *sheol*. It sometimes describes the condition of the lost between death and the resurrection, and it sometimes describes the condition of the saved.

I Corinthians 15:54-55 equates death and *hades*: "So when this corruptible shall have put on incorruption, and this mortal shall have put on immortality, then shall be brought to pass the saying that is written, Death is swallowed up in victory. O death, where is thy sting? O grave [*hades*], where is thy victory?" This passage quotes from the Septuagint translation of Hosea 13:14, a poetic passage in which, as is the case with Hebrew poetry, the rhyme is not one of sound but of thought. In this sense, *hades* "rhymes" with death; it is a restatement of the same point in a different word. As used by Paul, it is the righteous who have experienced and are delivered both from "death" and "*hades*." In this context, then, *hades* cannot refer to the abode of the wicked dead.

Peter's quote from the Septuagint version of Psalm 16:8-11 on the Day of Pentecost also demonstrates that *sheol* and *hades* may refer to the condition of the righteous dead. To explain that David prophesied of the resurrection of Jesus, that He would be "loosed from the pains of death" (Acts 2:24), Peter said, "For David speaketh concerning him, I foresaw the Lord always before my face, for he is on my right hand, that I should not be moved: therefore did my heart rejoice, and my tongue

Exhortations in View of Suffering

was glad; moreover also my flesh shall rest in hope: because thou wilt not leave my soul in hell [*hades*], neither wilt thou suffer thine Holy One to see corruption" (Acts 2:25-27). Peter reiterated David's prophecy of the resurrection of Jesus (Acts 2:31). The flesh of Jesus was in the grave, but His soul—His immaterial part—was in *hades* until His resurrection. Since Jesus was not wicked, He did not suffer the fate of the wicked dead. In this case, *hades* is the same place as paradise, for Jesus said to the thief on the cross, "Verily I say unto thee, To day shalt thou be with me in paradise" (Luke 23:43).

But the New Testament also uses *hades* to refer to the condition of the unsaved after death. To the unbelievers in Capernaum, Jesus said, "And thou, Capernaum, which art exalted unto heaven, shalt be brought down to hell [*hades*]" (Matthew 11:23). In the story of the rich man and Lazarus, Jesus said of the former, "And in hell [*hades*] he lift up his eyes, being in torments" (Luke 16:23).

Only an examination of the context will tell us whether the words *sheol* and *hades* refer to the condition of the unrighteous or righteous dead and whether they refer to death itself, as represented by the grave, or to the afterlife. By contrast, *gehenna* ("hell," as in Mark 9:43-47) consistently refers to the condition of the unrighteous dead.

The word translated "prison" (*phulake*) has a range of meaning that includes "the underworld or the place of punishment in hell."[268] The same word also describes the place where Satan will be imprisoned for one thousand years (Revelation 20:7). We may be certain that Christ did not visit this place during the time between His death and His resurrection or at any other time for the

First Peter

following reasons: (1) He was not a sinner and thus did not deserve to suffer in hell.[269] (2) There was no point in Christ's preaching to those suffering in hell, whether they were the spirits of human beings or whether they were angels. Angels cannot be redeemed under any circumstance. (See Hebrews 2:16.[270]) And there is no second chance for human beings (Hebrews 9:27). (3) Jesus declared that He would be in paradise after His death (Luke 23:43).

The words "by which" refer back to the phrase "by the Spirit" in verse 18. It is in the sphere of the Spirit that Christ preached to the imprisoned spirits. In other words, He did so by means of the Spirit. Since the "Spirit of Christ" testified through the Hebrew prophets (1:10-11), since the context describes the time "when once the longsuffering of God waited in the days of Noah" (3:20), and since Noah was a "preacher of righteousness" (II Peter 2:5), verse 19 apparently speaks of Noah's preaching as animated by the same Spirit that resurrected Christ from the dead. In this sense we can say that Christ Himself did the preaching. (See Galatians 2:20.)

This verse does not suggest that the "spirits" who received the preaching were in prison at the time of the preaching. They were certainly in prison when Peter wrote this letter. These "spirits" seem to be the spirits of human beings who rejected Noah's preaching. The possibility that they are angels is ruled out by the following considerations: (1) These spirits received some kind of preaching, but there is no point in preaching to angels, for they cannot be redeemed. (2) These spirits were disobedient while Noah was building the ark. Even if the "sons of God" of Genesis 6:2 are angels, their disobedience was not while Noah was building the ark, but prior to that time. (3) Scripture often uses the words "soul" and "spirit" interchangeably (e.g., Luke 1:46).[271] Those who received preaching but who disobeyed were "spirits"; those who were saved were "souls" (verse 20). Both were human beings.

In the larger context, the purpose for the reference to this preaching during the days of Noah is twofold: (1) It reminds the readers that their duty to "be ready always to give an answer to every man that asketh you" is not unprecedented; Noah had the same duty and fulfilled it admirably. His preaching to unbelievers in a hostile world is an example to us. (2) Even though those who heard Noah rejected his message, God delivered him and his family. Likewise, even though those who falsely accuse believers might reject their attempts to give an answer, God will ultimately deliver the believers from them. Their baptism is the assurance of this deliverance (verse 21).

Verse 20. While Noah was building the ark, possibly a period of 120 years (Genesis 6:3), the human population of the world, with the exception of his family, was disobedient to God. Jewish tradition embellished the story of Noah and his interaction with the unbelieving society of his day.[272] He was a "preacher of righteousness" (II Peter 2:5), so undoubtedly he proclaimed to those around him his faith in God and the impending judgment of God. None responded to his preaching, however, except his family.

As Noah constructed the ark, "the longsuffering of God waited." Even though the human race deserved immediate judgment for their pervasive wickedness and unswerving evil (Genesis 6:5-7, 11-13), God mercifully refrained from destroying them until the ark was completed. By equipping Noah with a message and a promise, God made a provision for the wicked, violent population of the earth to receive one final warning. But even though it took a long time to build the ark, and even though Noah was faithful as a proclaimer of righteousness, only a few souls (i.e., people) were saved. (See Genesis 7:13.)

I Peter deals with a similar situation. It addresses believers who are bitterly criticized by unbelievers and who should not be surprised if they are called on to suffer (3:16-17; 4:12, 19). Even though they may be thoroughly prepared to explain the reason for their hope to their critics (3:15), there is no guarantee that their critics will be convinced. Other passages of Scripture also compare Noah's experiences to those of people of faith who lived later. (See Ezekiel 14:14, 20; Matthew 24:37-38; Luke 17:26-27; Hebrews 11:7.)

Believers usually do find themselves living and working among those who are in rebellion against God. Noah's example here assures believers that regardless of the attitude of those around them, if they remain faithful they will ultimately be delivered from the world of unbelievers. (See 1:7, 13.) This will be true even if most or nearly all of the population of the world reject God.

Specifically, the eight people who were saved "were saved by water." The same water that was the agent of destruction for unbelievers was the agent of salvation for Noah and his family; the water caused the ark to float above the worldwide destruction.

One might protest that actually it was the ark that saved Noah and his family, but I Peter emphasized water in order to draw a parallel between the salvation of

Noah's family and the significance of water baptism in the new covenant. Grammatically, the Greek phrase translated "were saved by water" (*diesothesan di' hudatos*) could be translated to indicate salvation through water, with water as a threat to their lives, or, as it is ordinarily translated, to indicate salvation by means of water. The next verse indicates that the ordinary translation is correct, for it describes baptism as an agent of salvation.[273]

Verse 21. There is a corresponding relationship between the salvation of Noah's family by water and the significance of water baptism in the church. The word translated "figure" by the KJV is the Greek *antitypon*, which indicates that baptism is a fulfillment of what was typified by the role of water in saving Noah's family.[274] Obviously, baptism does not negate faith's role in salvation. (See Ephesians 2:8-9.) It was Noah's faith in God that caused him to obey God's command to build the ark (Hebrews 11:7). Likewise, it is the New Testament believer's faith that prompts him to obey the command of Christ to be baptized. (See Matthew 28:19; Mark 16:16.)

It is difficult for those who see water baptism as merely an outward symbol of an inner reality to accept at face value Peter's statement that "baptism doth also now save us." For example, Grudem offered a paraphrase: "Baptism now saves you—not the outward physical ceremony of baptism but the inward spiritual reality which baptism represents."[275] This, he says, "guards against any 'magical' view of baptism which would attribute saving power to the physical ceremony itself."[276] Hillyer wrote, "The significance of baptism is that it is the public acknowledgment of an inward spiritual purity brought about in the individual by the work of God in Christ."[277]

McKnight pointed out that this text has

> generated considerable discussion in the history of the church. What Peter apparently does is connect the "water delivery" of the ark with the "water delivery" of baptism. What is fundamental to understanding the early church's attitude toward baptism is (1) that early Christians were much more ritualistic than most moderns, and (2) that all early Christians were baptized. Thus, there was no such thing as an "unbaptized believer" in Peter's day. This approach to the rite permits Peter to say things about baptism that many modern Christians would not want to say.[278]

McKnight's observation is significant. There can be no question that the actual text compares the genuineness of the saving effect of the water for Noah's family to the genuineness of the saving effect of baptism for the church. In other words, any attempt to make baptism an option ignores that the water of Noah's flood was not an option in the saving of his family. That Noah's family went into the ark certainly was evidence of their faith, just as baptism is evidence of our faith, but it was also an essential act of obedience if they hoped to survive the flood. All of the faith in the world would not have saved Noah and his family from the flood if they had refused to enter the ark.

This reality does not mean the ark had "magical" powers; neither does baptism. Grudem's reference to a "magical" view of baptism implies sacramentalism, the idea that God imparts grace through sacraments apart from or prior to faith. The Bible does not teach this view. Any act

Exhortations in View of Suffering

of obedience is validated only by faith. For Noah and his family, the ark was God's means of delivering them from the flood, and they built and entered the ark as a consequence of their faith. For the church, baptism is God's means of delivering believers from an unbelieving world very similar to the world in Noah's day, and believers submit to baptism as a consequence of their faith in God.

McKnight's comment that "early Christians were much more ritualistic than most moderns" and that "all early Christians were baptized" is important in that it reflects the understanding of first-century Christians. As he pointed out, "There was no such thing as an 'unbaptized believer' in Peter's day." We should ask whether those closest to the origin of the church had a clearer understanding of baptism than those who look at the commands of Scripture from the distance of two thousand years. If, as McKnight suggested, the first-century "approach to the rite permits Peter to say things about baptism that many modern Christians would not want to say," it seems appropriate for modern Christians to reassess their perspective on baptism. In other words, any modern Christian should be able to wholeheartedly join Peter in his view of the significance of baptism.

It was, after all, Peter who responded to the queries of those who heard his sermon on Pentecost with the command, "Repent, and be baptized every one of you in the name of Jesus Christ for the remission of sins, and ye shall receive the gift of the Holy Ghost" (Acts 2:38). It was Peter who, at Cornelius' house, "commanded them to be baptized in the name of the Lord" (Acts 10:48).

Baptism is "not the putting away of the filth of the flesh." In the view of most commentators, this statement means that the purpose of baptism is not to cleanse a person physically. Some, however, suppose that it is a reference to "moral defilement."[279] The latter view, of course, strips from baptism any actual connection to salvation. This interpretation is contextually problematic because it would imply that there was no real connection between the water of Noah's flood and the salvation of his family. It is also problematic in that "moral defilement" is not a matter of the flesh only, but of the "flesh and spirit" (II Corinthians 7:1).

When verse 21 declares that baptism does not deal with the filth of the flesh, perhaps its primary purpose is to refute any idea that baptism is merely a ritual to cleanse a person from external defilement. This purpose would be especially important if the letter was originally written to a primarily Jewish audience. Ritual washing was practiced widely in Judaism, as is attested by the *mikvahs* (ritual baths) found in first-century Jewish homes. Devout Jews immersed themselves daily to be cleansed from defilement. Many other ritual washings were inherent to Judaism. (See Matthew 15:2; Mark 7:4, 8; John 2:6; 11:55; Hebrews 9:10.) The sacrifices of the Mosaic covenant were for the "purifying of the flesh" (Hebrews 9:13). Christian baptism was not in this category, however. The ritual washings of Judaism accomplished nothing; they were mere ceremonies that resulted in external cleansing. The sacrifices of the law of Moses were divinely ordained, but they did not purify the inner person (Hebrews 10:1-4).

Baptism is not merely an external ritual, but it is "the answer of a good conscience toward God." Noah's entrance into the ark was evidence that his conscience

Exhortations in View of Suffering

was clear with God. He did what he did because of his faith in God; nothing stood between him and obedience to God's command. Likewise, when a person comes to God in faith, turning away from sin, his baptism testifies that he is holding nothing in reserve; he is making a clean break with the past. I Peter 1:22 connects the purification of the soul with obedience to the truth. Only those whose conscience is not clear with God would have any reason to refuse baptism.

The statement "not the putting away of the filth of the flesh, but the answer of a good conscience toward God" is parenthetical. To discover the basis upon which baptism "saves us," we must read directly from the first phrase to the last, as follows: "The like figure whereunto even baptism doth also now save us . . . by the resurrection of Jesus Christ." This statement connects the significance of baptism with the resurrection of Jesus Christ. (See also Romans 6:3-5; Colossians 2:11-12.) Michaels points out that "Peter speaks of water baptism in a way that recalls his reference to the new birth in 1:3. Both are said to take place 'through the raising of Jesus Christ.'"[280]

The meaning of Christian baptism is wide-ranging. By means of baptism, we are united with Christ in his death, burial, and resurrection (Romans 6:3-5; Galatians 3:27). We are baptized into Christ because He was crucified for us (I Corinthians 1:13). Baptism is the new covenant counterpart of old covenant circumcision (Colossians 2:11-12). It was a primary response everywhere first-century people turned to Christ. (See Acts 2:38, 41; 8:12-13, 16, 36, 38; 9:18; 10:47-48; 16:15, 33; 18:8; 19:5; 22:16.) The doctrine of baptisms is one of the principles of the doctrine of Christ (Hebrews 6:2).[281]

First Peter

Verse 22. The theme of the ascent of Christ into heaven appears frequently in the New Testament. (See Mark 16:19; Luke 24:51; Acts 1:10-11; Ephesians 1:20; 2:6; 4:10; Hebrews 4:14; 7:26.) Ephesians 4:8 quotes Psalm 68:18 in reference to Christ's ascension, in conjunction with which Christ "led captivity captive, and gave gifts unto men." In ascending, Jesus returned to "where he was before" (John 6:62; see also John 3:13). In His ascension, "God also has highly exalted Him and given Him the name which is above every name" (Philippians 2:9, NKJV).

It seems that Christ has reached a position here which is in some way higher than what He occupied prior to the Incarnation.[282] But this cannot be an exaltation of deity, for that has always been the essential nature of Christ and it cannot be in any way enhanced. The exaltation must, therefore, refer to the exaltation of the authentic human existence that He willingly and permanently assumed in the Incarnation. The Incarnation is permanent. That is, from the moment of conception in the womb of Mary, Christ is and forever will be God manifest in the flesh (full and genuine human nature), although He now is manifest in glorified humanity.

As far as we can tell, the only difference in the preincarnate and post-resurrection existence of Christ is that now humanity has been permanently joined to the Godhead. Robertson agrees with this assessment: "What glory did Christ have after the Ascension that he did not have before in heaven? What did he take back to heaven that he did not bring? Clearly his humanity."[283] Grudem points out that "Jesus' ascension to heaven . . . was the occasion when he received new authority and power

Exhortations in View of Suffering

which he had not had before as God-man."[284] This statement may seem strange in that Jesus was and is God manifest in genuine and full human existence (I Timothy 3:16; Colossians 2:9), but though He retained His deity in the Incarnation, He willingly embraced the limitations inherent in human existence. (See Philippians 2:5-8; John 5:19; Mark 13:32.) Now that He has ascended, these limitations have been overcome, even though He retains His humanity. Christ's glorification has overcome the earthly limitations of Christ's human nature. (See John 7:39; Philippians 3:21.)

In conjunction with His ascension, Jesus "is on the right hand of God." The passage describes in spatial terms both His ascension and His current position. As in other places in Scripture, this is the language of accommodation to human thought. In other words, the Bible expresses spiritual realities in concrete human terms to enable the readers to grasp something of their significance. So far as we can tell, the biblical idea of "heaven" as the place of God's abode relates to another realm of existence. The point is not that "heaven" is straight up from any particular point on the globe, but that "heaven," though a real place, exists in what we might call—for lack of a better term—a parallel universe. To illustrate this point, many people have no problem believing that angels are all about us, even though we cannot see them. The angels, as spirit beings, exist in the realm of the spirit. Because of the limitations of our human existence, we cannot see into the spirit realm. Occasionally, this limitation is temporarily overcome by means of visions. (See, e.g., Acts 7:55-56.) It is also sometimes overcome by means of visible manifestations of spirit beings, including angels. (See, e.g., Genesis 18:1-2.)

When Jesus ascended, He was visible to His disciples until the clouds received Him out of their sight. (See Acts 1:9-11.) There is no reason to think, however, that His ascent would have continued to be visible to human eyes if powerful telescopes had been available at that time to track His progress through the skies. Likewise, although He will return visibly just as He went away, there is no reason to think that the Hubble telescope or some other technologically advanced tracking system will be able to monitor His descent from a specific point in space to some specific point above the earth. He will make Himself visible to those to whom He wishes to appear at the moment and place that He wishes to do so.

God is a Spirit who is invisible. (See John 1:18; Colossians 1:15; I Timothy 1:17; Hebrews 11:27.) When John saw a new heaven and a new earth, he was "in the spirit." (See Revelation 1:10; 21:1.) That is, what John saw was a vision that presented spiritual realities in concrete terms. This is the nature of visions. (See Acts 10:10-17.)

We must understand the description of Jesus' being "on the right hand of God" to represent a spiritual reality in concrete terms. The imagery, which has its roots in Psalm 110:1, appears frequently in Scripture.[285]

To use figurative language to describe something about God in human terms is an anthropomorphism. The word "anthropomorphism" is from the Greek words *anthropos*, meaning "man," and *morphe*, meaning "form." The word refers to the way the Bible uses human terms to communicate something about God's nature or attributes. We are not to take such terms literally any more

Exhortations in View of Suffering

than we are to suppose that God literally has feathers and wings. (See Psalm 91:4.) Bernard Ramm points out:

> The fact of God's almightiness is spoken of in terms of a right arm because among men the right arm is a symbol of strength or power. Pre-eminence is spoken of as sitting at God's right hand because in human social affairs the right hand position with reference to the host was the place of greatest honor. . . .
>
> [Quoting Seisenberger:] We must not be offended by anthropomorphic expressions, which seem to us out of keeping with our conception of God. It is with a well-considered design that the Holy Scripture speaks of God as a Being resembling man, and ascribes to Him a face, eyes, ears, mouth, hands, and feet and the sense of smell and hearing. This is done out of consideration for man's power of comprehension; and the same is the case when the Bible represents God as loving or hating, as jealous, angry, glad, or filled with regret, dispositions which apply to God not *per affectum* but *per effectum*. They show us that God is not coldly indifferent to loyalty or disloyalty on the part of man, but notices them well. Moreover we must not forget that man is made in the image and likeness of God, and that therefore in the divine Being there must be something analogous to the qualities of men, though in the highest perfection. [286]

What are the dangers of taking anthropomorphisms literally? "More than one unlettered person and cultist has taken the anthropomorphisms of the Scriptures literally and has so thought of God as possessing a body."[287]

In his comments on the phrase "the right hand of the Majesty on high" in Hebrews 1:3, F. F. Bruce wrote:

> That no literal location is intended was as well understood by Christians in the apostolic age as it is by us: they knew that God has no physical right hand or material throne where the ascended Christ sits beside Him; to them the language denoted the exaltation and supremacy of Christ as it does to us.[288]

The literal method of interpreting Scripture does not deny symbols, figures of speech, or spiritual truth. It simply insists that we must make all interpretation on the basis of the literal meaning of the Scriptures. If the passage is not clearly symbolic, we should not force symbolism upon it. If it is clearly symbolic, we must interpret the symbols literally; that is, we must discover their literal, concrete meaning.

To say that Christ is now at the right hand of God indicates that He occupies the ultimate place of majesty, power, and authority. Specifically, I Peter speaks of Christ's authority, for it links His presence at the right hand of God with "angels and authorities and powers being made subject unto him."

Ancient Jewish texts often use the terms "authorities and powers" to describe angels as rulers over the nations.[289] The idea that angels ruled the nations arose from implications in the Hebrew Scriptures and from the Septuagint translation of Deuteronomy 32:8, which indicates that God has put this present world in subjection to angels: "When the Most High divided the nations, when he separated the sons of Adam, he set the bounds of the nations according to the number of the angels of God." This may be the point in Hebrews 2:5, which declares that God "has not put the world to come . . . in subjection to angels."[290]

Rather than trying to distinguish between "angels," "authorities," and "powers," with the idea that each word represents a different kind of spirit being, it may be best to see in these words a hendiadys, a literary figure which would mean "angels, authoritative and powerful as they are."[291] The authority of Christ over angels, whether fallen or faithful, is the frequent subject of New Testament literature. (See Romans 8:38; Ephesians 1:21; Colossians 1:16; 2:10, 15.) The Bible presents the ultimate outworking of Christ's authority as yet future (I Corinthians 15:24-28; Hebrews 2:5-9).

There is no conflict between the "realized eschatology" of some New Testament passages, which describe Christ's authority as a present reality, and the "already/not yet" description of other passages, which see Him as in authority but with the ultimate finality of that authority not yet visible to human eyes. The authority that already exists in the realm of the spirit will ultimately be manifested in the visible world. This might be compared with historical situations in which individual members of an army at war do not receive word that their army has been defeated and has surrendered until long after the fact. They may continue their fighting alone or in small groups, but their effort is futile. Eventually, the authority of the conquering army will be brought to bear upon them, and they will be forced to submit.

The authority of Christ over the angelic realm is now a reality, and He is presently exercising His authority through those who believe on Him. (See Mark 16:17-18; II Corinthians 10:3-4; Ephesians 6:10-18; James 4:7; I Peter 5:9; I John 4:4.) In the future, He will express His authority by the binding of Satan for one thousand years (Revelation 20:1-3). Then, after He gives Satan a temporary reprieve, He will exercise final authority over him by casting Satan permanently into the lake of fire and brimstone (Revelation 20:3-10).

Chapter 4. I Peter 4:1-6 returns to the theme of suffering so typical of the letter and from which it makes a brief departure in 3:19-22. In 3:18, Christ is seen suffering for sins, "being put to death in the flesh but made alive by the Spirit" (NKJV). This language is similar to 4:6, where those to whom the gospel was preached "might be judged according to men in the flesh, but live according to God in the spirit" (NKJV).

We may observe other parallels of 3:18-22 with 4:1-6: (1) Just as Noah preached to the spirits in prison (see comments on 3:19), so those who had already died in the era of the new covenant had been recipients of preaching (4:6). (2) Just as those who rejected Noah's preaching were disobedient (3:20), so those who rejected the message of the gospel were guilty of a wide variety of idolatrous activities (4:3). (3) Just as Noah's family was saved from the wickedness of their generation (3:20), so those who have responded to the gospel no longer live "in the flesh for the lusts of men" (4:2, NKJV). Further, it is not difficult to see a parallel in the rejection of New Testament believers by their former cohorts (4:4) with the rejection Noah must have faced as he preached righteousness (see comments on 3:20).

Verse 1. The substitutionary suffering of Christ is a theme in this letter. (See comments on 2:21, 24; 3:18.) This verse specifies that Christ suffered "in the flesh," that is, in His human existence. In 2:24, Christ bore our sins "in His own body." The specific purpose for the Incarnation was that the Messiah, as a human being, might suffer on behalf of human beings, as one of them, in order to satisfy the righteous judgment of God against sin.[292]

Although the substitutionary suffering of Christ is redemptive, I Peter encourages the readers to "arm" themselves "with the same mind." In keeping with the theme of suffering that undergirds this letter, the point is not that the suffering of believers is redemptive, as was the suffering of Christ. But believers can expect to suffer, just as Christ did. In some cases, this suffering might even conclude in martyrdom. (Some were "judged according to men in the flesh," a possible reference to martyrdom.)

The idea of "arming" oneself is a military metaphor. It describes believers as "arming, training or otherwise preparing themselves for battle and possible death. The sense seems to be that those who died with Christ through faith (cf. 2:24) are genuinely prepared to suffer with him in any other way, including martyrdom."[293] Military metaphors appear in the New Testament in several places.[294]

To arm oneself "with the same mind" as Christ had regarding His suffering means to be willing to accept unjust suffering as part of God's larger plan by which He works out His purposes. It is not possible to have this mind by a simple attitude shift. To genuinely think as Christ, one must be sincerely convinced that suffering is an instrument in the hands of God that will ultimately bring good things to pass. (See 1:11; 2:20; 3:14, 17; 4:12-14, 16, 19; 5:1, 10; Romans 8:17-18; II Corinthians 1:7; II Timothy 2:12; Hebrews 2:10; 12:2-3; James 5:10-11.)

The phrase "he that hath suffered in the flesh hath ceased from sin" has been interpreted in a variety of ways. The most common view is that it is a proverbial statement expressing a general principle. Those who take the statement as proverbial tend to link it with Romans 6:7: "For he that is dead is freed from sin." A problem with this view is that personal suffering does not free believers from sin's dominion; identification with Jesus Christ's death does. Viewing the statement as proverbial also requires "reading the aorist participle [*ho pathon*, translated 'he that hath suffered'] as generic and the perfect indicative [*pepautai*, translated 'hath ceased'] as gnomic (i.e., they are not linked to a specific time frame but are universal in their application)."[295] Though this is possible, it seems unnatural and without support from other biblical sources to suggest that personal suffering is the key to freedom from sin's power. The Bible everywhere teaches that freedom from sin is a consequence of Christ's suffering, not of personal suffering. If personal suffering results in freedom from sin, it seems that the sufferer would at least in some way be his own redeemer.

Some commentators view this phrase as referring not to a specific act of suffering resulting in freedom from sin but to the sanctifying influence of suffering. Grudem puts it, "Whoever has suffered for doing right, and has still gone on obeying God in spite of the suffering it involved, has made a clear break with sin."[296] The problems here are much the same as with the first view. If that is the meaning of this statement, I Peter would stand alone in this teaching. Since the statement "hath ceased from sin" (*pepautai hamartias*) is in the perfect tense, it indicates action completed at some point in the past with effects continuing into the present. This seems to rule out the idea of continued suffering with an ongoing sanctifying effect.

Another view is that the statement refers to "the Christian's entire life on earth as a life of suffering."[297] In this case, the phrase "hath ceased from sin" refers to the believer's eternal reward rather than to any state during his lifetime on earth. The idea is that believers will share in the eternal victory of Christ. But contextually, the focus is not on the believer's eternal reward but on his continuing experiences in this life.[298]

Contextually, grammatically, and in comparison with other New Testament references, it seems best to view the phrase "for he that hath suffered in the flesh hath ceased from sin" as parenthetical, referring to the manner in which Christ suffered once for sin and is now "'through with sin' in the sense that he has finished dealing with it, once and for all; he has put it behind him."[299] (See Hebrews 9:28.) This view does require the reading of the critical Greek text, which the NIV translates as "he who has suffered in his body is done with sin." Michaels translates the phrase as "for he who suffered in the flesh is through with sin."[300] (Very few manuscripts, mostly late, insert the word "from" (*apo*) before the word "sin."[301]) If this is the meaning of the phrase, it puts I Peter 4:1 in agreement with other New Testament passages concerning the finality of the work of Jesus on the cross in dealing with sin. (See Romans 6:10; Hebrews 7:27; 9:12, 26, 28; 10:10, 12, 14.) It also harmonizes with I Peter 3:18.

Verse 2. The phrase "that he no longer should live the rest of his time in the flesh to the lusts of men" may make problematic the suggestion that the previous phrase is parenthetic. The connected phrases, without the parenthetic phrase, would read, "Forasmuch then as Christ hath suffered for us in the flesh, arm yourselves likewise with the same mind . . . that he no longer should live the rest of his time in the flesh to the lusts of men, but to the will of God." The personal pronouns "he" and "his" are missing from the Greek text, however. If the phrase "he that hath suffered in the flesh hath ceased from sin" is a reference to the finality of Christ's sufferings, it would be appropriate, with Michaels, to translate verse 2 as follows: "So as to live out [your] remaining time in the flesh no longer for human impulses but to do the will of God."[302] This translation would meaningfully connect verse 1 (excluding the parenthetical phrase) with verse 2. To do so, we must supply the pronoun "you" in verse 2, but doing so is no different from supplying the pronouns "he" and "his," which the alternate translation requires.

On the other hand, if we supply these pronouns, as the KJV does, they would tend to connect with the pronoun "he" in verse 1. They would make the previous phrase "he that hath suffered in the flesh hath ceased from sin" improbable as a reference to Christ. In this case, since verse 2 cannot describe Christ, another meaning would be forced upon the previous phrase.

Believers should arm themselves with the same mind as Christ so that for the remainder of their lives on earth they will live for the will of God and not for human lusts. For a discussion of the Greek word *epithymiais*, translated "lusts," see comments on 1:14. The word has to do with the strong passions inherent to the human condition. Contextually, it refers specifically to evil passions. (See verses 3-4.) These evil passions are connected with ignorance (1:14), and they war against the soul (2:11). The "world" consists of the strong passions of the flesh and eyes and of the pride of life (I John 2:16).

Believers should live "no longer" for the lusts of people, which indicates that up until the time of their coming to Christ that is precisely how they lived. Although verse 3 focuses on a specific dimension of human passion, it does not exhaust the manifestations of that passion. Human lusts are deceitful (see Jeremiah 17:9); they can disguise themselves in a multitude of ways, including apparent virtues. But anything other than the will of God is human passion. (See Galatians 5:17-21.) Apart from Christ, all people are dead in sins, and their lifestyle is characterized by the lusts of the flesh (Ephesians 2:1-3).

Throughout the letter, there is a concern for the will of God. (See 2:15; 3:17; 4:19.) It connects the will of God with submission to civil authorities and with suffering as a consequence of one's identification with Christ (2:15; 3:17; 4:19).

Verse 3. The translation of this verse in the NKJV is helpful: "For we have spent enough of our past lifetime in doing the will of the Gentiles—when we walked in lewdness, lusts, drunkenness, revelries, drinking parties, and abominable idolatries." To say that we have spent "enough" of our life doing the things listed does not mean, of course, that God approves of a certain amount of these sins. Rather, the word translated "enough" (*arketos*) "is used ironically, as a piece of understatement. 'Enough' is actually more than enough—too much in fact."[303]

Peter identified himself with his readers as having shared with them in the past in "doing the will of the Gentiles." To some, this reference to Gentiles (*ethnos*) indicates that this letter was written originally to a Gentile audience.[304] But as Hillyer points out, "it would be wrong to infer from the way [Peter] writes that they were all Gentiles. The many references to the Hebrew OT suggest otherwise, for Peter would hardly inject an important letter with frequent allusions which his readers might have little chance to appreciate."[305] As pointed out in the section on "Original Audience," the descriptions of the former sins of the readers does not require a primarily Gentile audience. Indeed, the most natural reading of this verse is that, though the original readers were primarily Jews, they lived like Gentiles before they came to Christ. That is, though they had a covenant with God and were the recipients of revealed knowledge, they behaved as though they had minimal revelation.

It would seem strange to address a primarily Gentile audience in the words of this verse. If the original readers were primarily redeemed Gentiles, and if Peter wanted to tell them that they had lived like unredeemed Gentiles long enough, it would seem reasonable for him to use a description like Paul used in a similar circumstance, when he referred to his readers as being "once Gentiles in the flesh" (Ephesians 2:11, NKJV). The only other explanation for Peter's terminology here would be if he intended to indicate that "Gentile Christian readers are actually Jews in God's sight."[306] Scripture does not support this idea; indeed, it specifically denies that Christians become Jews.[307]

As to why he used this reference to the Gentiles to describe his and his readers' past life, Peter's point seems to be that before they came to Christ, they lived a "Gentile kind of life." Those who believe that the original readers were Gentiles support their view by the supposed doubtfulness of Jewish people practicing Gentile sins like "abominable idolatries." But idolatry is a temptation of human passion, not of Gentile passion alone. (See Galatians 5:20, which was originally written to an audience of Jews and Gentiles.) Idolatry expresses itself in a variety of forms, including covetousness (Colossians 3:5). (See also I Samuel 15:23.) The darker chapters of Israel's history include the most despicable forms of idolatry. (See I Kings 14:24; 15:12; II Kings 23:7, 24; Zechariah 10:2.) Even in the first century, Jesus declared that the scribes and Pharisees, who claimed allegiance to the law of Moses, actually transgressed the law and worshipped God in vain (Matthew 15:1-9.) It is difficult to see any substantial difference between their sin and idolatry. Indeed, Jesus identified the religious leaders of His day as hypocrites who would not enter the kingdom of heaven, blind guides, fools, and serpents. (See Matthew 23:13-33.) Those who identify the original audience of this letter as Gentile on the basis that Jews have little or no inclination to commit the same sins as Gentiles are too optimistic about Jewish piety.

The sins in which the readers of this letter formerly walked are typical of those practiced among unbelievers in Asia Minor at the time.[308] Lewdness has to do with sexual excess that results in grossly indecent behavior. Lusts,

First Peter

as found in 1:14; 2:11 and 4:2, denote evil human passions. Drunkenness describes habitual intoxication.[309] Revelries result from drunkenness; they are wild parties, which the NIV describes as orgies. Drinking parties can include competitions to see who can drink the most. Abominable idolatries include those practices forbidden by the law of Moses; they outrage common decency.[310]

There is no place in the Christian life for any of these expressions of debased human passions.

Verse 4. Again, the translation of the NKJV is helpful: "In regard to these, they think it strange that you do not run with them in the same flood of dissipation, speaking evil of you." Those who had previously been companions of the original readers thought it strange that their former partners in sin would no longer "run with them." They could not understand the radical change that occurs in one's life when one is born again. (See 1:3, 23; 2:2.)

The word translated "dissipation" ("riot" by the KJV) is *asotia*, which appears also in Ephesians 5:18 and Titus 1:6. The cognate *asotos* describes the "riotous" living of the prodigal son (Luke 15:13). The description is of "a life given to profligacy . . . implying a waste of time, energy, and resources."[311]

Because of unbelievers' inability to understand the radically new behavior of their former friends, they spoke evil of them. The word that describes this evil speaking is *blasphemountes*, from which comes the word "blasphemy." This is one of several references in the letter to unbelievers speaking evil of believers. (See 2:12; 3:9; 4:14.) The word may indicate, however, that the former friends blasphemed against God. The Greek text does not specifically say that they spoke evil of the believers them-

Exhortations in View of Suffering

selves.[312] Though we could assume so from the context and from the other references to evil speaking by unbelievers, it may be that the word *blasphemountes* is a vocative, identifying these evil speakers as blasphemers.[313] If one thinks that a Jew would not be a blasphemer, we should note that Paul identified himself as a blasphemer in his preconversion days. (See I Timothy 1:13.)

Verse 5. Those who are blasphemers will answer to God for their evil words. Those who will answer to God include "the quick [living] and the dead." All who have ever lived and all those presently living will stand before God for judgment. (See comments on 1:17.) Through a series of four judgments over a period of time, every human being will give an account to God. (For a discussion of these four judgments, see the endnote.[314])

Some commentators are uncertain here as to the identity of the judge in this verse. From the perspective of trinitarianism, they cannot determine if the judge here is the Father or the Son.[315] This is a problem only for those who embrace the idea that the Father and the Son are distinct "persons" in the Godhead. But as Romans 2:16 points out, "God shall judge the secrets of men by Jesus Christ."

The statement that God will judge "by Jesus Christ" harmonizes with Jesus' own statements on this subject. (See John 5:22-23.) The mystery of the Incarnation is in view here (I Timothy 3:16). Jesus Christ Himself is fully God (Colossians 2:9; John 5:18), but He is God manifest in an authentic and complete human existence. (For further discussion, see the comments on I Peter 1:17 and the accompanying endnote 68.)

We can say with confidence that whenever the Bible

speaks of "Jesus Christ," it refers to the Incarnation. Thus, Romans 2:16 declares that God has determined to perform final judgment by means of the Incarnation. At the Great White Throne, men will not stand before an invisible Spirit, but before the visible manifestation of God, now in glorified humanity. (See Revelation 20:11.)

Although I Peter 1:17 declares that the Father judges each one's work, this does not contradict Peter's assertion that Jesus is the one who will judge the living and the dead (Acts 10:42). Other passages of Scripture also teach that Jesus is the judge. (See Romans 14:9-10; II Timothy 4:1.) When we recognize that Jesus is the Father Himself made known in genuine human existence, the problem of identifying the judge in this verse vanishes. (See John 1:18; 8:19; 14:7-11; I John 2:23.)

Verse 6. Some suppose that this verse describes the same event as 3:19, but a study of the Greek indicates that this is not the case. The word translated "preached" in 3:19 is *ekeruxen*, from *kerussein*, which means "to proclaim." The word translated "preach" in this verse is *euangelizesthai*, which means "to preach good news" or "to evangelize."[316] In 3:19, Noah apparently proclaimed the coming judgment of the flood to his hearers; in this verse, the gospel message was preached in an attempt to bring the hearers to a place of faith in Christ.

Blum points out the four most common views in interpreting this verse: (1) While His body was in the tomb, Jesus went to the abode of the dead, preaching salvation to all those who lived before His coming. (2) While His body was in the tomb, Jesus went to the abode of the dead, preaching salvation to those who lived before His coming and had been justified by their faith. (3) After the

Exhortations in View of Suffering

ascension of Christ, the apostles and others preached the gospel to those who were spiritually dead. (4) The dead are those who heard the gospel preached, believed, and then died (or were martyred for their faith).

Under the fourth view, the "dead" were not dead when the gospel was preached to them, but they were dead when Peter wrote his letter. They had been "judged according to men in the flesh," which could refer to martyrdom or simply to their dying as all people must die (Hebrews 9:27). But in the resurrection they would "live according to God in the spirit."[317] In other words, although all people, including believers, die, those who die in faith experience eternal life. The grammatical construction of the phrase translated "that they might be judged according to men in the flesh, but live according to God in the spirit" is the Greek *men . . . de*, which strongly contrasts the judgment according to men with the life according to God. A literal translation would be "that they might, on the one hand, be judged according to men in the flesh, but, on the other hand, live according to God in the spirit."

The fourth view seems most accurate for the following reasons: (1) It allows the word "dead" in verse 6 to have the same meaning as in verse 5. (2) It allows the words "flesh" and "spirit" to have the same meanings as in 3:18. (3) No problem is caused by the introduction of any "second chance" theology, the idea that people can have an opportunity for salvation after death. According to Hebrews 9:27, all that remains after death is judgment. There would be little impact to the warning of verse 5 if there is a second chance for salvation after death. Nor would it be an encouragement to believers to remain steadfast if they could capitulate to persecution in this life and then repent after death. (4) If the reference is to the spiritually dead, the word "also" has no meaning.[318]

An interesting parallel appears in the apocryphal *Wisdom of Solomon* 3:1-6:

> But the souls of the righteous are in the hand of God, and there shall no torment touch them. In the sight of the unwise they seemed to die: and their departure is taken for misery, and their going from us to be utter destruction: but they are in peace. For though they be punished in the sight of men, yet is their hope full of immortality. And having been a little chastised, they shall be greatly rewarded: for God proved them, and found them worthy for himself. As gold in the furnace hath he tried them and received them as a burnt offering.

To a large degree, as Michaels points out, verse 6 is a footnote on verse 5.[319] The phrase "for this cause" refers back to verse 5, explaining the reason for the preaching. Since God will one day judge all people, the Christian commission is to preach the gospel so people can receive eternal life. (See Matthew 28:19-20; Mark 16:15-16; Luke 24:47; Acts 1:8.)

B. Call to Mutuality in Ministry in View of the Critical Hour (4:7-11)

(7) But the end of all things is at hand: be ye therefore sober, and watch unto prayer. (8) And above all things have fervent charity among yourselves: for

charity shall cover the multitude of sins. (9) Use hospitality one to another without grudging. (10) As every man hath received the gift, even so minister the same one to another, as good stewards of the manifold grace of God. (11) If any man speak, let him speak as the oracles of God; if any man minister, let him do it as of the ability which God giveth: that God in all things may be glorified through Jesus Christ, to whom be praise and dominion for ever and ever. Amen

I Peter has previously focused on how believers are to relate to unbelievers (2:9-21; 3:1-2, 9-11, 13-17; 4:1-4). Here it turns our attention to how believers are to relate to each other, although it briefly addressed this subject previously (1:22; 2:1; 3:6-8). The encouragement to minister to one another is based upon the nearness of the end (verse 7). This awareness of the end should encourage believers to "serious and watchful" prayer (verse 7, NKJV), to fervent love for their brethren (verse 8), to willing hospitality (verse 9), and to mutual ministry arising out of each believer's unique giftedness (10-11). Such mutuality in ministry will glorify God (verse 11).

Verse 7. In that nearly two thousand years have elapsed since Peter wrote the words "the end of all things is at hand," we may be tempted to interpret these words to blunt the meaning that he intended and that the first readers would have understood. Hillyer comments, for example, that the "second coming is not in view here as much as is the transience of all that pertains to the closing present age."[320] According to Grudem, the phrase means "that all the major events in God's plan of redemption have occurred, and now all things are ready for Christ to return and rule."[321] But, as McKnight points out, "if we understand Jewish prophecy properly, then imminency can mean what it seems to mean (they believed the end of the world would come soon)."[322]

The word translated "is at hand" (*engiken*) is in the perfect tense, indicating that something has already occurred to cause the end to draw near at some point in the past, and it continues to be near. Whatever "the end" means, nothing else needs to occur before it can come. Although the eschatological (end-time) events flow in order, we can view them holistically as "the end." Once they begin, they cannot be restrained; every event foretold by the Scriptures will occur in order once they are triggered by the first event, the rapture of the church. (See I Thessalonians 4:13-18; 5:1-3; II Thessalonians 2:1-12; I Corinthians 15:51-55.)

James assured his readers that the coming of the Lord was drawing near (James 5:8). Though James was more specific ("the coming of the Lord") than Peter ("the end"), there is no reason to think that Peter had something in mind other than the Lord's appearing. If Peter's reference to "the end" was to something other than the appearing of the Lord, it seems he would have made that point clear, for up until now in his letter the "appearing of Jesus Christ" has been the focus. (See 1:5, 7, 13.)

How could Peter write "the end of all things is at hand," since nearly two millennia have passed without the end coming? The first-century church lived in hope of Jesus' return. (See I Corinthians 15:51-52; Philippians 3:20-21; I Thessalonians 1:9-10; 4:13-18; Titus 2:13.) It may seem to us that they were wrong, but for His own purposes and for the sake of the church's hope, God chose not to reveal the time of the Second Coming. (See Mark 13:32-37; Acts 1:6-7; I Thessalonians 5:1-6.) Thus, believers since the Day of Pentecost have been able to anticipate this glorious event in their own day. If God had revealed the time of the Second Coming, the only believers who could live in hope of that event would be those privileged to live at the prophesied time.

Since nothing else must occur before the event that triggers all other eschatological events (the rapture of the church), it is still correct to say, "The end of all things is at hand." This is the doctrine of imminence, which means that, so far as we know, the end can come at any moment. It also means that, as far as the writers of the New Testament knew, the end could have come at any moment. If this had not been the case, these writers would at least have known a time frame during which the end could not come, and many of Jesus' statements concerning the future would have been meaningless to them. (See, e.g., Mark 13:28-37; Acts 1:11.)

That the writers of the New Testament anticipated the coming of the Lord at the time they wrote does no damage to the doctrines of inspiration and inerrancy of Scripture. Rather, it illustrates the practical nature of Scripture and the manner in which inspiration is accommodated to the limitations of human understanding. The only way damage would have been done to the doctrines of inspiration and inerrancy is if the writers of Scripture had predicted the end by a certain date, and they did not. To say that the end is "at hand" or that the coming of the Lord is "near" is completely true, when viewed from God's perspective, in which "one day is as a thousand years, and a thousand years as one day" (II Peter 3:8, NKJV).

Contextually, we should understand "the end" in light of the statement of verse 5 that God "is ready to judge the quick and the dead." This reference apparently includes the judgment seat of Christ; verse 6 states that the gospel was preached to those who are now dead in order that they might "live according to God in the spirit." If so, we have further reinforcement that "the end" means all those events beginning with the rapture of the church. The judgment seat of Christ will follow the rapture of the church; at this judgment, believers will be judged for their works.

The hope of the coming of the Lord encourages us to patience and single-mindedness (James 5:8).[323] Similarly, the word "therefore" here indicates that the nearness of "the end" is reason for sobriety and watchfulness in prayer.

The word translated "sober" (*sophronesate*, from *sophroneo*) indicates the need for a sound mind. In the New Testament and other early Christian literature, it means to "be reasonable, sensible, serious," and to "keep one's head."[324] The NKJV translates the word "serious." Thus, the nearness of the end should not provoke frenzy or foolishness. Everything that God commands believers to do—including praying, witnessing, working, studying, caring for others—they are to do right up until the end. They are to be found doing these things when the Lord appears. A biblical approach to eschatology will never promote frantic behavior.

The word translated "watch" is translated from *nepsate*, which comes from *nepho*, a form of which appears also in 1:13 and 5:8. The word means "to be free from every form of mental and spiritual 'drunkenness,' from excess, passion, rashness, confusion."[325] Specifically, it addresses the need to exercise self-restraint.[326] In the context of the Second Coming, Jesus warned against deceiving oneself into thinking that the event is not imminent and being lured into drunken, and thus irrational, behavior. (See Matthew 24:48-51; Luke 12:35-48; 21:34.)

The reason believers need to practice clear thinking and self-restraint is to enhance the quality of their prayers: "therefore be serious and watchful in your prayers" (NKJV). (I Peter 3:7 also expresses an interest in the effectiveness of prayer.) There is an obvious connection here between the quality of prayer and clear, balanced thinking. There is certainly a place for praying "with the spirit," a reference to praying in languages one has never learned as the Holy Spirit gives the ability, but there is also a place for praying "with the understanding" (I Corinthians 14:15). To pray with the understanding means to involve one's mind in prayer. It means to think clearly with a biblically well-informed perspective. Believers should not expect God to answer in the affirmative when their prayers are outside His sovereign will.[327] Even Jesus, who sincerely prayed to be spared the shame of being made a sin offering on the cross (Hebrews 12:2; Isaiah 53:10), surrendered to the will of God (Matthew 26:39). In His ministry, He could do nothing but what He saw the Father do (John 5:19-20).

Another reason to practice clear thinking and self-restraint in prayer is that it is always possible for believers to be distracted by the circumstances of life. Specifically, it would have been possible for Peter's readers to be distracted by the suffering they had already experienced and by the even more intense persecution on the

First Peter

horizon. But believers must not allow the circumstances of life to have a negative impact on their relationship with God. As Hillyer points out, "Being too caught up with worldly affairs and being confused by their attendant worries can ruin prayer-life and spoil spiritual relationships, both with God and with fellow Christians."[328]

Verse 8 is not the letter's first call for believers to love one another. (See comments on 1:22.) A form of the Greek *agape* is translated "love" in the phrase "love one another" in 1:22 and "charity" here. This kind of love can be commanded, because it is not primarily emotional. It is volitional, an act of the will.[329] More than affecting one's feelings, it influences one's actions. (See I Corinthians 13:4-8.)

Believers are to have "fervent" (*ektene*) love for one another. The connotation is to be eager or earnest. Literally, the word means "strained."[330] Though we should not take it in a negative sense to infer that love is an unpleasant duty, the word does imply that love must be sincere and constant. Acts 12:15 uses the same word to say that the church prayed "without ceasing" for Peter when he was under arrest.

Believers are to have this fervent love "above all things." Love is the preeminent virtue in the New Testament. (See I Corinthians 13:13; Galatians 5:22-23.) It is the proof of genuine discipleship (John 13:35; 15:12, 17). Where love prevails, all other virtues will flow from it, including hospitality and a commitment to others in the exercise of one's ministry gifts (verses 9-11). If believers do not love, there is no need to call on them to be hospitable and to use their ministry gifts for the benefit of others.

One of the characteristics of love is to "cover a multitude of sins." (The definite article is not present in the Greek text.) This statement is an allusion to Proverbs 10:12, which reads, "Hatred stirreth up strifes: but love covereth all sins." (See also Proverbs 17:9.) Where there is love, a person will not look for opportunities to expose the errors of others to public ridicule; he will instead seek to restore as privately as possible those who err.[331] (See Matthew 18:15-17.)

James 5:19-20 also alludes to Proverbs 10:12 to encourage the restoration of believers who err from the truth. There, however, covering a multitude of sins does not mean refraining from the public exposure of sins; it means that the sinning brother's sins will be forgiven in conjunction with his restoration.[332]

These differing emphases illustrate the manner in which the Holy Spirit inspired New Testament writers to draw upon Old Testament references but to give them new or additional meaning. This does not mean that the New Testament writers misinterpreted Scripture; they were inspired equally with the writers of the Old Testament. Nor does it mean that all Old Testament Scripture carries more than one meaning or can be allegorized. Rather, it means that the Holy Spirit, who inspired the words of the Old Testament, can take those same words and use them in new contexts in the New Testament to mean different things. It is the context that gives meaning to words. The inspiration of Scripture means that every word in the Old Testament and New Testament exists in an inspired context. If the context in which a word or words appear in the New Testament is different from the context in which the same word or words appear in the Old Testament, we must seek the meaning in each specific context.[333]

Some suggest that "love will cover a multitude of sins" means the person who loves others will thereby "procure forgiveness from God at the end."[334] In the Jewish view, "deeds of love, especially almsgiving . . . helped to atone for an individual's own sins."[335] If this is what I Peter means, however, it is difficult to tie the latter part of verse 8 together with the first part. The only way the verse could hold together in this case would be if one's motivation for loving others was primarily selfish, that is, only because of the personal benefit to be obtained. This interpretation would disconnect the verse from its context, which focuses on mutuality in ministry so as to exercise good stewardship of the grace of God and to bring glory to God (verses 10-11). It would also make the individual his own co-redeemer, robbing Christ of the exclusivity of His work on the cross.

Verse 9. Hospitality is a concrete expression of love. In many places in the modern world, hospitality may refer primarily to one's social skills. In the world of the first century, however, hospitality involved taking others into one's home, providing lodging and food for two or three days to travelers. Though there were inns, they were sparse and often were occupied by violent and immoral people. Thus it was very important for believers to open their homes to other believers.

Other New Testament passages also call for believers to practice hospitality. (See Matthew 25:35; Romans 12:13; III John 5-8.) Though hospitality is to characterize all believers, it is a specific requirement for bishops (I Timothy 3:2; Titus 1:8). It is also a qualification for a

Exhortations in View of Suffering

widow to receive support from the church (I Timothy 5:10).

Since it is always possible for one to conform only outwardly, hospitality should be "without grudging." The word translated "grudging" (*gongusmon*) has to do with complaining, being displeased, or grumbling.[336] Someone could receive another into his home because he felt it was his duty, but privately he might complain to others about the hardship involved. This should not happen. Hospitality is to be shown with cheerfulness. When we realize that Jesus considers the hospitality we show to needy people to be hospitality we show to Him (Matthew 25:35), we will have genuine joy in being able to minister to others. Where there is "fervent love," we will not complain about the hospitality we extend to other believers.

Verse 10. Each believer is the recipient of a gift (*charisma*) or gifts. We sometimes categorize the gifts listed in Paul's epistles as spiritual gifts (I Corinthians 12:1-11), motivational gifts (Romans 12:6-8), and positional gifts (Ephesians 4:8, 11). I Peter emphasizes gifts that involve speaking and serving (verse 11), but the primary focus is on how believers are responsible to use their gifts to minister to one another.

The definite article ("the") is not in the Greek text, which leads to the translation of "a gift" in translations other than the KJV. "The" gift implies that a specific gift is in view when it is not. Whatever gift a believer receives from God, he is to use to minister to other believers. Elsewhere, Scripture presents the same idea in a lengthy analogy comparing gifted believers with the various members of the human body (I Corinthians 12:14-27). It also identifies the purpose of gifts as edification (I Corinthians 14).

Undergirding the responsibility of believers to minister to one another out of their giftedness is the responsibility of believers to be "good stewards of the manifold grace of God." *Charitos*, translated "grace," is related to *charisma*. Both words, by definition, have to do with something freely given.[337] Grace is often defined as the unmerited favor of God. Biblically, whatever gift that God gives is a "grace." Some have suggested that we might recognize the nature of spiritual gifts more readily if we identified them as "spiritual gracelets." Since the word "gift" reflects the biblical idea of "grace," we should understand that the gifts of God are completely free; He does not give them in response to some good deed of the recipient. Since this is true, we should use these gifts freely for the benefit of others. (See Matthew 10:1, 8.)

The grace of God is manifold (*poikiles*). This means that the grace of God is diversified; there is great variety in the way God manifests His grace in the lives of believers.[338] We see some of this diversity in the spiritual gifts of I Corinthians 12, the motivational gifts of Romans 12, and the positional gifts of Ephesians 4:8, 11. (See also I Corinthians 12:28-30.) Perhaps we can say that there is an infinite variety of ways the Holy Spirit combines spiritual gifts in believers so that each one is different and able to make a unique contribution to the growth and strengthening of the body of Christ.

In the New Testament era, a steward was a slave entrusted with the management of his master's household and estate.[339] The essential requirement of a steward was that he "be found faithful" (I Corinthians 4:2). To be faithful means to be trustworthy and dependable. Thus, each believer should carefully assess his spiritual giftedness

Exhortations in View of Suffering

and faithfully use his spiritual gifts to serve his brothers and sisters in the church, always recalling that God has freely given him these gifts for this very purpose. Believers should also keep in mind that others do not have to duplicate their gifts in order to be genuinely gifted. God has set each member in the body "just as He pleased," and He has done this so that there "should be no schism in the body, but that the members should have the same care for one another" (I Corinthians 12:18, 25, NKJV).

Verse 11. Unlike Romans 12 and I Corinthians 12, I Peter does not offer an extended list of gifts that believers can receive. It simply describes gifts in the categories of speaking and ministering. This list is not exhaustive; indeed, no list of gifts in the New Testament seems to be. There may be an endless variety of ways in which God bestows gifts upon His children.

The word translated "speak" is the Greek *lalei*, from *lalein*. Contextually, it does not refer to "ordinary conversation . . . but to authoritative speech in worship assemblies."[340] It could include any of the spiritual gifts involving vocalization, like prophecy, the word of wisdom, the word of knowledge, various kinds of languages, and the interpretation of those languages. There seems to be no reason why it could not include preaching and teaching. The point is that if anyone's gift falls into the category of a speaking gift, that person should "speak as the oracles of God."

To speak "as the oracles of God" (*hos logia theou*) means to speak as those who bring words from God.[341] This statement is problematic to some who think it would compromise the finality and authority of Scripture. Thus they attempt to soften the force of the words. Grudem, for example, suggests that the phrase "as the oracles of God" means that those who speak should speak "with the seriousness of purpose which one would use if one were speaking God's words."[342] In other words, the speaker is not actually speaking God's words, but he should speak as if he is.

But Romans 3:2 uses the words "oracles of God" in reference to the Hebrew Scriptures (although definite articles are employed with both "oracles" and "God"). In Hebrews 5:12, the phrase also appears, again with the definite articles. In Acts 7:38, Stephen referred to the revelation of God at Sinai as "living oracles." In precisely the same words used here, the Septuagint records Balaam as claiming to hear "the oracles of God" (Numbers 24:16).[343]

Consistently, whenever the Bible refers to the oracles of God, it means authoritative words from God. It will not do to soften this meaning by suggesting that those who speak are merely speaking "as" (*hos*) the oracles of God but that they are not actually speaking His oracles. Later in the verse, those who minister are to do so "as [*hos*] of the ability which God giveth." This phrase does not suggest that they are to minister "as if" God gave them the ability even though He actually did not. Neither does the believer's responsibility to speak "as the oracles of God" imply that he is to speak "as if" he is speaking God's oracles, though he is not actually doing so. The oracles are the "very words of God"; they are "utterances from God's mouth."[344] Although not specifically stated, the implication is that if a believer does not have an oracle of God, he is not to speak. This does not preclude normal speech, but it does preclude presuming to speak authoritatively without an oracle of God.

The possibility that believers will speak authoritative words does no danger to the authority and finality of Scripture. Scripture is the Word of God in a unique way and for a specific purpose. (See II Timothy 3:16-17.) To its very words, Scripture is inspired of God, infallible, and without error.[345] God does not give spiritual gifts, including those involving speech, for the same purpose as Scripture, and the New Testament does not indicate that these gifts render a person infallible. Even what prophets speak is to be judged by others (I Corinthians 14:29). Those who are spiritually gifted are in control of their utterances (I Corinthians 14:27-28, 30, 32). Spiritual gifts, including those involving knowledge and speaking, are only "in part" (I Corinthians 13:9).

By analogy, Paul wrote, "When I was a child, I spoke as a child, I understood as a child, I thought as a child; but when I became a man, I put away childish things. For now we see in a mirror, dimly, but then face to face. Now I know in part, but then I shall know just as I also am known" (I Corinthians 13:11-12, NKJV). This analogy allows for the possibility that spiritual gifts could reflect a believer's immaturity. Spiritual gifts exercised by one who is spiritually immature are not worthless, but we are to take into account the limitations reflected by a lack of spiritual maturity. In the natural realm, we do not prohibit children from speaking because they are immature, but we take their immaturity into account when they speak.

Spiritual gifts do not render the speaker infallible any more than the ability to speak renders a child infallible. If one thinks that no one who is spiritually immature could speak "as the oracles of God," he should ask, "Can a child share the gospel story?" A child who shares the gospel

First Peter

with another is speaking authoritatively, even though his witness will reflect his immaturity. His immaturity may be reflected in his vocabulary or his expressions or his limited comprehension, but that does not mean that his witness is to be shunned. Likewise, when a believer speaks "as the oracles of God," what he says will reflect the level of his spiritual maturity, but it can still be something given by God Himself, accommodated by God to the limitations of the individual's understanding. To the extent that a believer faithfully speaks what God has given him to speak, he is speaking "as the oracles of God."

The oracles of God in the Scriptures are, however, in another category. Scripture claims to be the very Word of God, completely authoritative and inerrant.[346] Scripture is the final authority, and all human utterances must yield to it.

The word translated "minister" (*diakonei*) has to do with serving. Paul also mentioned a specific gift of serving (Romans 12:7). Perhaps serving here includes all spiritual gifts that do not fall into the category of speaking, such as giving, leading, showing mercy, faith, gifts of healings, the working of miracles, and the discerning of spirits (Romans 12:8; I Corinthians 12:9-10). All of these gifts are, in some way, to be used in service to other believers. So are the speaking gifts, of course, but since not all gifts directly involve speech, this verse may incorporate the remaining gifts under this rubric.

Regardless of which gifts are included under the idea of ministry or serving, the verse describes the responsibility of believers to employ their gifts in service to one another. As they do so, they are to minister "as of the ability which God giveth." Ministry is to flow out of the desire and ability given by God. (See Philippians 2:13.) Ministry that is energized by the grace of God is not only fruitful and rewarding for the recipients, but it gives the person ministering a sense of fulfillment and joy. On the other hand, attempts to minister out of human strength will be limited in their effect and will leave the minister weary and disappointed.

We are to use our gifts in this way so that in all things we may glorify God through Jesus Christ. To be "glorified" (*doxazetai*) means to be praised or worshiped. Thus, the mutual ministry of believers to one another out of their spiritual giftedness is an act of worship; they praise God by this kind of ministry. (See the comments on 2:5 for a discussion of the idea that God is worshiped or praised "through Jesus Christ.") There, the same Greek phrase (*dia Iesou Christou*) here translated "through Jesus Christ" is translated "by Jesus Christ."

The verse concludes with the doxology "to whom be praise and dominion for ever and ever. Amen." Grammatically, the antecedent of the pronoun "whom" is Jesus Christ.[347] Some commentators, thinking it odd to ascribe glory to God in one breath and to Jesus Christ in the next ("praise" is translated from the Greek *doxa*, from which comes the previous *doxazetai*) prefer to see the antecedent to "whom" as being God. This problem arises from the view that God is more than one "person." From this perspective, one commentator sees in I Peter a "'binitarian' tendency to put Jesus Christ and God on the same plane as simultaneously the objects of Christian worship."[348] The problem is a consequence of a preconceived theology. Again in verse 13 there is a reference to Christ's glory (*doxes*), while 5:10-11 ascribes the glory to God.

When we approach the supposed problem from the monotheistic perspective of Scripture—which proclaims that there is but one LORD God (Deuteronomy 6:4) who is made known to us in the person of Jesus Christ (I Timothy 3:16; John 1:14, 18; Hebrews 1:3)—the problem vanishes. We can truly know God only through Jesus Christ (John 8:19; 14:6-10; 20:28; I John 2:22-23). To glorify Jesus is to glorify God. We cannot give praise to Jesus without at the same time giving praise to God. And, since God has manifest Himself in the flesh, we cannot give praise to God without at the same time giving praise to Jesus.

The word translated "be" in the phrase "to whom be praise and dominion" is the Greek *estin*, the third person singular form of *eimi*, the verb "to be." The pronoun *ho*, translated "to whom," is singular. The words express no concept of plurality. The NIV translates the phrase, "To Him be the glory and power." Literally, *estin* means "is." The NKJV translates the phrase, "To whom belong the glory and the dominion," which does not specify whether the referent is singular or plural.

The entire phrase translated "praise and dominion for ever and ever. Amen" is *he doxa kai to kratos eis tous aionas ton aionon amen*. The identical phrase appears in Revelation 1:6, where again it refers to Jesus Christ. Since the Incarnation is permanent, all that we may say of God throughout eternity we may say of Jesus. The ascription of glory and dominion (*kratos eis tous aionas ton aionon amen*) to God in I Peter 5:11 does not conflict with the ascription of glory and dominion to Jesus Christ here. The glory and dominion ascribed to Jesus is ascribed to God, and vice versa, for Jesus is none other than God Himself made known to us in complete and authentic humanity. Any attempt to ascribe glory and dominion to one "person" in the Godhead to the neglect of another is to create an artificial problem and to fragment God.

"Amen" is transliterated from the Greek *amen*, which means something like "so be it!" or "so it is!" The New Testament commonly uses the word to conclude doxologies.[349]

We should note that the word translated "man" in this verse does not indicate the masculine gender only. The word is *tis* and means "anyone" or "any person." No Scripture indicates that God gives any of the spiritual gifts on the basis of sexual gender. In this verse, it is not men alone who can be gifted to speak; it could be anyone, male or female. Neither is it males alone who can be gifted to minister.

C. Call to Accept Suffering As Normative (4:12-19)

(12) Beloved, think it not strange concerning the fiery trial which is to try you, as though some strange thing happened unto you: (13) but rejoice, inasmuch as ye are partakers of Christ's sufferings; that, when his glory shall be revealed, ye may be glad also with exceeding joy. (14) If ye be reproached for the name of Christ, happy are ye; for the spirit of glory and of God resteth upon you: on their part he is evil spoken of, but on your part he is glorified. (15) But let none of you suffer as a murderer, or as a thief, or as an evildoer, or as a busybody in other men's matters. (16) Yet if any man suffer as a Christian, let him not be

ashamed; but let him glorify God on this behalf. (17) For the time is come that judgment must begin at the house of God: and if it first begin at us, what shall the end be of them that obey not the gospel of God? (18) And if the righteous scarcely be saved, where shall the ungodly and the sinner appear? (19) Wherefore let them that suffer according to the will of God commit the keeping of their souls to him in well doing, as unto a faithful Creator.

At this point, I Peter returns to a direct discussion of trials. (See 1:6-7; 2:12, 15, 18-21; 3:9, 13-17; 4:1.) The believers' response to trials should not be surprise, but rejoicing (verses 12-14). Believers should be certain there is no basis for their suffering in wrongdoing (verse 15); the only suffering they should experience is what comes their way due to their identification with Christ (verse 16). All people, including both the persecuted and the persecutors, will answer to God in judgment (verses 17-18). Those who suffer in the will of God should commit their souls to Him as they continue to do what is right (verse 19).

Verse 12. I Peter 1:7 alludes to the idea of a "fiery trial." There, the word "fire" is translated from the Greek *pyros*, which is the source of the *pyrosis*, here translated "fiery trial." The New Testament uses *pyrosis* only twice more, both times in Revelation in reference to the destruction of a city called Babylon the great. In both Revelation 18:9 and 18:18, *pyrosis* is translated "burning." Considering that Peter identified his location when he wrote this letter as "Babylon" (5:13), it may be significant that he used a word to describe the trials of those in the church at "Babylon" that John would later use to describe the destruction of Babylon itself.

It may be that the use of *pyrosis* here reflects the Septuagint version of Proverbs 27:21, which uses the word to translate the Hebrew *kuwr*, which in turn refers to a furnace for the purification of gold.[350] Just as a furnace of fire purges the impurities from precious metals, so the fiery trials of believers have a cleansing effect. These trials come specifically "to try you" (*pros peirasmon*), a phrase that means "to put . . . to the test."[351]

There is substantial biblical evidence that God may allow painful circumstances into the life of a believer in order to accomplish some greater good. (See Job; II Corinthians 12:7; Hebrews 11:35-40; James 5:10-11; Romans 8:18, 35-39; Matthew 5:10-12; I Peter 4:13-16.) This good is accomplished only as the believer responds to suffering with faith and by committing himself to God. (See Romans 8:28; I Peter 4:19.)

Believers should not be surprised to experience a "fiery trial." It has always been the experience of people of faith who are "strangers" (1:1) in this world to be ridiculed and rejected by those who do not understand them. Christ Himself is the greatest example of this, and those who identify with Him will tend to be treated as He was (verses 13-16). (See John 15:20.)

As in 2:11, Peter addressed his readers as "beloved." There, he began a section dealing with proper Christian conduct in the face of those who spoke evil against them (2:12, 15, 19-20; 3:9, 14-17). Here he did much the same (4:14, 16; 5:10).

Verse 13. The right response to suffering for a believer is to rejoice because of the way suffering identifies the believer with Christ Himself. In similar statements in the

Sermon on the Mount, Jesus described the blessed state of those who are persecuted for the sake of righteousness. (See Matthew 5:10-12.) Those who suffer for doing right are blessed because the kingdom of heaven is theirs and because they have a great reward in heaven. Their persecution identifies them with the Hebrew prophets in their suffering.

To be a partaker of Christ's suffering does not mean that the believer's suffering is redemptive—that he in any way shares in procuring redemption for himself or others. (See Philippians 3:10; II Corinthians 1:5-7; Colossians 1:24.) Rather, it means to follow "the example of his behavior when facing similar circumstances."[352]

The word translated "inasmuch as" in the KJV (*katho*) is rendered "to the extent" by the NKJV. The point is that individual believers may partake more or less in the sufferings of Christ. Some suffering that believers experience may not be due to their identification with Christ, but to their own misdeeds. (See verse 15.) This is no cause for rejoicing. But to the extent that believers suffer because of their identification with Christ (verse 16), it is cause for rejoicing.

Greco-Roman society was obsessed with shame and honor. The idea that it was noble to suffer ridicule for doing good would have been shocking to those who embraced the ideals of the culture.[353] But, of course, biblical values are often at odds with those of society at large.

Believers are but human, and it is sometimes difficult to maintain the right attitude in the painful circumstances of life. But focusing on faith's ultimate reward can help the believer keep the right perspective. (See Hebrews 12:2.) In this case, believers can rejoice in the face of suffering as they anticipate even greater gladness at the revelation of Christ's glory.

The revelation of Christ is also the subject of 1:7, 13. The One who shall appear is the chief Shepherd (5:4); at His coming the ultimate outworking of salvation will be revealed (1:5).

Verse 14. It is not reproach itself that is cause for joy, but reproach resulting from one's identification with Christ. In Hebrew thought, the idea of "name" was much more than a label. Instead, "name" was virtually equivalent with "person." "Name" could also signify character, reputation, works, and worth. To be reproached for the "name of Christ" means to suffer reproach for the "person of Christ." (See also Acts 5:41; 9:16; 15:26; 21:13; III John 7; Revelation 2:3.

The subjunctive "if" is in the first-class condition, which affirms the reality of the condition. That is, I Peter acknowledges that the readers are indeed reproached because of their association with Christ.

On "happy," see comments on 3:14. The reason for the believer's happiness or blessedness is that "the spirit of glory and of God" rests on those who are reproached for Christ. Contextually, the glory is the glory of Christ that will be revealed at His coming (verse 13). Even now, however, the spirit of that glory rests on believers. The spirit of glory is, in fact, the Spirit of God.[354] John the Baptist prophesied that Jesus would baptize His followers with the Holy Spirit (Mark 1:8; John 1:33). Jesus promised that those who believed on Him would be baptized with the Holy Spirit (John 7:37-39; Acts 1:4-5). The fulfillment of this promise began on the Day of Pentecost and continued throughout the history of the early church

(Acts 2:1-4; 8:15-17; 9:17; 10:44-48; 19:1-6). Being filled with the Holy Spirit was one of the things that characterized first-century believers.[355] The coming of the Spirit upon all kinds of people signifies the inauguration of the new covenant. (See Isaiah 59:21; Ezekiel 36:27; 37:14; 39:29; Joel 2:28-29.)

Those who ridicule believers because of their identification with Christ are actually speaking evil of Christ Himself. The word translated "evil spoken of" (*blasphemeo*) appears also in verse 4. But as unbelievers blaspheme Christ, believers glorify Him. In this context, they glorify Him by their joyous identification with Him even in His sufferings. To glorify (*doxazo*) includes the ideas of honoring, extolling, and praising.

Verse 15. Although believers may expect to suffer because of their identification with Christ, their suffering should never be on account of their wrongdoing. The short list of prohibited behaviors here includes murder, thievery, evil doing, and being a busybody. Many other behaviors are obviously prohibited as well. No doubt this list is simply representative of all sinful activity.[356]

It may seem strange that I Peter would warn believers against murder, but so does James 4:2. Though it is not impossible that someone professing faith in Christ could resort to murder, perhaps the meaning here is like that of I John 3:15: "Whosoever hateth his brother is a murderer: and ye know that no murderer hath eternal life abiding in him." There may be some question, however, as to whether unbelievers intent on persecuting the church would be intimately acquainted with believers to the point of knowing their attitudes toward each other or would care how believers treated each other.

Before we are too quick to dismiss the possibility of believers resorting to murder, we should note that the prohibition on thievery has a precise counterpart where the prohibition seems clearly to be against actual theft: "Let him who stole steal no longer, but rather let him labor" (Ephesians 4:28, NKJV). Believers are not immune from temptation or sin, and no sin is in a category of temptation completely unknown to believers. (See I Corinthians 10:13.)

Third on Peter's list is a prohibition against being an evildoer. This is a more generic term that could imply a broad range of criminal behavior.[357] Whether or not believers were actually guilty of this sin, it was possible they would be accused of it. (See 2:12.) It is the God-given responsibility of civil government to punish evildoers (2:14). Again, however, it seems that the warning here anticipates actual evil doing, not just the accusation. If I Peter only envisions readers being persecuted as a result of false accusations, this verse would be meaningless. If they were falsely accused of these sins because of their identification with Christ, their suffering would actually be "for the name of Christ" and "as a Christian" (verses 14, 16). Believers have no real control over false accusations, but they do have the ability to avoid the types of behavior listed in this verse that result not only in God's displeasure but also in the displeasure of others.

The final prohibited behavior here is being a busybody in others' matters. The word translated "busybody" (*allotriepiskopos*) is an interesting one. It appears only here in the New Testament, and it has not been found in earlier Greek literature. It is found three times in later Christian literature.

Although Paul warned against being busybodies (II Thessalonians 3:11; I Timothy 5:13), he used a completely different word (*periergazomai* or *pereiergos*). Paul's word has to do with being busy about insignificant things and neglecting important matters, with a specific application to being busy with the affairs of other people.

The word here incorporates *episkopos* (a form of which is transliterated into English as "episcopal"), which means to be an overseer and which the KJV renders as "bishop." (See I Timothy 3:1-2; Titus 1:7.) The word also incorporates *allotrios*, which means "belonging to another." In the postbiblical Christian literature, Dionysius used the word to refer to a bishop who encroached on another's diocese. Epiphanius used the word twice, first in discussing I Corinthians 2:10 to indicate that the Holy Spirit does not probe into "alien" matters in searching out the "deep things of God," and second to explain that when Jesus broke the Sabbath, He was not abrogating "another's" work but doing His own work.[358]

Although "busybody" here definitely has to do with meddling, the Greek word seems to deal more specifically with those who, like the Cynic philosophers, thought it their duty to be guardians of public morality. It seems to be a warning to believers to refrain from trying to legislate morality for others. There may be a hint of this in 2:1 also.

Regardless of the specific meaning of the word here, it is interesting that I Peter groups busybodies together with murderers and thieves. The negative effect of a busybody's meddling is devastating. Just as a murderer may take one's life and a thief may take one's possessions so that they can never be recovered, so a busybody may

Exhortations in View of Suffering

destroy one's reputation, friendships, and family relationships.

Verse 16. If any believer suffers because of his identification with Christ, he should not be ashamed. Rather, he should view the suffering as an occasion to glorify God. (See verses 13-14; 3:14-17.) To glorify means to praise or worship.

The word "Christian" appears only three times in the New Testament. It is first used by unbelievers to describe those who follow Christ (Acts 11:26). It is used next by an unbelieving civil ruler, Agrippa, to describe Paul's attempt to bring him into agreement with those who believed on Christ (Acts 26:28.) The present use of the word is from the perspective of unbelievers who justify their persecution of believers by identifying them as Christians.

The word "Christian" is transliterated from the Greek *Christianos*. Like the words "Herodians" and "Caesarians," the word "Christian" describes those who adhere to a particular coalition somewhat like a political party.[359] It means something like "those of Christ's party." It is not the plural form of the singular "Christ."

In this case, to suffer for the charge of being a Christian is parallel to suffering for the charge of being a murderer, a thief, an evildoer, or a busybody in other men's matters. Although those who believe in Christ have come to treasure the identification "Christian," the unbelieving world never intended it to be a compliment. Because of the derogatory nature of the term, I Peter urges believers not to be ashamed for any suffering that arises from their identification as Christians. Contrary to the opinion of their persecutors, it was not shameful to be identified as a member of the party of Christ. To be so closely identified with Him as to suffer for that reason, was cause to praise and worship God.

Verse 17. Even when New Testament writers do not quote directly from Old Testament passages, it is often apparent that there is a parallel in their minds. Such is the case here. The background for this verse is the Septuagint translation of Ezekiel 9 and Malachi 3.

Ezekiel 9 records the vision of the slaying of all those in Jerusalem who do not "sigh and cry over all the abominations that are done within it" (Ezekiel 9:4, NKJV). All were slain except those who had a mark on their foreheads indicating their vexation over the sins committed in Jerusalem. We see the precise verbal parallels in the Greek text of I Peter 4:17 and the Septuagint Greek of Ezekiel 9:6.

The KJV translation of verse 17 reads, "For the time is come that judgment must begin at the house of God: and if it first begin at us. . . ." The words translated "begin at" (*arxasthai apo*) mean more precisely "begin from." The second word translated "at" is also *apo* ("from"). The word translated "house" is *oikos*. In the Septuagint text of Ezekiel 9:6, those who are slaying are ordered to begin from (*arxasthe apo*) the sanctuary, and they began from (*apo*) the elders (*presbyteron*) who were in the house (*oikos*). Shortly after I Peter discusses the judgment that begins from the house of God, it instructs the elders (*presbyterous*) as to their duty (5:1-4). Another parallel is that Ezekiel 9:3 mentions the departure of the glory of God from the cherub, and I Peter 4:14 points out that the glory of God rests upon believers.

As compared with Ezekiel's account of the cleansing

Exhortations in View of Suffering

of Jerusalem starting from the Temple, the point of I Peter is that the judgment of God begins in the church. (In the only other use of *oikos* in this letter, 2:5 refers to believers as making up a "spiritual house.") It spreads from there to the unbelieving society outside the church.[360]

Malachi 3 announces that the Lord will "suddenly come to His temple" as "the Messenger of the covenant . . . like a refiner's fire . . . like launderers' soap," and "He will sit as a refiner and a purifier of silver," purifying "the sons of Levi" and purging them "as gold and silver, that they may offer to the LORD an offering in righteousness" (Malachi 3:1-3, NKJV). Malachi 3:5 describes the fate of unbelievers.

The parallels between Malachi 3 and I Peter 4 are apparent. I Peter describes the "fiery trial which is to try you." (See comments on verse 12.) In Malachi, the sons of Levi, the priests, are purified. In I Peter, believers are "an holy priesthood" (2:5). In Malachi, the priests are purified so "they may offer to the LORD an offering in righteousness" (NKJV). In I Peter, believers "offer up spiritual sacrifices" (2:5). In Malachi, the Messiah purifies the priests and then moves in judgment against the unbelievers (Malachi 3:5). In I Peter, judgment begins with believers and moves from there to unbelievers.[361]

Judgment (*krima*) does not always refer to condemnation. (See Romans 11:33.) *Krima* is broader in meaning than *katakrima* (which refers to the punishment or doom following sentencing).[362] *Krima* can "refer to a judgment which results in good and bad evaluations, a judgment which may issue in approval or discipline as well as condemnation."[363] Thus, verse 12 identifies the "fiery trial" as the judgment of God intended to purify the believers. (See also I Corinthians 11:29-32; Hebrews 12:5-11.)

If God judges believers, it is certain that He will judge unbelievers who "obey not the gospel of God." (See II Thessalonians 1:7-9.) As in Ezekiel's imagery, there are some who are not troubled over the evil in the world, which indicates that they participate in it. As in Malachi's description, they are sorcerers; adulterers; perjurers; exploiters of wage earners, widows, and orphans; and those who turn aliens away. In short, they are people who do not fear the LORD. (See Malachi 3:5, NKJV.)

Verse 18. The word translated "scarcely" (*molis*) includes in its range of meaning the ideas of "with difficulty" and "not readily, only rarely."[364] The first meaning is appropriate here. I Peter does not mean that "only rarely" are the righteous saved. Neither does it mean that the righteous are "not readily" saved. (See John 6:37; Romans 8:29-30.) From the context, it is clear that the righteous are saved "with difficulty." Verse 18 does not mean that it is difficult for God to save them or that they must work hard to be saved; it means that the fiery trials sent to test them are difficult to endure.

Again, we readily see the influence of the Septuagint on Peter's letter, for this verse follows the Septuagint translation of Proverbs 11:31. The point is that if those who are righteous are saved only as they endure the difficulty of "fiery trials," the destiny of those who are unrighteous will be much more difficult for them.

Verse 19. Since the difficulty of fiery trials (verse 12) is a consequence of one's faith in God and the suffering associated with these trials is "according to the will of God," believers who experience this suffering should respond by committing "their souls to Him in doing good, as to a faithful Creator" (NKJV). The word translated "souls" (*psychas*) can mean "selves." The word translated "commit" (*paratithemi*) has to do with entrusting oneself to the care or protection of someone.[365] Jesus used the same word in Luke 23:46: "Father, into thy hands I commend [*paratithemi*] my spirit."

Believers must continue to do good, even in the face of suffering. Although we may endure pain, we may be sure that our Creator is faithful. He will not allow us to be tempted beyond our ability and will with each temptation provide a way of escape (I Corinthians 10:13).

Grudem sees this verse as summarizing the teaching of the entire letter.[366] The knowledge that suffering as a Christian is the will of God assures us that there is a limit set by God and that it is "only for our good: it is purifying us, drawing us closer to our Lord, and making us more like him in our lives."[367]

The more completely we recognize the hand of God in our suffering the more fully we can identify with Paul's words. Upon learning that his "thorn in the flesh" was an instrument in the hands of God to prevent him from being "exalted above measure," Paul wrote, "Therefore most gladly I will rather boast in my infirmities, that the power of Christ may rest upon me. Therefore I take pleasure in infirmities, in reproaches, in needs, in persecutions, in distresses, for Christ's sake. For when I am weak, then I am strong" (II Corinthians 12:9-10, NKJV).

VI

Exhortations to Elders and Younger Believers
5:1-9

As the letter draws to a close, I Peter addresses the elders and the younger believers as to their behavior in view of the coming of the Lord (verses 1, 4).

A. Call to Elders to Serve As Shepherds (5:1-4)

(1) The elders which are among you I exhort, who am also an elder, and a witness of the sufferings of Christ, and also a partaker of the glory that shall be revealed: (2) feed the flock of God which is among you, taking the oversight thereof, not by constraint, but willingly; not for filthy lucre, but of a ready mind; (3) neither as being lords over God's heritage, but being ensamples to the flock. (4) And when the chief Shepherd shall appear, ye shall receive a crown of glory that fadeth not away.

Contextually, Peter's exhortation to the elders reflects that when judgment begins at the house of God, it begins first with those who are spiritual leaders. (See comments on 4:17; Ezekiel 9:6.) God will judge elders on the quality of their service as shepherds, as reflected in the diligence of their oversight, their attitude toward materialism, and whether they are servant leaders or domineering.

First Peter

Verse 1. The word translated "elders" is *presbyterous*, which includes in its range of meaning those who are older than others, ancestors, and officials of some kind.[368] The meaning here is influenced by the admonition to "feed the flock of God" (verse 2). "Feed," which the NKJV renders as "shepherd," is from the Greek *poimen*. A form of this word appears in Ephesians 4:11, where it is translated "pastors." In verse 2, the majority of Greek manuscripts include the word *episkopountes* (from *episkopos*), translated "taking the oversight" by the KJV. This is doubtless the original reading.[369] *Episkopos* is translated "bishop" in I Timothy 3:1-2, Titus 1:7, and I Peter 2:25. As Grudem points out, the close connection of the term "elder" with the verbs related to "pastor" and "bishop" indicates that these terms were interchangeable at the time Peter wrote.[370] (See I Timothy 3:1-7 with Titus 1:5-9; Acts 20:17, 28.)

Peter identified himself as a "fellow elder" (NKJV) or "co-elder" (*sympresbyteros*) with those he exhorted. He did not view himself as superior to those to whom he wrote. He also declared himself to be "a witness of the sufferings of Christ." This must have been a humbling confession for Peter to make, for he witnessed the sufferings of Christ from the perspective of one who denied knowing Jesus. (See Matthew 26:69-75; Mark 14:66-72; Luke 22:55-62; John 18:15-18, 25-27.) Not long after Peter denied Christ, Christ commissioned him to the shepherding ministry. (See John 21:15-17.)

Perhaps Peter's oblique reference to his denial of Christ and then to his being a "partaker of the glory that shall be revealed" is intended to demonstrate that the judgment which begins at the house of God can result in

Exhortations to Elders and Younger Believers

full forgiveness and complete restoration.

The "glory that shall be revealed" has been previously identified as the glory of Christ that we will see at His return. (See 4:13; 1:5, 7, 13.) The word translated "partaker" is *koinonos*, which does not mean that Peter or anyone else deserves the glory or that the glory is actually theirs. The idea is that believers are associated with Christ so intimately that they will participate in the glory belonging to Him. Indeed, verse 4 promises the elders that they will "receive a crown of glory."

Peter's words to his fellow elders and to the younger people (verse 5) form an exhortation. To exhort (*parakaleo*) is to call one alongside, with the implication that the purpose is to make an appeal, to urge, to encourage, to implore, to comfort.[371] Here the word underscores Peter's equality with the other elders and describes the nature of his appeal.

Verse 2. The phrase translated "feed the flock" is a play on words: *poimanate to . . . poimnion*. Both words can be traced back to *poimen*, "a shepherd."[372] The NKJV translates the phrase as "shepherd the flock." It underscores the role of the elders (*presbyterous*) as pastors. The English word "pastor" comes from the Latin translation of *poimenas* (the accusative masculine plural form of *poimen*). The word "pastor," like *poimen*, means "shepherd."

The word "shepherd" provides a graphic and concise description of the pastor's responsibility. The biblical image of a shepherd "is that of a concerned guide, not of a severe ruler."[373] We see this meaning in the warning for elders not to exercise lordship, but to be examples (verse 3). Cultural factors tend to influence the pastoral role—in some societies the pastor is seen as a manager, a chief executive officer, a motivator, an executive—but the biblical ideal is that of a shepherd. As a shepherd, the pastor's primary responsibilities include feeding, watering, and protecting the sheep. (See Psalm 23; Acts 20:28.)

Believers are the "flock of God." They do not belong to the shepherds. Shepherds are responsible to the owner of the flock for the well-being of his sheep. In this case, the flock belongs to God; Christ is the "Chief Shepherd" (verse 4). The flock belongs to God because He purchased it with His own blood (Acts 20:28).

Although elders are not to exercise lordship over the flock (verse 3), they are to exercise oversight (*episkopountes*). Oversight involves the kind of watchful care a shepherd gives his sheep. It is not domination, but self-sacrificing investment of one's life in the well-being of others.

Pastors should take the oversight not by compulsion, but willingly. No one should enter pastoral ministry who feels forced into it. Those who attempt to minister out of compulsion will not adequately fulfill the responsibilities of the ministry, and they will tend to become frustrated quickly. It is not merely our deeds, but our motives, that are a concern to the Lord. (See Matthew 6:1-8, 16-18; I Corinthians 3:12-15.) Those who cannot enter the shepherding ministry joyously and with freedom from coercion would do better not to enter into it at all.

Those who are involved in the shepherding ministry must not do it "for dishonest gain but eagerly" (NKJV). In the ancient world, charges of illegitimate gain were often leveled against moral teachers.[374] The Christian community should be unmarked by greed, and those in leadership

Exhortations to Elders and Younger Believers

should set the example for financial integrity. It is perfectly acceptable and morally right for spiritual leaders to be supported by those to whom they minister. (See Matthew 10:10; I Corinthians 9:1-14; I Timothy 5:17-18; II Timothy 2:6.) The ancient Levites were supported by the tithes of the Israelites. (See Numbers 18:8-31; Deuteronomy 26:12.) But it is wrong for those in spiritual leadership to abuse their position of trust and responsibility.

This is a significant challenge, for there are no hard and fast rules in the New Testament governing the appropriate level of financial support for elders. But the same principles that apply to all believers apply to pastors as well. They must not be motivated to get rich. (See I Timothy 6:9-11.) They must learn contentment with the basic necessities of life. (See I Timothy 6:8.) They must accept abundance or poverty with equal grace. (See Philippians 4:11-13.) Any other attitude will reduce the shepherd to a hireling who will abandon the sheep and flee in times of trouble. (See John 10:12-13.)

Rather than being greedy, the elder must be distinguished by eagerness. *Prothymos*, translated "a ready mind" by the KJV, is a compound word formed from the word for "passion" or "ardor" (*thymos*) and the preposition *pro*, which means "before." The idea expressed by this word is that the elder does not need external motivation; he is ready, willing, and eager to perform his calling.[375]

Verse 3. This passage reveals three temptations that pastors must avoid: sloth, greed, and abuse of power.[376] Sloth will certainly result when ministry is done by some misguided sense of compulsion rather than willingly;

greed will increase when one's motivation is material prosperity rather than a heart of passion for God and His people; the lust for power overwhelms those who see their role as controlling rather than as providing an example.

The word translated "*God's* heritage" by the KJV is *kleron*, which the Septuagint version of Deuteronomy 9:29 uses in reference to Israel as God's "inheritance." This verse may have been in Peter's mind, for the Septuagint of Deuteronomy 9:29 refers to Israel's deliverance from Egypt by the "mighty hand" of God. Verse 6 urges the readers to humble themselves "under the mighty hand of God."

In some contexts, *kleron* refers to lots that were cast to make a determination. (See Matthew 27:35; Acts 1:26.) In secular Greek, the word meant an estate.[377] It is used in this sense in Acts 8:21; 26:18; Colossians 1:12; and here.

The word "God" does not appear in the Greek text; thus it is italicized in the KJV. But just as Israel was the heritage of the LORD, so is the church. It is His possession, and He entrusts the care of it into the hands of the elders. The NKJV translates the verse, "Nor as being lords over those entrusted to you, but being examples to the flock."

The word translated "lords over" by the KJV (*katakyrieuontes*) has the idea of harsh or excessive use of authority. Jesus used it in Matthew 20:25 to describe how His disciples were *not* to exercise authority. (See also Matthew 20:26-28.) Instead of "lording it" over others, New Testament leaders are to emulate Christ's example of servant leadership. Acts 19:16 uses the word in a very negative way to describe how a man with an evil spirit

Exhortations to Elders and Younger Believers

overpowered the seven sons of Sceva. The Septuagint uses it in the sense of military conquests; it always seems to deal with bringing something or someone into subjection by force.[378]

Rather than ruling by stark power or subtle manipulation, the elder is to be an example to the flock. We see the idea of spiritual leadership by example in I Corinthians 4:16; 11:1; Philippians 3:17; 4:9; II Thessalonians 3:7-9; I Timothy 4:12; Titus 2:7-8; Hebrews 13:7. It requires depth of character and it is much more of a challenge to lead by example than to manipulate people by coercion.

Verse 4. Those elders who exercise their responsibilities as verses 2-3 describe will receive a reward at the appearance of the Chief Shepherd, when they will "receive a crown of glory that fadeth not away."

The Chief Shepherd is the Lord Jesus, whom 2:25 identifies as the "Shepherd and Overseer of your souls" (NKJV). A "chief shepherd" is an overseer over a group of other shepherds.[379] (See Matthew 26:31; John 10:11-16; Hebrews 13:20.)

In Ezekiel 34:11-31, the LORD identified Himself as Israel's Shepherd. The passage is a Messianic prophecy with a change of pronouns in verse 23 from "I" to "he," indicating that the Messiah—David's greatest Son—will be the ultimate Shepherd.

In Micah 5:4, the Messiah "shall stand and feed His flock in the strength of the LORD, in the majesty of the name of the LORD His God" (NKJV). The One to be born in Bethlehem has been going forth (in activity) from everlasting, indicating His preexistence and deity (Micah 5:2).

These prophecies do not teach that the Messiah is a

person distinct from the LORD. They underscore, rather, the genuineness and fullness of His humanity. Both before and after the Incarnation, the Shepherd is the same. But in view of the coming day when God would add humanity to His identity (Philippians 2:5-8), it was necessary for Messianic prophecies to take into account the genuineness of the Messiah's human personality. Before the Incarnation, the LORD was Israel's Shepherd; after the Incarnation, the LORD was still Israel's Shepherd and the Shepherd of other sheep who were not of the fold of Israel (John 10:16). After the Incarnation, however, the LORD fulfilled His shepherding ministry through and by means of the human identity He took on when, as the Word, He was made flesh. (See John 1:1, 14.)

If God existed as more than one person, there would have to be a transition of God's shepherding ministry from one person to another, indicating a very real change in the identity of the Shepherd. But after the prophetic statement about the coming Shepherd in Ezekiel 34:23, the LORD declared, "Thus they shall know that I, the LORD their God, am with them, and that they, the house of Israel, are My people, says the Lord GOD. You are My flock, the flock of My pasture; you are men, and I am your God" (Ezekiel 34:30-31, NKJV).

In Matthew 26:31 Jesus applied to Himself the prophecy of Zechariah 13:7: "'Awake, O sword, against My Shepherd, against the Man who is My Companion,' says the LORD of hosts. 'Strike the Shepherd, and the sheep will be scattered'" (NKJV). (For further discussion, see the endnote.[380])

The reward for elders who faithfully fulfill their responsibilities will be the unfading "crown of glory." In the ancient world, garlands or wreaths were given as crowns to those who were victorious in athletic contests, to those who rendered distinguished public service, to benefactors, or to other heroes. There was also the golden crown of royalty.[381] The imagery frequently appears in the New Testament to describe the rewards awaiting faithful believers. (See I Corinthians 9:25; Philippians 4:1; I Thessalonians 2:19; II Timothy 4:8; James 1:12; I Peter 5:4; Revelation 2:10; 3:11.) All earthly crowns are temporal and fading, but the rewards awaiting believers will endure forever.

We should understand the words translated "crown of glory" (*doxes stephanon*) to mean "glorious crown." It is a mark of honor that faithful elders will receive as a reward for their service. (See I Corinthians 3:12-15.) It does not mean that they possess the honor belonging only to God, but that God honors them before all. In his heavenly vision, John saw twenty-four elders with golden crowns, but as they worshiped God, they cast their crowns before Him to demonstrate that ultimately all honor belongs to Him. (See Revelation 4:4, 10-11.)

The Greek text identifies the "crown of glory" as a specific crown by means of the definite article; it is "the crown of glory" rather than "a crown of glory." This wording indicates a specific reward is reserved in heaven for faithful elders.

B. Call to Younger Believers to Submit to Elders (5:5a)

(5a) Likewise, ye younger, submit yourselves unto the elder.

If the elders have specific responsibilities in the church, so do younger believers. I Peter now turns from the behavior that should characterize elders to the behavior that should characterize younger people.

Verse 5a. The word "likewise" (*homoios*), as in 3:7, means "continuing the same subject," not "act in the same way."[382] In 3:7, the word continues a discussion of relationship within marriage; here it continues a discussion of relationships between elders and younger people in the church.

The use of the words "elder" and "younger" may seem at first to indicate that only those who are advanced in age may serve in the shepherding ministry of verses 1-3. The word "elder," depending on the context, can refer to older people, ancestors, or officials of some kind. (See comments on verse 1.) Grudem argues convincingly, however, that the word "elder" here refers not to people of advanced age, but to those who are in positions of spiritual leadership in the church.

It is clear that verses 1-4 use the word "elders" to describe those in spiritual leadership. The focus is not on their age, but on their responsibilities. If the idea in verse 5 is that those who are younger must submit to those who are older, then the verse introduces a new subject. This is unlikely from the use of the word "likewise," which indicates a continuation of the same theme. There is no clear contextual evidence that we should understand the word "elder" in verse 5 differently from the immediately preceding verses.[383]

Why are only the younger called upon to submit to those in spiritual leadership? Does this suggest that those who are older need not submit?

Perhaps I Peter addresses younger believers because they are the specific category of believers who most need to be reminded to submit. Human nature does not change, and youth have always tended to a certain sense of independence and perhaps even rebellion. Peter may not have called on those who were advanced in age to submit because they were already submitting to their spiritual leaders. He directed his address toward those who needed to hear it.[384]

As I Peter uses the word "submit" (*hypotasso*), it has to do with respect or deference rather than unquestioning obedience. (See comments on 2:13.) We see this point not only in its use elsewhere in this letter, but also in the immediate context. The kind of submission in view here is the kind that one can give only to shepherds who exercise their loving and watchful care willingly rather than by coercion, whose reputations are unsullied by greed, and who lead by example rather than by domination. (See comments on verses 2-3.) Elders who violate these tenets disqualify themselves as spiritual leaders; we must not submit to them. To submit to those who violate biblical principles is wrong. (See Acts 5:29.)

C. Call to Mutual Submission and Humility (5:5b-7)

(5b) Yea, all of you be subject one to another, and be clothed with humility: for God resisteth the proud, and giveth grace to the humble. (6) Humble yourselves therefore under the mighty hand of God, that he may exalt you in due time: (7) casting all your care upon him; for he careth for you.

First Peter

Not only are younger believers to submit to the elders who exercise shepherding care; all believers are to submit to one another. The call for mutual submission is similar to that in Ephesians 5:21. In a culture where relationships are structured along clear lines of authority, it may be difficult to think in terms of mutual submission or deference. Indeed, the idea of mutual submission opposed Greco-Roman ideals in the first century.[385] Western society tends to be structured along hierarchical relationships. Although there has been some softening of this structure in the latter part of the twentieth century, for many people, leadership is still a matter of hierarchical authority rather than biblical servant leadership. The following poster sometimes observed in places of business depicts the authoritarian concepts that are still prevalent: "Rule One: The boss is always right. Rule Two: If the boss is wrong, see Rule One." This lighthearted approach is often closer to fact than fiction.

Verse 5b. We should note a textual variant here. The Received Text includes for the second time in the verse the word *hypotasso*, resulting in the translation, "Yes, all of you be submissive to one another" (NKJV). The critical Greek text omits *hypotasso*, resulting in the translation, "All of you, clothe yourselves with humility toward one another" (NIV). Because of this variant, Grudem suggests that a new verse should begin at this point with the translation, "Clothe yourselves, all of you, with humility toward one another."[386]

This commentary follows the Received Text, but even if the critical text reading is preferred, the meaning of the verse is not substantially different. Even the verse does not specifically call on all believers to submit to one another, mutual submission is a natural result of mutual humbling "toward one another." Humility that does not result in deference to others is not genuine humility.

The word translated "clothed" (*egkomboomai*) appears only here in the New Testament. The word describes slave garb, including a kind of overall slaves wore to keep their clothing clean as they worked. This word is a further indicator that believers are to humble themselves to serve one another. It underscores the idea of mutual submission.

Verse 5 encourages mutuality in humility by quoting from the Septuagint version of Proverbs 3:34. James 4:6 appeals to the same verse to emphasize the danger of pride and the value of humility.

The word translated "be subject" (*hypotasso*) comes from the preposition *hypo* and the verb *tasso*. The word translated "resists" (*antitassomai*) comes from the preposition *anti* and the middle voice of the verb *tasso*. Thus, within the verse, there is a play on words: believers are to defer to one another; God will oppose the proud.

Pride is the opposite of humility. The proud refuse to submit or defer to anyone. Pride prevents a person from being useful in God's service; humility makes a person useful to God. To be proud is to assert one's independence; to be humble is to acknowledge one's complete dependence on God.

The grace of God that He extends to the humble is the free, gracious influence of God working in the believer's life. Grace is the unmerited favor of God, but His favor is not static. By grace we are saved (Ephesians 2:8), and by grace we are able to do the things that glorify God. (See I Corinthians 15:10; Ephesians 3:7.) Believers must grow

First Peter

in grace (II Peter 3:18). They must not frustrate the grace of God by relying on human effort to please Him (Galatians 2:21; Hebrews 12:15).

The only condition to receiving grace is humility. When a believer confesses his complete dependence on God and his inability to help himself, God responds by extending His favor and strength to do what should be done. On the other hand, when a proud person stubbornly attempts to make his own way, God leaves him to his own resources.[387]

The verbs translated "resisteth" and "giveth" are both present indicatives, indicating that God keeps on resisting the proud and keeps on giving grace to the humble.

Verse 6. James and I Peter have in common not only the reference to Proverbs 3:34, but also the application of the proverb. (See James 4:10.) To humble oneself before God will result in being exalted or lifted up by Him. Both letters also share a concern with resisting the devil. (See verses 8-9 and James 4:7.)

The similarities between James 4:6-10 and I Peter 5:5-9 give rise to speculation about the relationship between the passages. Did James follow I Peter? Did I Peter follow James? Did they both follow a common exegesis of Proverbs 3:34 current in the church at that time? These questions are ultimately unanswerable.[388] It does seem that the "main point of similarity between Peter and James is the close association between humble submission to God and successful resistance to the devil."[389]

The word "therefore" connects verse 6 to verse 5 as the conclusion of the previous statement from Proverbs 3:34. Since God resists the proud but gives grace to the humble, believers should humble themselves under God's mighty hand so that He may exalt them in due time.

In Mary's magnification of the Lord following Elizabeth's Spirit-inspired blessing (Luke 1:41-45), she referred to the way in which the Lord has abased the proud and exalted the lowly. (See Luke 1:52-53.) In discussing appropriate behavior at a wedding feast, Jesus uttered a statement similar to that of James and I Peter: "For whoever exalts himself will be humbled, and he who humbles himself will be exalted" (Luke 14:11, NKJV). As He concluded the parable of the Pharisee and the tax collector, Jesus repeated this statement. (See Luke 18:14.) We also see this theme in the Old Testament in connection with the eschatological day of judgment. (See Isaiah 2:11-12, 17; Ezekiel 17:24; 21:26.)

In the Old Testament, the idea of humbling oneself had to do either with repentance (II Chronicles 7:14; 34:27; Isaiah 57:15) or with a recognition of one's complete dependence upon God (Exodus 10:3; Deuteronomy 8:2, 16; Psalm 34:2; 69:32; Proverbs 16:19; 29:23). In I Peter, it occurs in the context of submitting one to another and accepting the suffering associated with faith in Christ as the will of God. (See 4:19.)

The reference to the "mighty hand of God" recalls a common theme in the Old Testament. It frequently mentions God's "mighty hand" in connection with the deliverance of the people of Israel from Egyptian captivity. (See Exodus 32:11; Deuteronomy 3:24; 4:34; 5:15; 6:21; 7:8, 19; 9:26; 11:2; 26:8; 34:12; Daniel 9:15.) It also mentions God's "mighty hand" in connection with the regathering of Israel from their dispersion in the nations of the world. (See Ezekiel 20:34.)

The "mighty hand of God" imagery thus reflects the

First Peter

Old Testament theme of deliverance from oppression. Just as the ancient Israelites were freed from Egyptian captivity by "the mighty hand of God" as a result of their cry to God for deliverance (Exodus 3:7; Psalm 106:44), so will New Testament believers be delivered from their persecutors as they humble themselves under God's mighty hand. Verse 7 further defines this as "casting all your care upon him." This imagery is especially appropriate in a letter written originally to Jewish Christians. (See comments under "Original Audience.")

A dissimilarity between I Peter and James at this point is that James does not indicate the time of the exaltation of those who humble themselves before God. In James, humbling oneself and then being lifted up seems to be a maxim. I Peter, on the other hand, says the exaltation will occur "in due time." Given the general theme of I Peter, this is apparently a reference to the time of Christ's revelation. (See 1:5, 7, 13; 4:5, 7, 13; 5:4.) For the elders, the exaltation is contextually linked with the time when they will "receive the crown of glory" (verse 4). The nature of the exaltation of the younger people is not specified, but the ultimate exaltation of all believers will be at their identification with Christ in His glory. (See 1:7; 4:13; 5:1.)

Verse 7. We see the influence of the Septuagint again, for here I Peter apparently draws from Psalm 55:22. The word translated "burden" by the Septuagint appears here as "care" (*merimna*). The New Testament uses this word in a variety of contexts to describe things one is "anxious or worried about."[390] (See Matthew 13:22; Mark 4:19; Luke 8:14; 21:34; II Corinthians 11:28.) The related *merimnao*, which can mean "to be anxious and troubled with cares," appears in Matthew 6:25, 31; 10:19; 13:11; Luke

12:22. In each case, Jesus taught that those who have faith in God should not worry.

Verse 7 continues the sentence begun in verse 6 and explains exactly how a believer goes about humbling himself under the mighty hand of God: he does so by casting all his cares upon God. In the context, then, becoming humble refers not so much to repentance as to recognizing one's complete dependence upon God. (See comments on verse 6.)

The reason believers can cast all of their cares upon God is that God cares for them. Literally, the Greek text here reads, "It matters to Him about you." The same word translated "careth" (*melei*) appears in John 10:13, which describes the hireling as not caring for the sheep. Jesus is the Chief Shepherd (verse 4; 2:25); His sheep matter to Him to the point that He gave His life for them. (See John 10:11.)

D. Call to Spiritual Vigilance (5:8-9)

(8) Be sober, be vigilant; because your adversary the devil, as a roaring lion, walketh about, seeking whom he may devour: (9) whom resist stedfast in the faith, knowing that the same afflictions are accomplished in your brethren that are in the world.

After the use of Proverbs 3:34 in James, it continues, "Therefore submit to God. Resist the devil and he will flee from you" (James 4:7, NKJV). Following its use of Proverbs 3:34, I Peter says, "Therefore humble yourselves under the mighty hand of God. . . . Be sober, be vigilant; because your adversary the devil walks about like a

First Peter

roaring lion, seeking whom he may devour. Resist him, steadfast in the faith" (I Peter 5:6, 8-9, NKJV).

Both books tie the ability to resist the devil with submission to God.

Verse 8. There is a reason for sobriety and vigilance: believers have an adversary, the devil, who walks about like a roaring lion seeking to devour his prey. Although both the critical text and the majority text omit "because" (*hoti*) here, it clearly expresses Peter's meaning. Even without the word, we understand that the devil's activity is reason for sobriety and vigilance.

Peter previously advised sobriety by use of the same word (*nepho*) in 1:13 and 4:7. The word has to do with freedom from "every form of mental and spiritual 'drunkenness' . . . from excess, passion, rashness, confusion."[391] (See also I Thessalonians 5:8; II Timothy 4:5.)

The word translated "be vigilant" (*gregoreuo*) appears frequently in the New Testament, commonly translated with some form of "watch."[392] The figurative meaning of *gregoreuo* is to "be on the alert, be watchful [e.g., 'keep your eyes open']."[393]

Sobriety is conceptually connected with the humility of verses 5-6. To humble oneself under the mighty hand of God is an act of sobriety; it represents clear thinking to recognize one's complete dependence upon God and to cast all of one's cares upon Him. Vigilance is conceptually linked with resisting the devil "steadfast in the faith" (verse 9).

The devil is "your adversary" (*antidikos*). This description is appropriate, for the meaning of the word "Satan," which is transliterated from the Hebrew *satan*, is "adversary."

Elsewhere I Peter represents believers as having more than one opponent. (See 2:12; 4:4.) But behind these opponents is the ultimate adversary: the devil. He is the ultimate accuser of brethren (Revelation 12:10), but the charges he brings against God's elect fail because God has given all who believe right standing on the basis of the miracle of Christ's atoning work. (See Romans 8:33-34.) Satan makes all his accusations as if Jesus had never died for the sins of the world. (See I John 2:2.) In his accusations, Satan denies the reality of the Atonement.

The imagery of the devil walking about reflects the pacing of a lion as it stalks its prey. The background of Peter's description of the devil as a lion may be the Septuagint version of Psalm 22:13. In this Messianic psalm, the experiences of Christ in His crucifixion include "strong bulls of Bashan" gaping at Him with their mouths "as a raging and roaring lion." (See Psalm 22:12-13, NKJV.)

The word translated "devour" (*katapiein*) means "to swallow."[394] The word appears also in Matthew 23:24; I Corinthians 15:54; II Corinthians 2:7; 5:4; Hebrews 11:29; and Revelation 12:16. It may be significant that the Septuagint uses this word in Jeremiah 51:34, 44, where he who inhabits Zion declares that Nebuchadnezzar the king of Babylon "has devoured" him, but the LORD says that He "will punish Bel in Babylon, and . . . bring out of his mouth what he has swallowed" (NKJV). Peter wrote from a city he called Babylon; it is possible that he connected the way the king of Babylon swallowed the inhabitants of Zion, only to be forced to regurgitate them, and the way the devil sought to swallow New Testament believers in "Babylon" and elsewhere.[395]

The context indicates that one of the ways the devil seeks to swallow believers is by persuading them to live self-centered, independent lives characterized by worry and lack of trust in God.

Verse 9. The right response to the devil is to resist him from a position of steadfast faith and to keep in mind that the sufferings of believers in any locale are not unique; they are typical of the sufferings of believers everywhere.

Although not as detailed as the discussion of spiritual warfare in Ephesians 6:11-13 and II Corinthians 10:4-5, both I Peter and James recognize the reality and necessity of spiritual warfare in the commands to resist the devil. Believers cannot take a passive stance when it comes to the devil's attacks against them; they must be proactive in resisting him.

The grammar of the verse indicates that the way believers resist the devil is by being "steadfast in the faith." The definite article before the word "faith" indicates that a specific kind of faith is in view, not just some kind of generic trust or optimism. Specifically, the context of the letter makes it clear that the faith is specifically faith in Christ Jesus. (See 1:5, 7, 9, 21.) I Peter, like James, presents trust in God as the only effective way to resist the devil. (See 4:19; 5:6; James 4:7.)

Specifically, this passage connects the devil's efforts to "swallow" believers with his attempts to convince them that they are alone in their suffering, that God has abandoned them, and that they alone—of believers anywhere on earth—are suffering persecution. In what Michaels calls "perhaps the most important [information] in the entire letter,"[396] I Peter assures its readers that "the same sufferings are experienced by your brotherhood in the world" (NKJV). There is great comfort simply in knowing we are not alone in our pain.

If believers are to resist the devil, then "defeat is not inevitable."[397] Where there is unswerving trust in God, there will be victory over the enemy. (See comments on 4:19; 5:6.)

VII

Closing
5:10-14

As Peter concluded his letter, he reminded his readers that the gracious God who had called them, in Christ, to share in His eternal glory would perfect, establish, strengthen, and settle them, even though they would first experience suffering (verse 10).

After his second doxology (see 4:11), Peter acknowledged Silvanus as the person who bore the letter to its recipients, and he identified his brief letter as an exhortation to his readers and a testimony to the true grace of God that enabled them to stand (verses 11-12).

Peter sent greetings from the church in "Babylon" and from Mark (verse 13).

He concluded his letter by commanding his readers to great each other with "a kiss of love" and by wishing them peace (verse 14).

A. The Reward for Suffering (5:10)

(10) But the God of all grace, who hath called us unto his eternal glory by Christ Jesus, after that ye have suffered a while, make you perfect, stablish, strengthen, settle you.

Verse 10. The "God of all grace" immediately recalls I Peter's use of Proverbs 3:34. (See comments on verse

5.) But I Peter's perspective on the grace of God is not limited to God's gift of grace to the humble. The opening words of the letter wish grace for the readers (1:2.). It characterizes the Messianic age as "the grace" about which the prophets spoke (1:10). The coming revelation of Jesus Christ is the "grace" that would come to those who believe (1:13). Believing husbands and wives share in the inheritance of the grace of life (3:7). The giftedness of every believer is a result of the multifaceted grace of God (4:10). Believers are able to remain steadfast because of the grace of God (5:12).

The God who extends every aspect of grace to believers has called all who believe to "his eternal glory by Christ Jesus." I Peter's emphasis on glory is as consistent as its emphasis on grace. Those who endure the trial of their faith will be rewarded with praise, honor, and glory when Jesus Christ appears (1:7). The prophets of old saw the sufferings of Christ and the glory that would follow (1:11). Jesus was given glory in conjunction with His resurrection (1:21). God is glorified through Jesus Christ, and glory ("praise" in the KJV) belongs to Jesus (4:11). The revelation of Jesus Christ will be the revelation of His glory, which will bring gladness and exceeding joy to those who believe (4:13). The spirit of glory is the Spirit of God who rests upon those who are reproached for His name (4:14). Peter saw himself as a "partaker of the glory that shall be revealed" (5:1). When the Chief Shepherd appears, faithful elders will receive a crown of glory (5:4). Believers are called to share in the eternal glory of Christ (5:10). Eternally, all glory belongs to Him (5:11).

The preposition translated "by" in the phrase "by

Christ Jesus" is *en*, which can mean "in," "on," or "by." In the eight-case system of Greek, *en* is taken to mean "in" or "on" in the locative case and "by" in the instrumental case. In the five-case system, *en* is understood to be in the dative case, which can include the ideas of location and instrumentality. The believers' call to eternal glory *en Christo Iesou* ("in Christ Jesus") means essentially the same thing as their being "in Christ." (See Romans 8:1; 12:5; 16:3, 7, 9-10; I Corinthians 1:2, 30; 3:1; 15:18-19, 22, etc., where the same preposition appears.) That is, by their identification in His death, burial, and resurrection, believers are so intimately joined with Christ as to share with Him in the full range of His experiences, from His suffering to His glory. (See Romans 8:17.)

The eternal glory to which believers are called is contrasted with the temporary nature of their sufferings. The suffering is only for "a while," and it will conclude with believers being perfected, established, strengthened, and settled.

The word translated "perfect" is *kartartizo*, which the New Testament often uses with the idea of mending or repairing something that has been broken. (See Matthew 4:21; Mark 1:19; I Corinthians 1:10; Galatians 6:1; I Thessalonians 3:10.) As it is used in conjunction with the idea of suffering, that seems to be the point here. It may be the will of God for believers to suffer temporarily, but the suffering will be followed by restoration and mending of whatever may have been broken during the suffering.

The word translated "stablish" or "establish" (NKJV) is *sterizo*, which has to do with something being strengthened or made firm. (See Luke 22:32; Romans 1:11; 16:25; I Thessalonians 3:2, 13; II Thessalonians 2:17; 3:3; James

5:8; II Peter 1:12; Revelation 3:2.) Since the next word on the list specifically describes strengthening, perhaps we should take *sterizo* as specifically to make something firm. Again, in the context of suffering, this seems to be a promise that God will firmly establish those who have suffered "in any position, rightful privilege, or responsibility which this suffering has taken from them."[398]

The word translated "strengthen" is *sthenoo*, which has to do with making something strong, with specific application to the soul. Any weakness that may have resulted from suffering will be removed by God.

The word translated "settle" is *themelioo*, which has to do with laying a foundation or making something stable. (See Matthew 7:25; Luke 6:48; Ephesians 3:17; Colossians 1:23; Hebrews 1:10.) If any believer's stability has been damaged by suffering, God will correct it.

I Peter regularly uses the connective "but" (Greek, *de*) "to indicate a distinct contrast with a previous statement,"[399] and so it does here. Believers universally are now locked in spiritual battle with the devil, but the day is coming when that warfare will be over and any painful result will be removed.

B. Doxology (5:11)

(11) To him be glory and dominion for ever and ever. Amen.

Verse 11. This is the second and final doxology of I Peter. (See comments on 4:11.) I Peter 4:11 directs glory and dominion to Jesus Christ; this verse directs them to the "God of all grace." There is, of course, no inconsistency here; Jesus Christ is the God of all grace who has made Himself known to human beings in a genuine, full human existence. We should note that in neither doxology did Peter see a plural object of glory and dominion.

C. Delivery of the Letter (5:12a)

(12a) By Silvanus, a faithful brother unto you, as I suppose, I have written briefly.

Verse 12a. Silvanus is the lengthened form of Silas. Silas was connected with Paul's ministry as well as Peter's (II Corinthians 1:19; I Thessalonians 1:1; II Thessalonians 1:1). Together with Judas, Silas carried the letter from the church council in A.D. 50 to its Gentile recipients (Acts 15:27). He was a "chief" man among the brethren and a prophet (Acts 15:22, 32). Together with Paul, Silas sang in the Philippian jail (Acts 16:25). He is mentioned several more times between Acts 15:34 and 18:5.

Some commentators take this verse to mean that Silvanus actually wrote the letter of I Peter as Peter dictated it to him. This arrangement is not without precedent. (See Romans 16:22.) But Grudem argues convincingly that this is not what Peter meant. Rather, Peter meant that Silvanus would deliver this letter to its recipients; he mentioned Silvanus to assure his readers that he was a "faithful brother."[400]

Grudem's reasoning is as follows: "The Greek phrase meaning 'to write to someone by someone else' is nowhere else clearly seen to mean 'to dictate a letter with the help of someone else' . . . [but] there are clear cases where this same Greek construction is used to designate the messenger who carries a letter to someone."[401] Also, "the fact that Peter calls Silvanus *a faithful brother as I regard him*, argues strongly for Silvanus as the bearer of the letter: this expression would have no function if Silvanus were merely the secretary, but it would be very appropriate as a personal recommendation."[402] It was common for Paul to commend the bearers of his letters. (See Romans 16:1-2; I Corinthians 16:10-11; Ephesians 6:21-22; Colossians 4:7-9; Titus 3:12-13.)

D. Purpose of Composition (5:12b)

(12b) Exhorting, and testifying that this is the true grace of God wherein ye stand.

Verse 12b. Here Peter revealed his purpose in writing this brief letter: it is to exhort his readers and to testify to the true grace of God in which believers stand.

The word translated "exhorting" (*parakaleo*) appears three times in I Peter. (See 2:11; 5:1.) In these contexts, the range of meaning includes "to appeal to, urge, encourage, request, implore, entreat, comfort, cheer up."[403]

The "true grace of God in which you stand" (NKJV) refers to "the entire way of life described in the letter as a whole . . . [which] is one of *grace*."[404]

The phrase translated "in which you stand" (*eis en stete*) is actually an imperative of command. The idea is something like, "Stand firm in it!"

The persecution already being experienced and the greater persecution looming on the horizon apparently made it necessary for Peter to firmly exhort the original readers to stand fast in the grace of God. Otherwise, they may have been tempted to question the gospel message as they endured the suffering associated with it.

E. Greetings (5:13-14)

(13) The church that is at Babylon, elected together with you, saluteth you; and so doth Marcus my son. (14) Greet ye one another with a kiss of charity. Peace be with you all that are in Christ Jesus. Amen.

Verse 13. The NKJV translates the opening words of this verse as "she who is in Babylon." Though this is the literal meaning of the Greek, Peter certainly used the phrase as a reference to the church, as the KJV translates. It is very unlikely that Peter would have introduced at this point in his letter an anonymous woman whom his readers would have had no way of identifying. In the second century, Papias wrote that I Peter sent greetings from the church in Babylon. Early believers understood this phrase as a reference to the church rather than to an individual.

"Babylon" here is apparently "a symbolic way of referring to Rome, a name that expressed something of Rome's pride, luxury, immorality, and godlessness."[405] (For further discussion of this point, see the discussion under "Place of Origin" in the Introduction.)

The church in "Babylon" was elected, or chosen, together with the original recipients of this letter. Thus Peter again underscored his readers' solidarity with all believers everywhere. (See verse 9.) On election, see comments on 1:2.

Marcus is Mark, the John Mark of Acts 12:12. Here

we discover that Mark was Peter's convert or disciple in the same way that Timothy was Paul's. (See I Corinthians 4:17.) When Peter was miraculously released from prison, the first place he went was to the house of John Mark's mother, Mary, where a prayer meeting was underway for him. (See Acts 12:5-17.)

Mark was Barnabas's cousin (Colossians 4:10), and he accompanied Saul and Barnabas on their first missionary journey. (See Acts 12:25; 13:5.) John Mark returned to Jerusalem before the completion of the trip (Acts 13:13). When Paul and Barnabas prepared for their second missionary trip, Barnabas "was determined to take with them John called Mark" (Acts 15:37, NKJV). Paul strongly disagreed, saying that one who had not completed the previous trip should not go with them. The disagreement between Paul and Barnabas was so sharp that they parted company; Paul chose Silas to go with him, and Barnabas took Mark and sailed to Cyprus. (See Acts 15:38-40.) Later, Paul recognized the usefulness of Mark and asked for him to come to him in prison. (See II Timothy 4:11.) Mark is the author of the Gospel of Mark.

Verse 14. In the first century, it was customary for close friends and relatives to greet one another with a kiss.[406] There were, however, no romantic overtones to this customary greeting.

Four times Paul recommended that believers greet one another with a holy kiss. (See Romans 16:16; I Corinthians 16:20; II Corinthians 13:12; I Thessalonians 5:26.) It was customary among Christians in the first century to greet one another this way, just as it is today in Western society to greet one another with a handshake.

> The holy kiss . . . was primarily a symbolic expression of the love, forgiveness, and unity which should exist among Christians. As such, it became associated with the celebration of the Lord's Supper as a prelude to its observance. . . . There is no indication that it was restricted to one's own sex in the New Testament era. . . . The suggestion to separate the sexes for the exchange of the kiss arose in the late second century due to concern about criticism from non-Christians and the danger of erotic abuse. . . . By the third century it seems that the sexes were separated . . . and by the fourth century the clergy and laity were also kept apart.[407]

Paul did not emphasize the kiss as much as that the greeting was to be "holy." No doubt, out of sheer social convention, the believers were greeting one another with a kiss; Paul's concern was to make the greeting with the awareness of their mutual separation unto God and in the fear of God. Since he focused on the holiness of the greeting and not so much on the form of the greeting itself, the latter is not normative for all time. Believers in cultures where kissing is not a socially acceptable form of greeting are not obliged to practice it. In each culture, believers can use the normative cultural greeting, but whatever it is, it should be "holy."

Instead of a "holy" kiss, Peter spoke of a "kiss of love." (The KJV translates "charity" from *agapes*, which means "love.") Like Paul, Peter did not merely command his readers to greet one another with a kiss. This was a common greeting in the first century, and such a command would have been relatively meaningless. Instead, he commanded them to greet one another with a certain kind of kiss, a "kiss of love," which means essentially the same thing as the "holy kiss."

Peter's final wish for his readers was that they would have peace. This was a typical greeting in first-century letters. (See the comments on 1:2b for a discussion of "peace.") Once again, he identified his readers as being "in Christ Jesus." (See discussion on verse 10.)

"Amen" appears twice previously in the letter at the conclusion of the doxologies. (See 4:11; 5:11.) Now, however, it concludes the entire letter. Peter had exhorted his readers and testified to them about the life of grace, urging them to stand fast in it, regardless of the painful circumstances they experienced at the hands of unbelievers. Now, he wrote, "So be it!"

Endnotes

[1] This outline has been adapted from Gary Tuck, "The Arguments of the Books of the New Testament" (unpublished work presented to the Department of Bible Exposition at Dallas Theological Seminary in June 1987), 225-26; Scot McKnight, *The NIV Application Commentary, I Peter* (Grand Rapids, MI: Zondervan Publishing House, 1996), 34.

[2] See James and Marti Hefley, *By Their Blood: Christian Martyrs of the Twentieth Century*, 2d ed. (Grand Rapids, MI: Baker Book House, 1996).

[3] See T. F. Tenney, "Persecution Fires in 1996," *Pentecostal Herald*, September 1996: 5-6.

[4] See the July 15, 1996, and August 12, 1996, issues of *Christianity Today*.

[5] Edwin A. Blum in Frank E. Gaebelein, ed., *The Expositor's Bible Commentary* (Grand Rapids, MI: Zondervan Publishing House, 1976) 12:213.

[6] Tenney.

[7] This summary of patristic evidence follows Blum, 215.

[8] For patristic evidence concerning Peter's authorship, see the discussion under "Inspiration and Place in the Canon."

[9] See the author's unpublished dissertation, "Education in Transition: From Judaism to Christianity."

[10] Clement of Rome wrote: "Through envy and jealousy, the greatest and most righteous pillars [of the church] have been persecuted and put to death. Let us set before our eyes the illustrious apostles. Peter, through unrighteous envy, endured not one or two, but numerous

labors, and when he had at length suffered martyrdom, departed to the place of glory due to him. Owing to envy, Paul also obtained the reward of patient endurance, after being seven times thrown into captivity, compelled to flee, and stoned. After preaching both in the east and west, he gained the illustrious reputation due to his faith, having taught righteousness to the whole world, and come to the extreme limit of the west, and suffered martyrdom under the prefects."

[11] Blum, 212.

[12] McKnight, 29.

[13] D. A. Carson, Douglas J. Moo, and Leon Morris, *An Introduction to the New Testament* (Grand Rapids, MI: Zondervan Publishing House, 1992), 424.

[14] Ibid.

[15] Eusebius, *Ecclesiastical History* 2.15.2.

[16] Bruce M. Metzger, *A Textual Commentary on the Greek New Testament* (Stuttgart, Germany: United Bible Societies, 1971), 698.

[17] McKnight, 23.

[18] Ibid.

[19] Ibid., 24.

[20] For an exploration of this view and an explanation as to why it is unlikely, see Carson, Moo, and Morris, 426-28.

[21] Blum, 214.

[22] See the discussion on Hebrews 1:4 in Daniel L. Segraves, *Hebrews: Better Things* (Hazelwood, MO: Word Aflame Press, 1996) 1:40-41.

[23] See R. P. Martin in Geoffrey W. Bromily, gen. ed., *The International Standard Bible Encyclopedia* (Grand Rapids, MI: William B. Eerdmans, 1986) 3:804.

[24] Walter Bauer, *A Greek-English Lexicon of the New*

Testament and Other Early Christian Literature, trans. William F. Arndt and F. Wilbur Gingrich, revised and augmented by F. Wilbur Gingrich and Frederick W. Danker, 2nd ed. (Chicago: University of Chicago Press, 1979), 99 [hereinafter BAGD].

[25] See discussion under "Original Audience."

[26] Craig S. Keener, *The Bible Background Commentary, New Testament* (Downers Grove, IL: InterVarsity Press, 1993), 711.

[27] There is some textual evidence to suggest that Ephesians may have been a circular letter. See the discussion in Metzger, 601.

[28] Keener, 709.

[29] See discussion by McKnight, 52-53.

[30] See the discussion on the meaning of "holiness" in Daniel L. Segraves, *Themes from a Letter to Rome* (Hazelwood, MO: Word Aflame Press, 1995), 173-74.

[31] See Romans 1:5; 4:12; 6:16; 14:23; 15:18; 16:26; I Corinthians 16:13; II Corinthians 4:13; 7:15; 10:6; Galatians 2:20; 5:6; Philippians 2:17; I Thessalonians 1:3; II Thessalonians 1:8; I Timothy 6:12.

[32] See John 1:12; 3:15-18, 36; 5:24; 6:35, 40, 47; 7:38; 11:25-26; I John 5:1; Acts 10:43; 16:31.

[33] See, for example, Roger M. Raymer, in John F. Walvoord and Roy B. Zuck, *The Bible Knowledge Commentary*, New Testament edition (Wheaton, IL: Victor Books, 1983), 840.

[34] For Paul's insight on grace, see Romans 1:5; 3:24; 4:4; 5:15, 17; 11:6; 12:3, 6; I Corinthians 3:10; 15:10; II Corinthians 9:8; 12:9; Galatians 2:21; Philippians 2:13.

[35] See discussion in McKnight, 68-69.

[36] Keener, 709.

First Peter

[37] It is common for trinitarian theologians to explain the passages indicating the subordination of the Son to the Father as speaking of functional or economic subordination rather than essential or real subordination. In other words, the Son is not actually subordinate in terms of deity, identity, value or worth; He has simply chosen a subordinate role.

[38] See comments on Hebrews 1:5 in Segraves, *Hebrews: Better Things* 1:42-45.

[39] See Gene Getz, *The Measure of the Church* (Glendale, CA: Regal Books, 1975).

[40] For example, Paul commended the Philippians for their faith (1:25; 2:17) and prayed that their love would abound more (1:9). Though they apparently had a measure of love, it needed development and maturing (2:2). He did not commend them for their hope.

The church in Ephesus was a relatively mature church, and Paul commended the believers there for their faith and love (1:15). They were apparently deficient in hope, however, and Paul prayed that they would grow in that area (1:18). By the time John wrote the final book in the New Testament, the Ephesian church had turned away from the love they formerly had (Revelation 2:4).

The churches of Galatia were being swayed from their exclusive faith in Christ to a form of Judaism (1:6-9). It is no surprise, then, that Paul did not commend them for faith, hope, or love. Instead, he encouraged them to develop these qualities: he encouraged faith in 3:2, 5, 7-9, 11, 14, 23-26; 5:5-6, 22; hope in 5:5; and love in 5:6, 13-14, 22.

In his first letter to the Thessalonians, Paul commended them for their faith, hope, and love (1:3), but in

Endnotes

his second letter he commended them only for their faith and love (1:3). Their hope had apparently been damaged by a letter forged under Paul's name claiming that the day of Christ had already come (2:2).

Paul did not commend the Corinthian church for faith, hope, or love in his first letter to them. The word "faith" appears in seven verses in I Corinthians (2:5; 12:9; 13:2, 13; 15:14, 17; 16:13). In no case is there a clear commendation of their faith. Paul discussed the spiritual gift of faith in 12:9 and 13:2, held up faithfulness as a desirable virtue in 13:13; acknowledged their salvific faith in 15:14 and 15:17, and exhorted them to stand fast in the faith in 16:13, an apparent reference to faith as doctrine or a body of belief. But 2:5 implies that to at least some extent their faith was in human wisdom. The word "hope" appears in only three verses in I Corinthians (9:10; 13:13; 15:19). In no case did Paul commend the Corinthians for their hope. He mentioned the right of ministers of the gospel to hope for support from those to whom they minister in 9:10, described hope as a desirable virtue in 13:13, and asserted the misery of hope in Christ only for this world in 15:19. The word "love" appears in ten verses of I Corinthians (4:21; 8:1; 13:1; 2, 4, 8, 13; 14:1; 16:14, 24). None of these references is a commendation of the love of the Corinthians. Paul questioned whether he should come to them in love (4:21), listed the characteristics of love (13:4-8), described love as superior to even faith and hope (13:13), and mentioned his love (16:24). All the other references to love imply the Corinthians' inadequacy in this virtue. Love edifies, but knowledge puffs up (8:1). The implication is that the Corinthians had knowledge, but not love. (Compare with I Corinthians 13:2, 8, 9, 12.) Paul described the incompleteness of spiritual gifts apart from love (13:1-2). He urged the Corinthians to pursue love (14:1) and to do everything with love (16:14). The only commendation they received is that they did not come behind in any gift (1:7). Paul, then, urged them to grow in these qualities, and especially in love.

That the Corinthians heeded Paul's advice is evident from a lexical study of II Corinthians. The book has only fifty-nine percent of the content of I Corinthians, but it contains far more references to faith, hope, and love proportionately. Though there is no commendation for hope, Paul commended the Corinthians for standing by faith (1:24) and for abounding in faith and love (8:7). The following references indicate that their abundant love was newly acquired: Paul urged them to reaffirm their love (2:8), tested their love (8:8), and urged them to show proof of their love (8:24). In what seems a plaintive cry, Paul complained that they did not properly reciprocate his love (12:15).

Paul commended the church at Rome for its faith, which was so well known as to be the topic of discussion among believers everywhere (1:8). Again in 1:12, Paul commended the Romans for this quality. Although he mentioned hope ten times in Romans, in no case did he commend the church at Rome for its hope. Instead, Paul prayed that they would abound in hope (15:13). He mentioned love eleven times in the letter, but as with hope, there is no commendation for the Romans' love. There are, however, repeated encouragements to love (8:28; 12:9, 10; 13:8-10). Like most of the first-century churches, the church at Rome needed to mature in these biblical measurements of maturity and spirituality. Specifically, the believers in Rome were deficient in hope and love.

Paul commended the Colossians for their faith, hope, and love (1:4-5). The essential message of the book is that the believers should stand fast in their relationships with Jesus Christ and not be moved by legalists, mystics, or ascetics.

[41]Blum, 220.

[42]See comments on faith, hope, and love in 1:3.

[43]Raymer, 841.

[44]For the Jewish perspective on trials, see Daniel L. Segraves, *James: Faith at Work* (Hazelwood, MO: Word Aflame Press, 1995), 33-34.

[45]See Blum, 221.

[46]Ibid.

[47]Ibid.

[48]See Genesis 3:15 (with Galatians 4:4); 12:3 (with Luke 3:34; Matthew 1:2; Acts 3:25; Galatians 3:16); 49:10 (with Luke 3:33; Matthew 1:2); Numbers 24:17, 19 (with Matthew 1:2; Luke 3:34); Deuteronomy 18:15-19 (with Matthew 21:11; John 1:21, 45; 6:14; Acts 3:22-23; 7:37); Psalm 132:11 (with Matthew 1:6; Acts 2:30); Psalm 2; 8; 16; 22; 23; 24; 40; 41; 45; 68; 69; 72; 89; 102; 110; 118; Isaiah 2:4; 7:14 (with Matthew 1:22-23); 9:6-7; 11; 49; 52:13-15; 53; 61:1-3; 63:1-6; Jeremiah 23:5-6; 31:31-34; 33:15; Ezekiel 36:24-28; 37:14; 39:25-29; Daniel 9:25-26; Joel 2:28-32; Amos 9:11-12; Micah 4:1-4; 5:2; Zechariah 9:9; 12:10; Malachi 3:1.

[49]See McKnight, 73, n. 16.

[50]The Greek *doxas*, translated "glory" in the KJV, is plural.

[51]See Jay E. Adams, *Trust and Obey: A Practical*

Commentary on First Peter (Grand Rapids, MI: Baker Book House, 1979), 22.

[52]Stephen's "church in the wilderness" (Acts 7:38) was simply the assembled Israelites gathered to receive the law of Moses. *Ekklesia*, translated "church," has to do with an assemblage of people whether for secular (Acts 19:32, 39, 41) or other reasons. In the New Testament, the word came to mean the universal church (e.g., Colossians 1:18) and local groups of Christians (e.g., Acts 13:1).

[53]Blum, 222.

[54]Ibid.

[55]See McKnight, 85.

[56]See discussion in Keener, 710.

[57]There are three categories of references to wine or drinking in Scripture: (1) where wine is mentioned, but neither endorsed nor condemned; (2) where wine is a source of misery and an emblem of the wrath of God; (3) where wine is a blessing in conjunction with corn and bread.

Some religious movements today permit or even encourage the use of intoxicants in moderation. A careful examination of Scripture will reveal, however, that alcoholic beverages are never spoken of favorably and that partaking of such beverages in any quantity is harmful to the human body. Intoxicants poison or fill the body with toxins. The intentional poisoning of our body is abusive of the temple of God. For these reasons, drinking is certainly a sinful practice in God's eye.

One cannot appeal to the references to wine that fall under the first category just mentioned in order to support drinking. Scripture often mentions practices without condemning or endorsing them, purely in the larger context of describing human actions.

The references in the second category clearly condemn the use of wine in any quantity. One of these denunciations of wine was written by Solomon, who had been blessed of God with great wisdom. He wrote, "Who hath woe? who hath sorrow? who hath contentions? who hath babbling? who hath wounds without cause? who hath redness of eyes? They that tarry long at the wine; they that go to seek mixed wine. Look not thou upon the wine when it is red, when it giveth his colour in the cup, when it moveth itself aright. At the last it biteth like a serpent, and stingeth like an adder. Thine eyes shall behold strange women, and thine heart shall utter perverse things. Yea, thou shalt be as he that lieth down in the midst of the sea, or as he that lieth upon the top of a mast. They have stricken me, shalt thou say, and I was not sick; they have beaten me, and I felt it not: when shall I awake? I will seek it yet again" (Proverbs 23:29-35).

This passage graphically describes the evils of drinking intoxicating beverages. The sure result is sorrow, woe, contention, senseless talk, and wounds. Drinking produces no good result. It breaks down moral restraints and causes a person to say things he would never say otherwise. A person who drinks is in danger of immediate death due to the effects of intoxication, not to mention the long-term, addictive results of alcohol.

"Woe unto them that rise up early in the morning, that they may follow strong drink; that continue until night, till wine inflame them!" (Isaiah 5:11). "But they also have erred through wine, and through strong drink are out of the way; the priest and the prophet have erred through strong drink, they are swallowed up of wine, they are out of the way through strong drink; they err in vision, they stumble in judgment" (Isaiah 28:7). These verses show the addictive nature of intoxicating beverages and that those who partake of them will err in matters of judgment; their senses are polluted.

The third category of references prompts some to excuse alcoholic beverages, often with the hopeful intention to drink in moderation. There is no way to know how many have fallen into the treacherous trap of drunkenness by prefacing their tippling with, "After all, didn't Paul tell Timothy to take a little wine for his stomach's sake?"

There are two kinds of wines mentioned in Scripture. As William Patton has pointed out, "There were . . . two kinds of wine in ancient use. The one was sweet, pleasant, refreshing, unfermented; the other was exciting, inflaming, intoxicating. Each was called wine." William Patton, *Bible Wines or Laws of Fermentation and Wines of the Ancients*, reprint (Oklahoma City, OK: Sane Press, n.d.), 132.

Patton meticulously documented that unfermented beverages called wines existed and were commonly used by the ancients. He gave abundant proof of the generic nature of the two Hebrew words, *yayin* and *shakar* (pp. 56-58). The Hebrew *yayin* (translated "wine") "designates grape-juice, or the liquid which the fruit of the vine yields. This may be new or old, sweet or sour, fermented or unfermented, intoxicating or unintoxicating" (p. 56). The Hebrew *shakar* (translated "strong drink") "signifies 'sweet drink' expressed from fruits other than the grape, and drunk in an unfermented or fermented state" (pp. 57-58). These two words are generic. In other words, they are used in Scripture to refer both to fermented and unfermented drink. The context determines which meaning is meant.

Other relevant Hebrew words always carry the same meaning. One of the most common is *tirosh* (translated "wine," "new wine," and "sweet wine"): this "wine" is an unfermented drink that generally refers to the juice of something other than the grape; for example, corn and olives.

The New Testament makes use of a generic Greek word, *oinos*, to correspond exactly to *yayin* in the Old Testament. It too designates the juice of the grape in all its stages. The context will determine whether fermented or unfermented beverage is meant.

The English word "wine" is from the Latin *vinum*, which is equivalent to the Greek *oinos*. *Vinus* is a generic word that refers to the juice of the grape in all its forms, as was the English "wine" during the era of the Authorized Version. Modern dictionaries define "wine" as a fermented beverage, but we must not allow the modern usage of a word to be retroactive.

John Stuart Mill in his *System of Logic* explained why restricted meanings of words typically develop: "A generic term is always liable to become limited to a single species if people have occasion to think and speak of that species oftener than of anything else contained in the genus. The tide of custom first drifts the word on the shore of a particular meaning, then retires and leaves it there" (Patton, 63-64).

What did Paul mean when he said to Timothy, "Drink no longer water, but use a little wine for thy stomach's sake and thine often infirmities" (I Timothy 5:23)? Did he command Timothy to indulge in fermented alcoholic beverages for the sake of a weak stomach and other ongoing sicknesses? Fermented wine would seem to be precisely the wrong prescription. Indeed, the fermented wines of that day produced "headaches, dropsy, madness, and stomach complaints" (Patton, 112). At the same time there were unfermented wines that were "exceedingly wholesome and useful to the body" (Patton, 113). Surely Paul, who had earlier told Timothy that a bishop must not be given to wine (I Timothy 3:3), and who knew the inherent evil of fermented wine from the law ("wine is a mocker," Proverbs 20:1), would not have recommended to Timothy such a forbidden, dangerous substance to drink in the place of water.

Some make their plea for moderate use of alcohol on the basis of a misunderstanding of Ephesians 5:18: "And be not drunk with wine, wherein is excess." They suggest that one is not to drink to excess, or until he is drunk. The literal meaning of the Greek word translated "excess" is, however, "dissolution, dissipation." In this case the word "excess" does not refer to quantity, but to what is inherent in fermented wine. The phrase, "wherein is," reveals that the "excess" is *in the wine.* In other words, the use of fermented wine dissipates. The translation of the NKJV is clear on this point: "And do not be drunk with wine, in which is dissipation; but be filled with the Spirit."

Physicians have pointed out that the first drink of alcohol intoxicates. After that, the drunkenness is only a matter of degree.

Twenty-five percent of the American people are directly affected by alcoholism. Ninety percent of college students and seventy percent of high school students drink. These amazing statistics contributed to nearly 22,000 alcohol-related deaths in one recent year among those in the fifteen- to twenty-four age group. (Statistics from *Christian School Comment* 12:9.)

The only consistent Christian position is total abstinence from all alcoholic beverages. Moderation is the first step toward immoderation. The person who refuses to drink will never have to concern himself with fears of drinking too much. He will never be tempted to drunkenness. He will live his life free from the ravages of liquor.

[58]See discussion in McKnight, 85, n. 1.

[59]See comments on faith, hope, and love in 1:3.

[60]Keener, 710.

[61]B. C. Caffin, in H. D. M. Spence and Joseph S. Exell, eds., *The Pulpit Commentary* (Grand Rapids, MI: William B. Eerdmans, reprint 1977), 22:8.

[62]Ibid.

[63]II Peter was apparently written to the same audience as I Peter. (See II Peter 3:1.)

[64]See Romans 2:17, 23; 3:27; 4:15; 5:20; 7:8-11; 8:3; 9:31-32; 10:3 (with Philippians 3:9); 11:7-10; I Corinthians 15:56; Galatians 3:19 (where "because of transgressions" means "to bring transgressions about").

[65]Blum, 224.

[66]See Deuteronomy 10:17; Matthew 22:16; Romans 2:11; Galatians 2:6. Compare with Romans 3:29-30; 10:12-13.

[67]See, e.g., Matthew 15:21-28; 27:54; John 4:46-53; Luke 7:1-10; Acts 10:1-4. Compare with Matthew 12:38-50. In this passage, following the Pharisees' rejection of Jesus, Jesus pointed out that the people of Nineveh, who were Gentiles, and the queen of Sheba, a Gentile, would "rise

First Peter

up in the judgment" to condemn unbelieving Jews. He characterized the unbelieving Jews as spiritually barren and pointed out that His family extended to include anyone who did the will of God.

[68]God, who is an omnipresent Spirit, existed before the Incarnation without any of the limitations inherent to human existence. But when He humbled Himself to permanently add full humanity to His existence as God, of necessity He voluntarily embraced the limitations of human existence. (See Philippians 2:5-8.) For example, although God is omnipresent (everywhere present), the physical body of Jesus cannot be omnipresent, even though it is now glorified. In the Incarnation, God humbled Himself to spatial limitations. Although God is omniscient (He knows everything), there are things that Jesus confessed He did not know as a man (e.g., Mark 13:32). In the Incarnation, God humbled Himself to limitations of knowledge. Although God is omnipotent (He has all power), Jesus confessed that He could do nothing of Himself (John 5.19, 30).

We cannot fully comprehend this integration of deity and humanity in Christ, because the Incarnation is the greatest miracle ever to occur. By definition, a miracle defies human understanding or explanation. Regardless of the doctrine of God one embraces, ultimately we cannot fully explain how God is manifest in the flesh. We must accept the doctrine of the Incarnation by faith; we cannot comprehend it by human intellect.

There are, however, certain ideas we must believe and confess to be true, even if we do not fully comprehend how they could be, simply because Scripture declares them to be true. We human beings must realize, after all, that God is infinite and we are finite. There is simply no way that finite humans can understand everything that the infinite God knows and understands. For this reason, faith plays an integral role in salvation. Faith does not ask us to believe things that are irrational, but it does ask us to believe things that are suprarational. For example, it would be irrational to say that Jesus is God but that He is not God. To say, however, that Jesus is fully God but that He is also fully man, is suprarational. The former statement contradicts itself; the second makes two positive assertions, neither of which contradicts the other. Though, from our perspective, we cannot comprehend how Jesus could be both God and man at once, this is the teaching of Scripture, and nothing in our experience tells us such a thing could not be, given the right circumstances.

The term "Son of God" is a reference to God manifest in human existence. Jesus Christ is the Son of God. This does not mean that He is a "person" other than God or other than the Father. Attempts to define God in human terms—like "persons"—will always fail. But the permanent incorporation of a complete human nature into God's transcendent deity does require a different way of speaking and thinking about God from the way people spoke and thought about Him prior to the Incarnation.

Essentially, whenever we see a reference to "Jesus Christ," it is a reference to the Incarnation. God assumed the name "Jesus" in the Incarnation, and "Christ" is the Greek equivalent of the Hebrew "Messiah." In other words, "Jesus Christ" is the Messiah, God in human nature. For this reason, it is not strictly accurate to use the name "Jesus Christ" for God prior to the Incarnation, in the era of the Old Testament. On the other hand, since the Incarnation did not terminate God's omniscience, omnipresence, omnipotence, or any of God's attributes, it is still appropriate to speak of God as "Father" or "Holy Spirit." (We do not mean that "Father" and "Holy Spirit" are merely attributes of God. God actually is our Father, and the Holy Spirit actually is God.) Though Jesus Christ is God made visible, and He is all of God we will ever see, the humanity that God assumed in the Incarnation is not present in all that God does as an omnipresent Spirit. For example, we are now filled with the Holy Spirit, but that does not mean the human nature of Jesus dwells within us.

For centuries, many in Christendom have struggled to formulate theological statements, but always without complete success due to the limitations of human comprehension and vocabulary. In some cases, theological statements have been limited largely to negative declarations; because it is difficult to formulate precise statements about what and how God *is*, the focus is on what He is *not*.

Scripture does not declare that Jesus is "God the Son" manifest in the flesh. It declares that He is God Himself manifest in the flesh. (See I Timothy 3:16; John 1:14.) As an omnipresent Spirit, God is invisible (John 1:18). But Jesus said, "He who sees Me see Him who sent Me" (John 12:45, NKJV). He also said, "If you had known Me, you would have known My Father also; and from now on you know Him and have seen Him" (John 14:7, NKJV). Knowing the Father is bound up with knowing Jesus; seeing the Father is bound up with seeing Jesus.

When Philip responded, "Lord, show us the Father, and it is sufficient for us" (John 14:8, NKJV), Jesus answered, "Have I been with you so long, and yet you have not known Me, Philip? He who has seen Me has seen the Father; so how can you say, 'Show us the Father'? Do you not believe that I am in the Father, and the Father in Me?" (John 14:9-10, NKJV). To know Jesus is to know the Father, and to see Jesus is to see the Father.

[69]Caffin, 9.

[70]Proverbs 1:7; Matthew 10:28; II Corinthians 7:1; Ephesians 5:21; Philippians 2:12; I Timothy 5:20.

[71]McKnight, 89.

[72]Ibid.

[73]A. T. Robertson, *Word Pictures in the New Testament* (Grand Rapids, MI: Baker Book House, 1960) 6:89.

[74]For a discussion of atonement theories, see Daniel L. Segraves, *Hebrews: Better Things*, vol. 2 (Hazelwood, MO: Word Aflame Press, 1997).

[75]See the discussion on the redeeming relative in C. I. Scofield, ed., *The New Scofield Study Bible*, New King James Version (Nashville, TN: Thomas Nelson Publishers, 1989), 849, n. 1.

[76]See discussion under "Original Audience."

[77]Keener, 711.

[78]See John 11:13; Romans 5:6, 8, 10; 6:3; 8:34; 14:9, 15; I Corinthians 8:11; 11:26; 15:3; II Corinthians 5:14-15; I Thessalonians 4:14; 5:10; Matthew 26:38, 59, 66; Philippians 2:8; 3:10; Colossians 1:22; Hebrews 2:9, 14; 5:7; 9:15-16.

[79]Caffin, 10.

[80]See discussion of *prognosis* in Wayne Grudem, *I Peter, Tyndale New Testament Commentaries* (Grand Rapids, MI: William B. Eerdmans, 1988), 85.

First Peter

[81] See discussion on verse 2.

[82] J. Ramsey Michaels, *I Peter, Word Biblical Commentary* (Waco, TX: Word Books, 1988), 49:67.

[83] Grudem, 85.

[84] Frank Stagg, *The Holy Spirit Today* (Macon, GA: Smyth & Helwys Publishing, Inc., 1995), 3.

[85] Grudem, 85.

[86] Michaels, 67.

[87] Raymer, 843.

[88] See Acts 2:24, 32; 3:15, 26; 4:10, 33; 5:29-32; 10:39-40; 13:29-31, 33-34, 37; 17:31; Romans 1:4; 4:24-25; 6:4, 9; 7:4; 8:11, 34; 10:9; I Corinthians 6:14; 15:1-4, 15-17; II Corinthians 4:14; Galatians 1:1; Ephesians 1:20; Colossians 2:12; I Thessalonians 1:10; II Timothy 2:8; I Peter 1:3, 21; 3:18; 5:1.

[89] Michaels, 69-70.

[90] A. Plummer, assisted by T. Randell and A. T. Bott, "Revelation," *The Pulpit Commentary* (Grand Rapids, MI: William B. Eerdmans, 1977), 22:333.

[91] Michaels, 70

[92] Grudem, 87.

[93] Ibid., 87-88.

[94] BAGD, 837.

[95] Caffin, 11.

[96] See Michaels, 74, for a discussion of the phrase "your souls."

[97] See discussion in ibid.

[98] See discussion in Metzger, 688.

[99] Blum, 227.

[100] Ibid., 226.

[101] See discussion in Grudem, 89.

[102] Caffin, 11.

[103] See Grudem, 90.
[104] This paragraph follows Grudem, 57.
[105] See discussion in Michaels, 76.
[106] Grudem, 91. For an alternative explanation of the change in preposition, see Michaels, 76.
[107] Caffin, 12.
[108] See Earl D. Radmacher, gen. ed., *The Nelson Study Bible* (Nashville, TN: Thomas Nelson Publishers, 1997), 2118.
[109] See Blum, 227; Grudem, 90.
[110] See Grudem, 91.
[111] See Grudem, 92 and n. 2.
[112] See discussion in Michaels, 78-79.
[113] See ibid., 79.
[114] Grudem, 93.
[115] See discussion in Grudem, 93; Michaels, 83. See Romans 13:12; Ephesians 4:22, 25; Colossians 3:8; Hebrews 12:1; James 1:21.
[116] BAGD, 397.
[117] Ibid., 203.
[118] Ibid., 845.
[119] Grudem, 94.
[120] BAGD, 412.
[121] See discussion in Grudem, 94.
[122] See Romans 1:11; II Corinthians 5:2; 9:14; Philippians 1:8; 2:26; I Thessalonians 3:6; II Timothy 1:4.
[123] BAGD, 476.
[124] See Grudem, 95-96.
[125] See McKnight, 104, n. 6.
[126] BAGD, 886.
[127] Keener, 712.
[128] Grudem, 97.

[129] See Leviticus 9:5-8; 10:4-5; Deuteronomy 4:11; 5:27; Exodus 12:48; 16:9; Hebrews 4:16; 7:25; 10:1, 22; 11:6; 12:18, 22.

[130] See the discussion of God's foreknowledge in the comments on 1:20.

[131] BAGD, 269.

[132] Grudem, 100.

[133] Ibid.

[134] Michaels, 101.

[135] See discussion in Grudem, 101-2.

[136] Another possible translation of the Greek text behind the words "Unto you therefore which believe he is precious" is "Therefore, to you who believe there is honor." See McKnight, 108; Grudem, 104-5. However, the NKJV, NIV, and NASB all translate the phrase in a way similar to the KJV. The alternate translation indicates that those who believe on Jesus share in some way in the honor belonging to Him.

[137] See Grudem, 107-10.

[138] Caffin, 71.

[139] Ibid.

[140] Michaels, 109.

[141] Blum, 231.

[142] Grudem, 114.

[143] See Grudem's discussion on page 115, n. 1.

[144] See comments under "Original Audience."

[145] A confusion of the church and Israel results from failure to rely strictly on a literal hermeneutic, and it results in a blurring of the distinctions between dispensational ages, a confusion of the covenants, and a denial of God's future dealings with the nation of Israel. The roots of this point of view reach back into church history to

Endnotes

Origen's allegorism ("spiritualizing" Scripture, e.g. the church is Israel), Augustine's *The City of God* (asserting that the Millennium is fulfilled in the present church age and failing to see any future for the Jewish people), and the amillennialism of the Roman Catholic Church.

A literal interpretation of Scripture, however, reveals a clear distinction between the church and Israel. I Corinthians 10:32 is pivotal to understanding the distinction between Jews, Gentiles, and Christians: "Give none offence, neither to the Jews, nor to the Gentiles, nor to the church of God." Here we see three distinct groups: (1) the Jews, (2) the Gentiles, and (3) the church of God.

A careful study of the word "Jew" in Scripture reveals that it was originally a nickname or abbreviation for those of the tribe of Judah. But its use soon expanded to include all the Hebrew race. Mordecai, of the tribe of Benjamin, was a Jew (Esther 2:5). Hebrews are known as Jews in Jeremiah 34:9. In Ezra 4:12, descendants of the tribes of Judah, Benjamin, and Levi are called Jews. The implication is strong that the term includes representatives of all twelve tribes. (See Ezra 2:70; 6:17; 8:35.) Throughout Ezra and Nehemiah they are called Jews. Throughout the Book of Esther, all Israelites in the kingdom of the Medes and Persians are called Jews. Thus the word "Jew" came to be a synonym for "Israelite." This is reasonable in that Judah was the leading tribe. It was the tribe through which the Messiah would come. It was the tribe that always led in battle. When the northern tribes rebelled against the house of David, Judah retained its loyalty.

But with the rejection of the Messiah by the nation of Israel at large, and with the continued persecution of the early believers by the Jewish leaders, there came a gradual shift in the meaning and significance of the word "Jew." Throughout the Gospels and the Book of Acts, both the godly and the ungodly who were physically descended from Jacob were called Jews. (See John 4:9; Acts 10:28; 13:6; 18:2, 24; 19:14; 21:39.) A clear shift occurs in Romans 2:28-29: "For he is not a Jew, which is one outwardly; neither is that circumcision, which is outward in the flesh: but he is a Jew, which is one inwardly; and circumcision is that of the heart, in the spirit, and not in the letter; whose praise is not of men, but of God" (Romans 2:28-29).

This passage is often misinterpreted to mean that Christians are "spiritual Jews." This is not the point at all. No passage in the entire New Testament suggests that Gentile Christians become "spiritual Jews" or "spiritual Israel." Such an idea confuses the hermeneutical principles concerning dispensations, covenants, and ethnic divisions. The logical outgrowth of this erroneous interpretation is to deny the nation of Israel any future in God's dealings and to reinterpret all the Old Testament prophecies having to do with Israel as referring in some spiritual way to the church.

Actually, Romans 2:28-29 reveals that physical ancestry alone is not enough to qualify one to be a true Jew (Israelite). Sincerity of heart must be coupled with physical descent. This is what Romans 9:6 means: "Not as though the word of God hath taken none effect. For they are not all Israel, which are of Israel." In other words, not all who are physically descended from Israel are actually true Israelites. True Israelites are those who have both physical and spiritual descent.

Endnotes

This point clarifies Paul's statement in Romans 11:26: "And so all Israel shall be saved: as it is written, There shall come out of Sion the Deliverer, and shall turn away ungodliness from Jacob." This prophecy is yet to be fulfilled in God's future dealings with Israel. It certainly does not mean that every physical descendant of Israel who has ever lived will be saved, nor even that all of them living at the time the prophecy is to be fulfilled will be saved. Rather, it means that all the physical descendants of Israel who are living at that time and who have a true heart after God, responding in faith to the Messiah, shall be saved. They will be those who, from faith, call on the name of the Lord; they are the remnant. (See Joel 2:32.)

It is evident that God has always had a true remnant within the nation of Israel. Asaph wrote, "Truly God is good to Israel, even to such as are of a clean heart" (Psalm 73:1). The statement of God's goodness to Israel is qualified by the phrase "to such as are of a clean heart." Not all of national Israel could be described by these words. They were thus excluded from the blessing Asaph had in view.

Paul said, "And as many as walk according to this rule, peace be on them, and mercy, and upon the Israel of God" (Galatians 6:16). The "Israel of God" in this New Testament sense refers to believing Israel, Jews who had embraced Jesus as their Messiah. No doubt Paul added this blessing in view of the nature of the Book of Galatians. In it he had dealt firmly with Judaizers, Jews professing Christianity who wanted to require Gentile believers to keep the law of Moses as a condition of salvation. Paul's unequivocal rebuke of these erring Jews must have prompted him to reassure the sincere Jewish

Christians of his love for them.

In his letter to the church at Smyrna, the Lord Jesus said, "I know the blasphemy of them which say they are Jews, and are not, but are the synagogue of Satan" (Revelation 2:9). This statement is similar to what Jesus declared to Jews, Abraham's seed, "If God were your Father, ye would love me. . . . Ye are of your father the devil" (John 8:42, 44). (See also John 8:31, 33, 37-41).

A key, then, to understanding the word "Jew" is to examine the context closely. The following chart illustrates this diversity of meaning:

Various Uses of the Word "Jew"

The tribe of Judah or the two tribes of the southern kingdom	II Kings 16:6; 25:25
The tribe of Benjamin	Esther 2:5
Hebrews	Jeremiah 34:9
Jesus, of the tribe of Judah	John 4:9
A sorcerer and false prophet	Acts 13:6
Aquila	Acts 18:2
Apollos	Acts 18:24
Sceva, a chief priest	Acts 19:14
Paul, of the tribe of Benjamin	Acts 21:39
As distinguished from Gentiles	Romans 1:16
The tribes of Judah, Benjamin, and Levi	Ezra 4:12

All of the converts to Christianity prior to Acts 10 were Jewish by birth, with the possible exception of some proselytes (Acts 2:10). These converts retained their Jewish identity. The Gentiles converted beginning with Acts 10 retained their Gentile identity.

And yet Paul wrote that in Christ, there are no racial, social, or gender barriers: "There is neither Jew nor Greek, there is neither bond nor free, there is neither male nor female: for ye are all one in Christ Jesus" (Galatians 3:28). Obviously Christianity does not erase gender distinctions: men are still men and women remain women. Neither does it negate social status: those who were converted as bondmen remained bondmen; those who were freemen remained freemen (I Timothy 6:1-2; I Corinthians 7:20-24). It follows, therefore, that conversion does not erase the ethnic distinctions between Jews and Gentiles. Jews are physically still Jews; Gentiles are physically still Gentiles.

The point is that "in Christ Jesus" all are one. That is, the Jew has no advantage over the Gentile; the man has no advantage over the woman; the freeman has no advantage over the bondman. As someone said, "The ground is level at the foot of the cross."

It is obvious, in certain cases, that both the terms "Jew" and "Gentile" carry negative connotations. In these cases, both terms refer to unregenerate members of both ethnic groups. For example, Paul wrote, "Wherefore remember, that ye being in time past Gentiles in the flesh, who are called Uncircumcision by that which is called the Circumcision in the flesh made by hands" (Ephesians 2:11). Romans 2:24 says, "For the name of God is blasphemed among the Gentiles through you, as it is written." Again, I Corinthians 10:20 declares, "But I say, that the things which the Gentiles sacrifice, they sacrifice to devils, and not to God: and I would not that ye should have fellowship with devils." In the same book, Paul said, "Ye know that ye were Gentiles, carried away unto these

First Peter

dumb idols, even as ye were led" (I Corinthians 12:2).

The word "Jew" and derivations of it are used in the same sense, speaking of unregenerate members of the Jewish race. Paul, himself a Jew, warned Titus that he should "not give heed to Jewish fables," an obvious reference to the Jewish oral traditions. (See Titus 1:14.) He also referred to Judaism, as distinguished from Christianity, as "the Jews' religion." (See Galatians 1:13-14.)

In I Corinthians 10:32, then, the term "Jew" refers to unregenerate members of the Jewish nation. The term "Gentiles" refers to the unregenerate members of all nations other than the Jewish nation. The term "the church of God" refers to all who by one Spirit have been baptized into the one body of Christ, regardless of their ethnic background, whether they are Jews or Gentiles. (See I Corinthians 12:13.) This unity in the church was the mystery Paul discussed in Ephesians 3:2-6.

The mystery in the Old Testament was never that Gentiles would one day come to the Messiah through the redeemed nation of Israel. The mystery was that in Christ the ethnic distinctions would be dissolved and both the Jew and Gentile would be "of the same body" and "fellowheirs."

In the future dealings of God with the nation of Israel, Gentiles will come to the Messiah through the redeemed nation. (See, for example, Revelation 7:4-14; Isaiah 60:3.) But this future work will be separate and distinct from the church, in which Jew and Gentile stand on equal footing. Though the Gentiles will have opportunity for redemption, the nation of Israel will still retain distinct privileges and status.

There is no clearer explanation of the oneness of Jew

and Gentile in the church than Ephesians 2:11-19. Let us notice carefully what this passage does and does not say.

What it does not say:
- Gentiles are "spiritual Jews."
- Gentiles are now part of the commonwealth of Israel.
- Gentiles are now partakers of the covenants of promise (those with eschatological implications).

What it says:
- Gentiles are now "made nigh" by the blood of Christ.
- The "middle wall of partition" between Jew and Gentile is broken down. (This is a reference to the wall that separated the Court of the Gentiles from the areas of the Temple reserved for the Jews. But the breaking down of this wall did not make the Gentiles into Jews any more than it made the Jews into Gentiles.)
- The "law of commandments contained in ordinances" was abolished. (This is a reference to the law of Moses.)
- In Christ both Jew and Gentile are made "one new man."
- Both Jew and Gentile are reconciled to God by the Cross.
- Both Jew and Gentile have access to the Father by the same Spirit.
- Gentiles are no more strangers and foreigners.
- Gentiles are fellow citizens with the saints.
- Gentiles are members of the household of God.

While a quick reading of this passage might suggest that believing Gentiles have become part of national Israel, a careful study will reveal this is not the case. The most accurate scriptural statement that we can make is not that believing Gentiles become "spiritual Jews" (a term that appears nowhere in Scripture), but that *believing Jews and Gentiles together become "one new man,"* a new man that is, spiritually, neither Jew nor Gentile. (See Galatians 3:28.)

The distinctions of I Corinthians 10:32 help us determine whether a specific scriptural passage concerns Jews as a nation, Gentiles (sometimes called "heathen" or "the nations"), or the church. If the passage concerns the nation of Israel, we should not interpret it as referring to the church. If it refers to the church, we should not interpret as referring to Israel. Obviously, if it refers to the heathen nations, we should interpret neither as relating to Israel or the church. Nor should we interpret statements referring to the church as applying to unregenerate peoples, whether Jewish or Gentile.

[146]See discussion in Blum, 232.

[147]Keener, 713. See also McKnight, 127-28.

[148]Keener, 713.

[149]The sentiment that "children should be seen, and not heard" was certainly current in the first century. Although children were loved in the Jewish community, they had no legal status or rights. The Jewish people connected status to age. (See Galatians 4:1-3.) Outside of the Jewish communities, children were commonly devalued. The death of children by exposure was common. Jesus' elevation of children as a model of faith and humility was undoubtedly shocking to His disciples. (See Matthew 18:1-6.)

[150] For a fuller discussion of these issues see Klyne Snodgrass, *The NIV Application Commentary, Ephesians* (Grand Rapids, MI: Zondervan Publishing House, 1996), 293-96.

[151] Michaels, 124.

[152] BAGD, 456.

[153] Michaels, 125.

[154] Grudem, 119.

[155] Grudem thinks the phrase translated "by him" should be translated "through him" and that the reference is not to the emperor sending governors but to God sending governors through the emperor. If this is the case, however, there is no antecedent for the pronoun "him."

[156] Grudem, 120.

[157] Paul acknowledged the legitimacy of the role of civil government in capital punishment when he expressed his willingness to die at the hand of civil government if he had done anything to deserve death (Acts 25:10-11).

[158] Michaels, 127.

[159] The Temple tax was originally one-half shekel; after the exile, it was reduced to one-third of a shekel (Nehemiah 10:32).

[160] See Grudem, 121, n. 2; McKnight, 148, n. 17.

[161] McKnight, 148.

[162] Grudem, 123, n. 1.

[163] BAGD, 817.

[164] See John 13:34; 15:12, 17; Romans 13:8; I Thessalonians 4:9; I Peter 1:22; I John 3:11, 23; 4:7, 11, 12; II John 1:5.

[165] Grudem, 123.

[166] Keener, 642.

[167] Ibid.

[168] Ibid, 714.
[169] See Keener, 642, 714.
[170] Grudem, 124.
[171] Keener, 643.
[172] Ibid.
[173] Keener, 714.
[174] Grudem, 124.
[175] Michaels, 138.
[176] Wesley J. Pershbacher, *Refresh Your Greek* (Chicago: Moody Press, 1989), 933.
[177] Keener, 643.
[178] Michaels, 139.
[179] Perschbacher, 933.
[180] Michaels, 142.
[181] See discussion in Michaels, 143.
[182] BAGD, 843.
[183] See McKnight, 168, n. 11; Michaels, 144.
[184] Michaels, 144.
[185] The critical text reads, "Sanctify Christ as Lord."
[186] Michaels, 142-43.
[187] See discussion in ibid., 145.
[188] See comments on verse 15 and in the introduction to "Responsible Conduct toward Civil Authority."
[189] Grudem, 130.
[190] See Michaels, 145.
[191] See discussion in ibid., 147.
[192] BAGD, 549.
[193] Ibid., 174.
[194] Romans 6:2 indicates that those who have died to sin can no longer live under its domination. Death has to do with separation. (See James 2:26.) Paul did not mean that sin is extinct for the believer, that he can no longer

be tempted, or that he can no longer yield to temptation. What he meant is that the believer has been separated from sin's ruling power. (See Romans 6:7.) If believers have died (aorist tense, indicating an action completed in the past) to sin, they can no longer draw from sin as the source of their life. Though a believer may be tempted and may succumb to a specific temptation, sin is no longer his life. Whereas prior to his regeneration the believer sinned as a way of life and thought little or nothing of it, the believer who sins senses that his sin has an aura of death about it, and he has a desire to confess his sin to God and to be cleansed from the effects of sin. Since sin's ruling power over him is broken, the believer can no longer live in sin.

In Romans 6:3, Paul wrote, "Know ye not, that so many of us as were baptized into Jesus Christ were baptized into his death?" Although the context does not mention water, there is little doubt that Paul referred to water baptism. Where Holy Spirit baptism is unquestionably in view, we see something other than identification with Jesus Christ in His death and burial: "For by one Spirit we were all baptized into one body—whether Jews or Greeks, whether slaves or free—and have all been made to drink into one Spirit" (I Corinthians 12:13, NKJV).

Spirit baptism identifies the believer with the body of *believers*, the church; water baptism identifies the believer with the *person* of Jesus Christ in His death and burial. Spirit baptism is a baptism from which the believer is never raised, for if he were raised, he would be disassociated from the body of believers, the church. Water baptism is a baptism from which the believer is raised. This does not mean the believer is no longer identified with Jesus Christ, but it does mean that, having been identified with Jesus in his death and burial, he is now identified with Him in his resurrection.

Since the baptism in Romans 6:3-4 is not the same as that of I Corinthians 12:13, and since I Corinthians 12:13 without question has to do with Spirit baptism, the baptism of Romans 6:3-4 must be water baptism. As further support for this idea, Romans 6:3-4 speaks of baptism into Christ, and the New Testament church always invoked the name of Jesus at water baptism, for it identifies the believer with Jesus Christ in His death and burial. (See Acts 2:38; 8:16; 10:48; 19:5; I Corinthians 1:13; 10:2; Galatians 3:27; I Peter 3:21.)

We should not confuse the process of "dying out to sin," which is a sanctification issue, with personal identification with Jesus Christ in *His* death, which is a salvation issue. No matter how devout a believer may be, he could never "die out to sin" so completely and thoroughly that he would merit salvation. Salvation is a gift of God made possible not by the believer's devotion or success in sanctification, but by the work of Jesus Christ on the believer's behalf. The only hope a believer has for salvation—and the only hope he needs—is to identify with Jesus Christ in His death, burial, and resurrection.

People sometimes speak of "dying out to sin" in repentance and appeal to Romans 6:2 in support of this idea. But in the context, the believer's death to sin ultimately occurs when the believer is by baptism united with Christ Jesus in His death (Romans 6:3-4). Repentance is necessary for salvation, but, in addition to confession of sins, repentance has to do with a radical reorienting of one's thoughts (about God, life, and sin), values, and purposes. Though, at repentance, a believer confesses his sins and declares his intention to turn away from them, he does not have within himself the moral strength to permanently keep this commitment. The removal of sin's dominating power is available to the believer, not merely by how sincere or complete his repentance is, but by the death of Christ on his behalf, and the believer identifies with Christ in His death by water baptism.

The significance of the name of Jesus Christ in water baptism is not merely the verbal formula, although the name of Jesus must be called over the baptismal candidate. Rather, the verbal formula is necessary because of baptism's purpose: the identification of the baptismal candidate with the person of Jesus Christ in His death and burial. We are baptized in the name of Jesus Christ because baptism unites us with Jesus in His death and burial.

In Romans 6:4-5, Paul wrote, "Therefore we are buried with him by baptism into death: that like as Christ was raised up from the dead by the glory of the Father, even so we also should walk in newness of life. For if we have been planted together in the likeness of his death, we shall be also in the likeness of his resurrection."

Water baptism identifies us with Jesus Christ in His death so that we may subsequently be identified with Jesus in His life. The "newness of life" in which we walk stands in contrast to the spiritual death we experienced before our regeneration. Whereas we previously were separated from fellowship with God (a state of spiritual death), we are now united with God by His Spirit (a state of spiritual life). Christ was resurrected by the "glory of the Father," which means the power of God effected His resurrection. Glory is a synonym for the power of God at work. (See Psalm 63:2; Matthew 6:13; Ephesians 1:19-20; Colossians 2:12; Jude 1:25; Revelation 5:13.) The "power" of God and the "glory" of God are also terms for the "Spirit" of God. (See Luke 1:35; Romans 1:4; 8:11.) Just as certainly as Jesus Christ was raised from the dead, so the believer who has been united with Christ in His death is enabled by the same Holy Spirit that raised Christ from the dead (Romans 8:11) to live in fellowship with God.

Romans 6:5 may allude to the bodily resurrection of the believer, but the context indicates that the more direct reference is to the spiritual life that believers experience as a consequence of their identification with Christ in His death.

[195] Grudem, 132.

[196] For references where *iaomai* refers to physical healing, see Matthew 8:8, 13; 15:28; Mark 5:29; Luke 5:17; 6:17, 19; 7:7; 8:2, 47; 9:2, 11, 42; 17:15; 22:51; John 4:47; 5:13; Acts 3:11; 9:34; 28:8; James 5:16.

[197] For references where *iaomai* refers to spiritual healing, see Matthew 13:15; Luke 4:18; John 12:40; Acts 28:27; Hebrews 12:13; I Peter 2:24.

[198] For references where *rapha'* refers to physical healing, see Genesis 20:17; 50:2 (translated "physicians"); Exodus 15:26; 21:19; Leviticus 13:18, 37; 14:3, 18; Numbers 12:13; Deuteronomy 28:27, 35; 32:39; I Samuel 6:3; II Kings 8:29; 9:15; 20:5, 8; II Chronicles 16:12 (translated "physicians"); 22:6; Job 5:18; 13:4 (translated "physicians"); Ecclesiastes 3:3.

[199] For references where *rapha'* refers to spiritual healing, see II Chronicles 7:14; 30:20; Psalm 6:2; 30:2;

41:4; 103:3; 107:20; 147:3; Isaiah 6:10; 19:22; 30:26; 53:5; 57:18, 19; Jeremiah 3:22; 6:14; 8:11, 22 (translated "physician"); 15:18; 17:14; 30:17; 33:6; 51:8, 9; Lamentations 2:13; Ezekiel 34:4; Hosea 5:13; 6:1; 7:1; 11:3; 14:4.

[200] See I Kings 18:30; II Kings 2:21, 22; Psalm 60:2; Jeremiah 19:11; Ezekiel 47:8, 9, 11; Zechariah 11:16.

[201] See Segraves, *James: Faith at Work*, 186-91.

[202] For examples of sheep-shepherd imagery, see Numbers 27:17; I Kings 22:17; Psalm 23:1; 100:3; 119:176; Isaiah 40:11; 63:11; Jeremiah 3:15; 10:21; 50:6; Ezekiel 34:6, 23; 37:24; Micah 5:2-9; Nahum 3:18; Zechariah 11:4-9, 15-17; 13:7; Matthew 10:6; Mark 6:34; John 10:1-18; Hebrews 13:20; Revelation 7:17.

[203] Keener, 715.

[204] See discussion in Norman Hillyer, *New International Biblical Commentary, 1 and 2 Peter, Jude* (Peabody, MA: Hendrickson Publishers, 1992) 16:91.

[205] Keener, 715.

[206] See discussion in Michaels, 156-57; Hillyer, 92.

[207] McKnight, 183.

[208] This statement does not suggest that the submission of Christian citizens, slaves, or wives is in any way redemptive. Only the work of Christ on the cross redeems. The point is that insofar as one person can have influence with another, it is usually the result of voluntary submission rather than forceful dominance.

[209] See discussion in McKnight, 186; Hillyer, 92; Michaels, 167-68.

[210] See comments on Hebrews 13:4 in Segraves, *Hebrews: Better Things* 2:223-24.

[211] Grudem, 138.
[212] See discussion in Michaels, 157.
[213] Ibid.
[214] See discussion in McKnight, 181-82.
[215] See BAGD, 12; Michaels, 158.
[216] Keener, 716.
[217] Ibid., 610.
[218] Hillyer, 91.
[219] Ibid., 93.
[220] Ibid.
[221] Grudem, 139.
[222] See ibid., 140.
[223] Edersheim, *Sketches of Jewish Social Life*, in Hillyer, 96.
[224] I. Epstein, *Judaism*, in Hillyer, 96.
[225] Keener, 716.
[226] Michaels, 165.
[227] Grudem, 141, n. 1.
[228] If this is the case, however, we are left to wonder why he did not use the stronger word in 2:13, 18 and certainly in 3:1, 5.
[229] Michaels, 166.
[230] Ibid., 167.
[231] Ibid.
[232] Hillyer, 97.
[233] Keener, 717.
[234] Michaels, 168; Hillyer, 98.
[235] McKnight, 186.
[236] Hillyer, 97.
[237] Michaels, 169.
[238] Ibid., 170.
[239] BAGD, 817.

Endnotes

[240]Ibid., 569.

[241]See Job 16:13; 19:27; Psalm 7:9; 16:7; 26:2; 73:21; 139:13; Proverbs 23:16; Isaiah 11:5; Jeremiah 11:20; 12:2; 17:10; 20:12; Lamentations 3:13.

[242]Hillyer, 104-5.

[243]Ibid., 101.

[244]Michaels, 178.

[245]Ibid.

[246]See discussion in ibid.

[247]See discussion on Psalm 34 and Genesis 26:1 in Charles C. Ryrie, *The Ryrie Study Bible*, King James Version (Chicago, IL: Moody Press, 1978), and on Psalm 34 in Earl D. Radmacher, gen. ed., *The Nelson Study Bible* (Nashville, TN: Thomas Nelson Publishers, 1997).

[248]See the discussion in Segraves, *Themes from a Letter to Rome*, 18-19.

[249]Michaels, 180.

[250]Hillyer, 104.

[251]Keener, 717-18.

[252]BAGD, 486.

[253]Grudem, 152.

[254]Some of the information on the conscience is from the "Acceptance Seminar: God's Change Agent for the Inner Life," conducted by David Eckman, Ph.D.

[255]The Corinthian church wrote Paul a series of questions (I Corinthians 7:1). One of them was whether it was right to eat meat that had been offered to idols (I Corinthians 8:4). Paul's inspired response identified those who were condemned by the eating of such meat as having a weak conscience. He carefully pointed out that the believer whose conscience is stronger should not exercise his liberty so as to encourage his weaker brother to violate

his conscience. (See I Corinthians 8:1-2, 9-13.) No believer should ever engage in any activity he believes to be a sin (I Corinthians 8:10-11; Romans 14:14, 22-23). This teaching does not mean that the stronger brother must abandon his weaker brother to live forever in weakness. Paul's statements revealed the error of the weaker brother's position. Stronger Christians can use these passages to help a weaker brother grow in grace so that he is no longer condemned by neutral things like eating meat and so that his conscience no longer compels him unnecessarily to observe certain days as holy. (See Romans 14:2, 5-6.) But until he reaches this place of greater maturity, they should respect his weakness.

A person with a weak conscience will tend to live under unnecessary condemnation. He will struggle with the temptation to judge those who do not share his weakness. In the worst case, he could eventually lose his faith in Christ. The best case is for his conscience to be strengthened by scriptural truth so that its instincts fit what is biblically true.

We could say that a person with a weak conscience is the victim of bad, incorrect information. His instincts do not fit reality.

The discussion of the wounded conscience occurs in the same context as the teaching about a weak conscience (I Corinthians 8:12). The weak conscience is a candidate to become a wounded conscience, and this occurs when a person with a weak conscience, following the example of someone with a stronger conscience, goes ahead and participates in some behavior he believes to be wrong. (See I Corinthians 8:9-12.) Scripture also describes this wounded conscience as being defiled (I Corinthians 8:7).

When a person's conscience does not condemn him for his behavior, he is a happy person. But a person who is condemned by what he does is not living by faith, and this is sin. (See Romans 14:22-23.) It is important to note that the "sin" occurring when a person with a weak conscience participates in behavior he believes to be wrong may not be a sin as far as God is concerned. The Greek word translated "sin" (*hamartia*) simply means "to miss the mark." Sin in the eyes of God is disobedience to specific commands of Scripture. It is falling short or missing the mark of perfect obedience to God's Word. (See I John 3:4.) But the weak conscience is an ill-informed conscience; its instincts are not in perfect harmony with the Word of God. What the weak conscience thinks is sin is not actually sin, as far as God is concerned.

The condemnation that comes on the weak conscience is self-condemnation; it is not from God. We see this point contextually in Romans 14:22-23, for verse 22 describes as happy the person who does not condemn *himself*. Thus the condemnation of the weak conscience in verse 23 is self-condemnation. The reason the weak person's conscience condemns him is because he knows he is not acting from the principle of faith at that point, but from the principle of doubt. Thus his actions are "missing the mark" of faith, and faith should be the motivating factor behind all believers do. In this sense his actions are "sin."

We can say that a wounded conscience occurs when a stronger brother flaunts his liberty before a weaker brother, encouraging the weaker brother to participate in behavior for which his weak conscience condemns him.

The ultimate solution to a wounded conscience is for

the person with the weak conscience to grow in grace and in the knowledge of the Lord and Savior Jesus Christ. (See II Peter 3:18.) A well-informed conscience comes from consistent and accurate study of Scripture. But in the meantime, stronger brethren must be careful to avoid doing anything that would encourage a weaker brother to violate his conscience.

Some people will leave the faith and heed deceiving spirits and demonic doctrines. These people are lying pretenders (hypocrites) whose conscience is "seared with a hot iron" (I Timothy 4:1-2). These people have once been in the faith; they have departed from it. This means they have rejected known truth. Not only have they rejected truth they once believed, they have also embraced false teachings.

False beliefs and teachings may not come merely as the result of intellectual misunderstanding; they may, in some cases, be the direct result of spiritual deception. This is one reason the gift of the discerning of spirits is important (I Corinthians 12:10). And all believers are to test spirits by the standard of biblical truth (I John 4:1-3).

In the discussion of beliefs typical of those who have a seared conscience, we find specifically those who forbid marriage and who command abstinence from certain foods. The only thing the Bible commands believers to abstain from is what is destructive and harmful. Some people reject the clear and helpful teachings of Scripture only to embrace confusing teachings that forbid people to enjoy the good gifts of God. (See Genesis 2:18; Mark 7:18-19.)

There are consequences of denying the truth one knows. Specifically, the person who does so will eventually embrace a lifestyle that is destructive and void of the good gifts God has given. Those who reject the true teachings of Scripture may think they are going to enjoy great liberty, but in the end they will wind up captive to relationships, lifestyles, substances, or beliefs that will destroy them (II Peter 2:19). Only the truth makes one free (John 8:32).

We can say that the person with the seared or burned-out conscience has so consistently rejected his inner standards that he no longer feels the normal pain that conscience produces when one does evil.

The person with the seared conscience must repent of his sin, forsake his false beliefs and destructive behaviors, and learn again the truth of God's Word. Only by doing so is there hope for his salvation.

Hebrews 10:22 mentions the evil conscience. The immediate context and the larger context of Hebrews indicate that those who have an evil conscience are those who have rejected the finality and sufficiency of the blood of Jesus to return to the shadowy imperfections of Moses' law.

The evil conscience is trained to believe that Christ plus obedience to the law of Moses gives us acceptance before God. It cheapens the work of the Cross by counting it insufficient to make a believer fully acceptable to God on a daily basis. The writer of Hebrews pointed out that when anyone adds to the Cross in an attempt to be acceptable to God, he tramples underfoot the Son of God, he counts the blood of the covenant to be common, and he insults the Spirit of grace.

There is a fourfold antidote to an evil conscience: (1) Boldly rely only on the blood of Jesus for entry into the most intimate relationship with God (Hebrews 10:19-22). (2) Believe completely in the faithfulness of God to keep His promises so as to hold fast to the biblically assured hope without wavering (Hebrews 10:23). (3) Vividly recall the time of first understanding that God's love is unconditional and confidently await the final fulfillment of His promise (Hebrews 10:32-36). (4) Refuse to draw back from a life of justification by faith into an attempt to be justified by works (Hebrews 10:37-39).

[256] Michaels, 190-91.
[257] Ibid., 192.
[258] Ibid., 202.
[259] Ibid.
[260] This is contrary to Michaels, who makes the distinction. (See Michaels, 203.)
[261] Michaels, 204.
[262] Ibid.
[263] Ibid., 205.
[264] Ibid.
[265] Ibid.
[266] See McKnight, 215, n. 9.
[267] Grudem, 204.
[268] BAGD, 867.
[269] Some have taught that Jesus atoned for sin by suffering in hell as a sinner. This notion is completely without scriptural support and opposes the clear teaching of Scripture that Jesus atoned for sin by His death on the cross.
[270] See comments on Hebrews 2:16 in Segraves, *Hebrews: Better Things* 1:78-79.
[271] "Hebrew poetry commonly uses synonymous parallelism (in which a second line reiterates the statement of the first); thus 'soul' and 'spirit' are used interchangeably

here [in Luke 1:46], as often in Scripture" (Keener, 191).

[272] See Keener, 729.

[273] See discussion in Michaels, 213.

[274] See BAGD, 76.

[275] Grudem, 163.

[276] Ibid.

[277] Hillyer, 116.

[278] McKnight, 215, n. 8.

[279] Michaels, 216.

[280] Ibid., 221.

[281] See comments on Hebrews 6:2 in Segraves, *Hebrews: Better Things* 1:156-61.

[282] Kennedy, 438.

[283] Robertson, *Word Pictures* 4:445.

[284] Grudem, 165.

[285] See Matthew 22:44; 26:64; Mark 12:36; 14:62; 16:19; Luke 20:42; 22:69; Acts 2:34; 5:31; 7:55-56; Romans 8:34; Ephesians 1:20; Colossians 3:1; Hebrews 1:3, 13; 8:1; 10:12; 12:2.

[286] Ramm, *Protestant Biblical Interpretation*, 3d rev. ed. (Grand Rapids, MI: Baker Book House, 1970), 100-1.

[287] Ibid., 101.

[288] F. F. Bruce, *The Epistle to the Hebrews*, *The New International Commentary on the New Testament* (Grand Rapids, MI: William B. Eerdmans, 1964), 7.

[289] Keener, 718.

[290] For further information on the concept of angelic rulership over the nations of the world, see comments on Hebrews 2:5 in Segraves, *Hebrews: Better Things* 1:68-70.

[291] Hillyer, 119.

[292] See John 3:16; Galatians 3:13; 4:4-5; Ephesians 1:7; Colossians 1:14; II Timothy 1:10; Hebrews 2:9-11,

14, 17; 7:26, 28; 9:12, 14, 26, 28; 10:5, 10, 19-20; 13:12; I Peter 1:18-20; I John 2:2; 3:5, 16; Revelation 5:9.

[293] Keener, 718.

[294] See Romans 6:13 (where the Greek *hopla*, translated "instruments," suggests weapons or armor); 13:12; II Corinthians 6:7; 10:4; Ephesians 6:11-17; I Thessalonians 5:8; I Timothy 1:18; 6:12; II Timothy 2:3-4; Revelation 12:17.

[295] Michaels, 226.

[296] Grudem, 167.

[297] McKnight, 226.

[298] See discussion in ibid.

[299] Michaels, 228.

[300] See discussion in ibid., 224-29.

[301] Ibid., 223, n. c.

[302] Ibid., 223.

[303] Ibid., 230.

[304] For example, see discussion in ibid., 230; Grudem, 168.

[305] Hillyer, 121.

[306] Michaels, 230.

[307] See endnote 145.

[308] See Keener, 718-19.

[309] See endnote 57.

[310] These descriptions are from Hillyer, 123.

[311] Ibid., 124.

[312] The word "you" is in italics in both the KJV and the NKJV.

[313] See discussion in Michaels, 233-34.

[314] First, there is the judgment seat of Christ (Romans 14:10; I Corinthians 3:11-15; II Corinthians 5:10). It will

occur in heaven after the rapture of the church and prior to the second coming of Christ to this earth at the end of the Great Tribulation. (See I Corinthians 4:5; II Timothy 4:8; Revelation 19:7-8; 22:12.) Only redeemed members of the church will be present at this judgment. It is not a judgment to determine salvation, but to determine rewards for deeds subsequent to salvation. Works categorized as gold, silver, or precious stone will be rewarded; those categorized as wood, hay, or stubble will not. (See Ephesians 6:8; Colossians 3:24-25.) Under the symbol of fire, each believer's work will be tested to determine "what sort it is" (I Corinthians 3:13), which indicates a test to ascertain the quality of the work. It may be that the determining factor is the motivation behind one's deeds. In describing the religious ostentation of the first century, Jesus said that some gave, prayed, and fasted out of a desire for others to see them. (See Matthew 6:1-18.) Thus all they would ever receive is the commendation of people. But those who engaged in these good works with pure motives, doing them secretly as to the Lord, would be rewarded openly.

The second judgment is the judgment of the Gentiles. Also known as the judgment of the nations, it will occur at the end of the Great Tribulation at the second coming of Christ. (See Matthew 25:31-46; Joel 3:2.) This judgment, which will occur on earth in the Valley of Jehoshaphat, will determine the fate of the Gentiles then living on the basis of their treatment of Christ's brethren, the Jewish people, during the preceding Tribulation. Those Gentiles whose faith in Christ prompted them to minister to the persecuted Jews during the Great Tribulation are the sheep. Their reward will be to enter

First Peter

into the kingdom, also known as the Millennium. (See Revelation 20:4-6.) Those Gentiles whose lack of faith in Christ caused them to fail to minister to the persecuted Jews during the Great Tribulation are goats. Their fate is to be cast into the lake of fire. This judgment will be a dramatic demonstration of the blessing and cursing of the Abrahamic covenant described in Genesis 12:3.

The third judgment is the judgment of Israel. (See Ezekiel 20:37-38.) This judgment will occur on the earth at the second coming of Jesus at the end of the Great Tribulation. It will involve the Jewish people who are living on the earth at that time and will be based upon their acceptance of or rejection of Jesus as the Messiah. (See Psalm 50:1-7; Ezekiel 20:33-44; Malachi 3:2-5; 4:1-2.) Those who have believed on Jesus will enter into the kingdom blessing of the millennial era; those who have rejected Him will not.

The last of the judgments pertaining to people (angels will also be judged) is the Great White Throne Judgment. (See Revelation 20:11-15.) This judgment, which occurs after the Millennium, involves all who have not previously been resurrected. It is based upon each individual's works. Those whose names are not in the Book of Life will be cast into the lake of fire.

This description of judgments is adapted from Segraves, *Hebrews: Better Things* 1:166-68.

[315]See discussion in Michaels, 235 (although Michaels confesses that "the distinction between God and Christ is not of paramount importance to Peter at this stage of his argument"); Hillyer, 121; McKnight, 227, n. 13; Blum, 245.

[316]See discussion in Hillyer, 122.

[317]See discussion in Blum, 245.

Endnotes

[318]See discussion in Grudem, 172.
[319]Michaels, 235.
[320]Hillyer, 125.
[321]Grudem, 172.
[322]McKnight, 236, n. 3.
[323]See comments in Segraves, *James: Faith at Work*, 173-74.
[324]BAGD, 802.
[325]Ibid., 538.
[326]Ibid.
[327]See Matthew 6:10; Acts 18:21; Romans 1:10; 8:27; 12:2; 15:32; II Corinthians 12:8-10; Colossians 4:12; Hebrews 2:4; 6:3; 10:36; James 4:15; I Peter 2:15; 3:17; 4:2, 19; I John 2:17; 5:14-15.
[328]Hillyer, 125.
[329]See Blum, 246.
[330]BAGD, 245.
[331]See comments on Proverbs 10:12 and 17:9 in Daniel L. Segraves, *Proverbs: Ancient Wisdom for Today's World* (Hazelwood, MO: Word Aflame Press, 1988), 99, 176-77.
[332]See Segraves, *James: Faith at Work*, 196.
[333]For further discussion on the use of the Old Testament in the New Testament, particularly the way the New Testament gives new meaning to Old Testament words, see Segraves, *Themes from a Letter to Rome*, 54-55; *Hebrews: Better Things* 1:55-57, 94; 2:98-100.
[334]McKnight, 238.
[335]Hillyer, 125.
[336]BAGD, 164.
[337]See BAGD, 877-79.
[338]BAGD, 683.

First Peter

[339] Hillyer, 128.
[340] Michaels, 250.
[341] Ibid.
[342] Grudem, 176.
[343] See discussion in Michaels, 250.
[344] Blum, 247.

[345] Article X, Section 11, paragraph 13 of the General Constitution of the United Pentecostal Church International, Inc. consists of this statement: "Trustees and administrators of all endorsed schools of the United Pentecostal Church International or other schools affiliated with or supported by the United Pentecostal Church International only employ and continue the employment of faculty members and professional staff members who sign annually that they believe in the divine inspiration of the whole Bible, the infallibility of the original writings and that the Bible is truth without any error and is inspired even to the very words and is therefore the inscripted Word of God."

[346] See Deuteronomy 4:2; Proverbs 30:5-6; Psalm 119:8-9; Isaiah 40:8; II Timothy 3:16; II Peter 1:20-21; I Corinthians 14:37; II Peter 3:2, 15-16; Revelation 22:18-19.

[347] See the discussion in Michaels, 253.
[348] Ibid.
[349] See 5:11; Romans 11:36; 16:27; Galatians 1:5; Ephesians 3:21; Philippians 4:20; I Timothy 1:17; 6:16; Hebrews 13:21; II Peter 3:18; Jude 25; Revelation 1:6; 7:12. See Hillyer, 129.

[350] See discussion in Michaels, 260-61.
[351] Ibid., 261.
[352] Ibid., 262.

[353] Keener, 720.

[354] See discussion in Michaels, 264, on the identification of the terms "Holy Spirit," "Spirit of your Father," "Spirit of God," and the "spirit of Christ's glory." All refer to one Spirit.

[355] See Romans 8:9-11, 15-16, 23, 26; I Corinthians 12:13; II Corinthians 3:6, 8, 17-18; 5:5; Galatians 3:2-3, 5; 4:6; 5:5, 16-18, 22, 25; Ephesians 1:13; 2:18, 22; 3:16; 4:30; 5:9, 18; Philippians 1:19; 2:1; I Thessalonians 4:8; 5:19; II Thessalonians 2:13; II Timothy 1:7; I Peter 1:2, 22; I John 3:24; 4:13; Jude 19.

[356] See, e.g., Galatians 5:19-21; Romans 13:9-10; Ephesians 4:25-31; 5:3-12, 15, 18; I Corinthians 6:9-11; 10:21; II Corinthians 6:14-18; II Timothy 3:1-7; Titus 2:3, 9-10; Hebrews 13:4-5; James 1:26-27; 2:1, 9; 3:10, 14; 4:1-4, 11; 5:1-6; I Peter 2:1; I John 2:15-16; 3:15, 17.

[357] Michaels, 266.

[358] The discussion of *allotriepiskopos* here follows ibid., 267.

[359] See comments on Acts 11:26 in Keener, 354.

[360] This discussion follows Grudem, 182, who follows Dennis E. Johnson, 181, n. 1.

[361] This discussion follows Grudem, 182-83, who follows Johnson, 181, n. 1.

[362] BAGD, 412.

[363] Grudem, 181.

[364] BAGD, 526.

[365] Ibid., 623.

[366] Grudem, 184.

[367] Ibid.

[368] BAGD, 699-700.

[369] See comments in Michaels, 276, n. b; Grudem, 187.

[370] Grudem, 187.
[371] BAGD, 617.
[372] Ibid., 684.
[373] Keener, 720-21.
[374] Ibid., 721.
[375] BAGD, 706.
[376] John Calvin identified the three sins as sloth, desire for gain, and lust for power. (See Grudem, 187-88.)
[377] Hillyer, 142.
[378] Grudem, 189.
[379] Keener, 721.
[380] Here, the LORD spoke concerning the Messiah. Still, this does not indicate that the Messiah is a divine person distinct from the LORD. The Messiah is a man (Hebrew, *geber*; a hero, warrior, male human being) who is the "companion" (Hebrew, *'amiyth*) of the LORD. The Hebrew Scriptures use *'amiyth* in reference to neighbors, relations, associates, or fellows. (See Leviticus 6:2; 19:11, 15, 17; 24:19; 25:14-15, 17.) If Zechariah 13:7 indicated that the Messiah-Shepherd is a person in the Godhead distinct from the LORD, these would be inappropriate words to use. From the perspective of classical trinitarianism, the three persons who exist as God are not "companions" in any meaningful sense as described by *'amiyth*. It is better to see this verse as focusing on the Messiah's human existence in the same sense as does Psalm 45:7.

From the standpoint of His human existence, the Messiah is the LORD's "fellow" or "companion." To deny this relationship would undercut or compromise the genuineness and fullness of the Messiah's human existence and suggest that His humanity was overwhelmed, or for all practical purposes obliterated, by His deity. But the relationship between the Messiah and the LORD does not arise from shared deity; it arises from the reality of the Messiah's human existence. If two or more divine persons can speak to or of each other as "companions," this would seem dangerously close to a fragmentation within God that would border on ditheism or tritheism. All study of God must have as its base the Shema, which Jesus identified as the first of all the commandments: "Hear, O Israel: The LORD our God is one LORD" (Deuteronomy 6:4; Mark 12:29). We cannot explain the oneness of the LORD merely as a oneness of "companionship." If we do, we compromise the meaning and significance of *echad* ("one"), turning God into a kind of committee whose members share equality of rank.

[381] See Hillyer, 143; Keener, 721.

[382] Grudem, 192.

[383] Ibid.

[384] See discussion in ibid., 193.

[385] Keener, 721.

[386] Grudem, 193.

[387] This follows the discussion in Segraves, *James: Faith at Work*, 147.

[388] See discussion in Michaels, 293-94.

[389] Ibid., 294.

[390] Grudem, 195.

[391] BAGD, 538.

[392] See Matthew 24:42-43; 25:13; 26:38, 40-41; Mark 13:34-35, 37; 14:34, 37-38; Luke 12:37, 39; Acts 20:31; I Corinthians 16:13; Colossians 4:2; I Thessalonians 5:6; Revelation 3:2-3; 16:15.

[393] BAGD, 167.

[394]Ibid., 416.
[395]See discussion in Michaels, 299.
[396]Ibid., 301.
[397]Grudem, 197.
[398]Ibid., 198.
[399]Ibid.
[400]See discussion in ibid., 23-24.
[401]Ibid., 23.
[402]Ibid., 24.
[403]BAGD, 617.
[404]Grudem, 201.
[405]Carson, Moo, and Morris, 424.
[406]Keener, 722.
[407]Walvoord and Zuck, eds., *The Bible Knowledge Commentary, New Testament Edition*, 548.